The Complete Idiot's Reference Card
Negotiation Preparation Worksheet

Use this handy worksheet to prepare for any negotiation. Write [...] opponent will discuss during the bargaining, and refer to it durin[...] to make sure you're staying on track.

tear here

What Are My Objectives?

Money: How much do I want to make? How much am I willing to spend?_____
_____

Payment Schedule: What is the best way to structure payment? _____
_____

Time: Within what time frame does this transaction need to happen?_____
_____

Service: What services might I want after the deal is closed? _____
_____

Improvements: What add-ons or upgrades might I need in the future?_____
_____

Returns: What return policy, if any, protects me if the product is flawed? _____
_____

Future Business: What kind of future business might I conduct with this opponent? _____
_____

Volume Deals: Will the terms of the negotiation improve if the deal involves larger quantities?
_____
_____

Other: Are there any other terms that affect my negotiation? _____
_____

What Are My Opponent's Objectives?

Money: How much does my opponent want to make? How much is my opponent willing to spend?
_____
_____

Payment Schedule: What is the best way to structure payment?_____
_____

Time: Within what time frame does my opponent need this transaction to happen? _____
_____

Service: What services might my opponent want after the deal is closed? _____
_____

Improvements: What add-ons or upgrades might my opponent need in the future? _____
_____

Returns: What return policy, if any, protects my opponent if the product is flawed? _____
_____

Future Business: What kind of future business might my opponent conduct with me? _____
_____

Volume Deals: Will the terms of the negotiation improve if the deal involves larger quantities?_____
_____

Other: Are there any other terms that might affect my opponent's negotiating position? _____
_____

alpha books

Satisfying Both Sides

Money:
My goal:_____
My opponent's goal: _____
Compromise that suits both: _____
_____

Payment Schedule:
My goal:_____
My opponent's goal: _____
Compromise that suits both: _____
_____

Time:
My goal:_____
My opponent's goal: _____
Compromise that suits both: _____
_____

Service:
My goal:_____
My opponent's goal: _____
Compromise that suits both: _____
_____

Improvements:
My goal:_____
My opponent's goal: _____
Compromise that suits both: _____
_____

Returns:
My goal:_____
My opponent's goal: _____
Compromise that suits both: _____
_____

Future Business:
My goal:_____
My opponent's goal: _____
Compromise that suits both: _____
_____

Volume Deals:
My goal:_____
My opponent's goal: _____
Compromise that suits both: _____
_____

Other:
My goal:_____
My opponent's goal: _____
Compromise that suits both: _____
_____

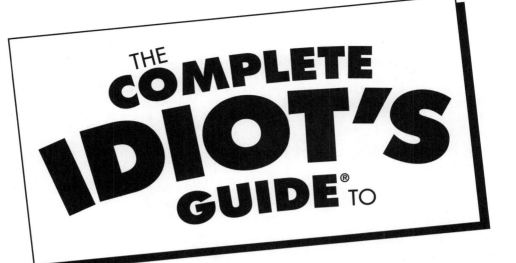

THE COMPLETE IDIOT'S GUIDE® TO

Winning Through Negotiation

Second Edition

by John Ilich

alpha books

A Division of Macmillan General Reference
A Pearson Education Macmillan Company
1633 Broadway, New York, NY 10019

Macmillan General Reference books may be purchased for business or sales promotional use. For information, please write: Special Markets Department, Macmillan Publishing USA, 1633 Broadway, New York, NY 10019.

International Standard Book Number: 0-02-863393-8
Library of Congress Catalog Card Number: 99-64699

01 00 99   8 7 6 5 4 3 2 1

Interpretation of the printing code: The rightmost number of the first series of numbers is the year of the book's printing; the rightmost number of the second series of numbers is the number of the book's printing. For example, a printing code of 99-1 shows that the first printing occurred in 1999.

Printed in the United States of America

Note: This publication contains the opinions and ideas of its author. It is intended to provide helpful and informative material on the subject matter covered. It is sold with the understanding that the author and publisher are not engaged in rendering professional services in the book. If the reader requires personal assistance or advice, a competent professional should be consulted.

The author and publisher specifically disclaim any responsibility for any liability, loss or risk, personal or otherwise, which is incurred as a consequence, directly or indirectly, of the use and application of any of the contents of this book.

Contents at a Glance

Contents

xiii

Foreword

Successful negotiation in all matters results in time saved, reduction of stress, and energy directed into more constructive projects. Your decision to purchase this book is one well negotiated, as you will benefit from John Ilich's advice on effective negotiating in everyday situations to those more complicated situations.

The Complete Idiot's Guide to Winning Through Negotiation, Second Edition will help you develop the skills to succeed in any type of negotiation from simple to complicated. You can learn how to negotiate the dinner of your choice to the salary you deserve all in a tactful, effective manner.

As an attorney and owner of a medium-sized legal practice, I already negotiate everyday with clients, prosecutors, opposing counsel and judges. As a result, I thought that this book would not benefit me. However, I was pleasantly surprised and I found that John Ilich's tactics enhanced my ability to get excellent results for my cases. This book is not just for first *idiot* negotiators—even distinguished professionals will reap its benefits.

This new and improved second edition is packed full of examples and strategies to show you how to become a master negotiator. John Ilich takes his first book to a new level, as he prepares you for negotiating in the new millennium. Updated forms and internet information are included in this new edition. With its easy-to-understand format and plain and simple language, you can quickly learn how to take control of any situation to get what you want from your opponent.

John Ilich's advice can have a profound effect on your personal and professional life. Specifically you will learn to negotiate competently, without becoming emotional, such that you will gain a greater sense of control and satisfaction. You can learn to remain calm, cool and collected as you bargain in the most heated situations. Gain the negotiating confidence that everyone needs with *The Complete Idiot's Guide to Winning Through Negotiation, Second Edition*.

Read the book, understand the techniques, and negotiate into your future!

—Sheri Paige

Sheri B. Paige, Esq. is owner of Sheri Paige & Associates, a medium-sized law firm in Norwalk, Connecticut. The firm specializes in legal matters in the areas of family, bankruptcy, criminal, and immigration.

Introduction

Here's a surprising fact: You were born a negotiator. At that moment in your crib when you first cried for your bottle, you were making your first opening bid to get something you wanted from someone else. You weren't particularly sophisticated in your negotiating skills—but you got the job done. And you've been negotiating, in one way or another, ever since.

So, if this is something you've been doing since your days in the cradle, why would you need anyone to teach you how? Simple—basic negotiating is not the same thing as negotiating well!

Let me share a story with you: In one of my earliest experiences as a novice negotiator, back in Chicago some 35 years ago, I faced a couple of old pros who negotiated me into a corner. As we shook hands, they looked me over like hungry lions sizing up a helpless lamb. Then they hauled out all the evidence they had prepared—reports, witness statements, and a truckload of supporting documents. When the discussions began, their language flowed as beautifully as a Shakespearean sonnet. I was outmatched and in awe. I remember thinking, "Wow! Those guys are good—really good! They're major leaguers."

My second reaction was: "I'm going to do whatever it takes to be better than them." From that time on, I dedicated myself to honing my negotiating skills and techniques. Several years later, I negotiated a settlement that saved my client more than $9 million. I had arrived. I, too, was a major leaguer.

That's what I want this book to do for *you*! In these pages, you'll learn the difference between asking for what you want and getting it. You'll learn the skills you need to sit down at the bargaining table with confidence, and you'll discover the techniques to swing even the most determined opponent around to your position. You, too, will enter the major leagues of negotiating.

This is the fifth book I've written on the subject of negotiating success. I wrote it for you: a person who's not a professional negotiator, yet whose entire life is influenced by negotiation. Think of all the times you've settled disputes with your family, friends, coworkers, clients, or customers. Think about how many times you've bought a car, sold a house, signed a lease, or asked for a raise. Think about how many times you'll do all this again in the future. Wouldn't it be easier if you knew how to bargain like a pro?

The tactics and techniques in this book will help you even when you're not sitting down to a formal bargaining table—like the couple with six young children who were having a new home built. The contractor promised that the home would be finished by the summer, when the kids were out of school, but it didn't look like the job would be anywhere near complete by that time. The husband hit on a brilliant solution. He sent the contractor a note: "After June 1st, you will be working for six full-time supervisors under the age of 12." The contractor rushed to complete the job. (The husband was using a simple technique I'll describe in detail in Chapter 17, "Fear and Trembling.") That shows you how a little bargaining knowledge can bring you great results!

Like that couple, you'll be able to use the knowledge you gain from this book to handle every situation in which things aren't going your way. That's what negotiation is all about.

Here's what's waiting for you in the pages to come:

Part 1: Negotiation Basics. In this part of the book, I'll show you that you were born with the instinct for negotiation, and I'll teach you how to make that instinctive knowledge work for you while you prepare for negotiation. You'll learn how to determine your own position, figure out the other side's bargaining strategy, and arrange the negotiation to give you negotiating power.

Part 2: Bargaining Table Techniques. Here's where you'll discover how to present your case in the most powerful and persuasive way possible—how to use the language of negotiation, how to speak with body language, how to use questions and correspondence as bargaining tools, and more.

Part 3: Making Minds Meet. This section shows you how to tailor your negotiation to suit the specific traits and styles of your opponents. By understanding how he or she is likely to respond to the bargaining process, you can determine the best ways to appeal to your opponent. With the information in these chapters, you'll learn how to discover negotiating solutions that give both you and your opponent exactly what you want.

Part 4: Increasing Your Negotiating Power. This part of the book explains how you can increase and maintain your personal power in a negotiating situation. You'll learn how to enhance your negotiating power through eliminating bad habits and employing mental techniques before and during the bargaining process. You'll also learn how to take—and keep—control over the negotiating session, and how to boost your confidence and competence when it comes time to negotiate.

Part 5: Problem Solving. Every negotiator, no matter how experienced, runs into a situation where everything seems to go wrong. But a pro knows that you don't just give up—you turn the situation around. In this part, you'll learn how to save a negotiation that has gone awry. Here's where you'll learn what to do to recoup when fear, anger, or personality or principle conflicts threaten to derail your negotiation.

Part 6: Sealing the Deal. This part gives you the tips you need to cruise through those delicate final stages of negotiation. It shows you how—and when—to make an offer, and it leads you through the ins and outs of making counteroffers. Finally, it teaches you the delicate art of closing—a crucial element of negotiation that even experienced negotiators often fail to master.

Part 7: Real-Time, Real-World Negotiating. This section brings together everything you've learned and shows you how you can use these skills to deal with the many common bargaining situations you'll face. You'll discover how to use the techniques when buying or selling a home, car, or property; when negotiating a loan or raise; when bargaining as a consumer; and when settling disputes. You'll also learn about negotiating in that brave new world of the Internet where, by all reports, we'll all be spending a great deal of our working, playing, and purchasing life in the near future.

So let's get started. I think you'll like what you read in these pages—and I *know* you'll benefit from it.

Extras

In addition to packing this book with pointers, worksheets, checklists, and examples, I've included sidebars that will alert you to important tips, warnings, sayings, case studies, and definitions. Look for these signposts as you read through the text:

Negotiable Terms

Basic words and terms in every negotiator's lexicon.

Talking Points

Aphorisms and quotables that highlight and reinforce basic negotiating truths.

Dealmaker

Bargaining tips you can use and profit from when you're at the bargaining table, raring to persuade your opponent to give you what you want.

Dealbreaker

Pitfalls to avoid that can derail your negotiation.

The Art of the Deal

Stories and anecdotes that illustrate a particular point or technique featured in the chapter.

Acknowledgments

Special thanks to my wife, Marjorie, for her fine editing assistance.

Special thanks also to the crew at Macmillan Publishing for making this book possible: Kathy Niebenhaus, Robert Shuman, Jessica Faust, and Nancy Gratton in New York, and Jena Brandt, Krista Hansing, and the entire production team in Indianapolis.

Special Thanks from the Publisher

The Complete Idiot's Guide to Winning Through Negotiation was reviewed by an expert in the field who not only checked the technical accuracy of what you'll learn here, but also provided insight to help us ensure that this book gives you everything you need to know to become a successful negotiator. Our special thanks are extended to Sara Adler, a graduate of the University of California at Los Angeles School of Law, and a member of the National Academy of Arbitrators.

Trademarks

All terms mentioned in this book that are known to be or are suspected of being trademarks or service marks have been appropriately capitalized. Alpha Books and Macmillan General Reference cannot attest to the accuracy of this information. Use of a term in this book should not be regarded as affecting the validity of any trademark or service mark.

Part 1
Negotiation Basics

Almost every day of your life, you have to negotiate—sometimes in unexpected ways. What do you do when you need a loan, but your budget just won't cover a high interest rate? You negotiate! How about when your car decides not to start—and it's the day after the warranty expires? You negotiate! What about when your teenager wants an increased allowance but hasn't done any chores? Or when you arrive at the airport only to find you've been bumped off your flight? That's right, you negotiate!

In all these situations, the key is this: There's something you want, and there's an opponent (your lender, your mechanic, your teenager, or the airline personnel) who can give you what you want. In such situations, you've got three choices. You can surrender and accept your fate without complaint. You can use intimidating bully tactics to try and get what you want. Or, you can successfully negotiate.

As with any other art, negotiation has certain basic preparation skills that are easy to learn. A painter, for example, must have a good grasp of colors, paints, brushes, and techniques to paint a picture—and possibly even create a masterpiece. In this part, you learn the basics you need to handle any negotiation—and even negotiate yourself a masterpiece.

Chapter 1

The Natural Negotiator

In This Chapter

➤ Born to negotiate!

➤ Wheeling and dealing for dollars

➤ People power through negotiation

➤ Negotiate unto others . . .

What images come to mind when you think of negotiation? Perhaps a tense room packed with sweaty business people shuffling papers, crunching numbers, and carving out the details of a crucial deal. Maybe a pair of suave diplomats coolly resolving affairs of state over cigars and brandy. Or, maybe a fast-talking car salesperson praising the virtues (and sugarcoating the price) of the latest lemon on the lot.

The truth is, negotiation isn't a complicated art best saved for business moguls, union bosses, or international leaders. It's for all people who try to get what they want—and that includes you. In this chapter, you'll learn that you're a natural-born negotiator. You'll discover why negotiating is an essential part of your everyday life, and you'll learn the basic premise beneath every successful negotiation.

The Meaning of It All

Negotiating is something you do naturally. But have you been doing it as effectively as you could? Probably not. That's because you've likely never really paid attention to the process—it seems to come as naturally as breathing. So you never took the time to hone your skills at it.

But all that's about to change! And your first step in making that change is to get a clear idea of just what negotiating is all about.

Negotiable Terms

To **negotiate** is to arrange for or bring about some desired outcome through reaching an agreement with another party, through discussion and sometimes compromise.

Simply put, *negotiating* is a way (often the *only* way) to get what you want. It's a way to deal with people and to increase your skills in human understanding and interaction. Negotiation is not the same as *manipulation*, in which you use unfair or under-handed means to reach your goals. Negotiation encourages a cooperative relationship, in which both sides want to reach an agreement.

A Born Dealmaker

You began your negotiating career the moment you were born and let out your first wail, even though you weren't consciously aware of it. Crying was your way of seeking food, attention, or affection. More often than not, you probably succeeded in getting what you wanted.

Gaining in Years, Gaining in Effectiveness

As you got older, your methods of negotiation became more sophisticated—and the results grew more satisfying. When you were a child, you persuaded your family to buy you toys and give you an allowance. As a teenager, you coaxed privileges from parents and teachers. You also learned how to balance your personality and interests with those of your friends. During all these experiences, you were trying to get your own way. You were *negotiating*. Successful negotiating simply means knowing how to motivate people to give you what you want.

Negotiating Through Adulthood

As an adult, your negotiations are even more serious. Are you thinking of renting an apartment or buying a home? Are you in the market for a car? Do you dream of starting your own business, or would you love to bring home a little more bacon by winning a raise or promotion? The stakes may be higher, but you're still trying to get what you want. You're still negotiating.

At every stage of your life, the importance of good negotiating skills is clear: If you know how to negotiate, you'll enjoy greater success, smoother relationships, and a happier life. You're already a negotiator—and will be one for the rest of your life—so why not perfect your negotiating skills? If you do, you'll reap enormous benefits.

A Mark, a Yen, a Buck, or a Pound

Some of the best benefits of successful negotiation are those that show up in your paycheck or in your wallet. Once you master the art of wheeling and dealing, you'll discover plenty of opportunities to increase your cash flow—whether by boosting your salary or whittling down the price tags on major purchases.

Talking Points

"If you would be wealthy, think of saving as well as getting."
—Benjamin Franklin

Raking It In

If you've ever tried to muster up the courage to confront your boss about a raise or promotion, you know how nerve-wracking it can be—and today's streamlined corporate climate doesn't make it any easier. Any kind of discussion about your worth can lead to a knotted stomach, a dry throat, and trembling fingers. But once you learn the right approach (which is covered in Chapter 26, "Becoming a Savvy Consumer"), you can handle the discussion coolly and confidently—and that in itself will boost your chances of getting a raise or promotion.

Likewise, if you're selling your home, car, or property, you'll command top dollar if you know how to negotiate for it. (You'll learn more about each of these specialized negotiations in Part 7, "Real-Time, Real-World Negotiating.")

Socking It Away

It's simple: Every time you save money, you make money—and the more you save, the more you make.

I once helped a client buy an $80,000 property for $40,000—half the asking price. Several years later, my client sold the property for $140,000. Thanks to some savvy negotiating, my client was able to make a sweet $100,000 profit.

Another way to increase your wealth is by decreasing your expenses. Every time you buy a car, furniture, clothes, property—anything your heart desires—you'll save money if you know how to negotiate. The money you save can add up to hundreds or even thousands of dollars.

Not only will negotiating a lower price make you richer, but it will also give you a wonderful feeling of accomplishment. You'll enjoy your negotiating conquests, your power of persuasion, and your ability to get your way. The victory is especially sweet when you're confronted with difficult situations and the odds are stacked heavily against you.

Dealbreaker

Adolescents are notoriously difficult to negotiate with—they're very good at pushing a parent's emotional buttons. But Chapter 18, "When Principles or Personalities Collide," will give you the insight you need to keep cool, calm, and in control whenever tempers threaten to flare.

The Personal Touch That Means So Much

Almost every day you try to get your way with those closest to you—your family, friends, and coworkers. Your ability to negotiate can make all these relationships easier.

It's a Family Affair

If your family is anything like mine, I'll bet that every day you find yourself trying to coax those closest to you to do what you want—and your family members likely are equally determined to watch out for their own interests. In fact, you probably find yourself negotiating at home as often—if not more often—than you do on the job.

Nearly every facet of family life, from deciding who cooks dinner to choosing the ideal vacation spot, involves negotiation. As you hone your negotiating skills, you'll find these everyday discussions becoming a lot easier to handle.

Children can be especially tough to negotiate with. Say you've got a demanding teenager who begs to use the family car. If you are concerned about your child's safety (not to mention the condition of the car), your first instinct might be to put your foot down and say no. But that will drive a wedge between you and your child and will strain your relationship.

This is where skillful negotiation can mean the difference between a harmonious household and a trip to the set of *Family Feud*. You can easily head off an argument with the knowledge you'll gain from this book.

You Know You Gotta Have Friends

Friendships offer plenty of opportunities for give and take. But what do you do when a friend asks for more than you are willing to give?

Let's say that a close friend stops by and asks to borrow a lot of money. She says she needs it to make some urgent repairs on her house. You're sympathetic, but you've also heard that your friend has borrowed from others and hasn't made an effort to pay them back.

What are your choices here? You can hand the money over to your friend and just hope that you get it back. Or, you can bluntly say no and destroy the friendship for good. But once you've read this book, you'll know how to maintain the friendship *without making the loan*. There is a way to do it—if you're savvy about negotiation.

Workplace Wheeling and Dealing

If you're a salesperson, you know how difficult it can be to impress a potential client—and then close a deal at a profitable price. If you own your own business, you know it's tough to work out terms with your suppliers and customers. But if you're a powerful negotiator, you can work out the best deals for you and your company.

Skillful negotiation can improve even everyday business situations. The next time you're in a committee meeting discussing business strategy, your ideas will be more influential and more powerful if you know the best way to present and defend them. If you need a crucial report on a tight deadline, your coworkers will be more likely to oblige if you know how to negotiate with them. When an important customer yells at your boss because a promised order hasn't come in on time, your smooth maneuvering can save the situation and boost your prestige.

Talking Points

"It is not the shilling I give you that counts, but the warmth that it carries with it from my hand."
—Miguel de Unamuno

The examples in this chapter are just the tip of the iceberg of the challenges you'll face with your family, friends, and coworkers that can be successfully resolved through negotiation. And every time you succeed, your life will be simpler, more profitable, and more enjoyable—I promise.

The Negotiator's Golden Rule

But how do you get to be a master negotiator? Here's a little mind-opening exercise to try: Look into the mirror. What you see, of course, is yourself. Now assume that you're negotiating with that person in the mirror. How do you want that person to treat you?

The Golden Rule, Defined

You're already familiar with the original Golden Rule: Do unto others as you'd have them do unto you. The Golden Rule of Negotiating derives from that age-old bit of wisdom: Treat your opponent the way you want your opponent to treat you. If you do that, it becomes very difficult for your opponent to resist agreeing with your bargaining position, because it's always difficult to resist agreeing with a decent person.

The Gold in the Golden Rule

You'll gain a number of benefits from treating your opponent the way you'd want to be treated:

➤ You'll eliminate much of the bargaining tension present in many negotiations, such as settling disputes.

➤ You'll not provide your opponent any basis for resenting you, thus freeing your opponent to focus on what you're saying and doing. By gaining your opponent's undivided attention, you can be much more effective in the presentation of your position.

➤ You'll eliminate your need to remedy the situation by such means as apologizing. That frees your mind for concentrating on the bargaining issues. Remember that negotiation is, in the final analysis, mind versus mind. Therefore, there is a great premium on you having a clear, unburdened thought process so you can fully and clearly make your best pitch to your opponent.

➤ Your opponent will like you and will thus be much more apt to go along with your bargaining position.

Strength Through Graciousness

When you encounter an opponent who tries to bully you or gain the edge through threats or intimidation, you can usually safely assume that his or her bargaining position is weak. Negotiators with a strong bargaining position have no need to employ such foolish tactics. On the contrary, they have enough common sense and savvy to stay focused on the issues and not venture into the murky waters of threats and intimidation.

Similarly, if you feel tempted to lash out at your opponent during a bargaining session, don't! Even if there's cause, you're wiser to bite your tongue or silently count to 10 until the feeling goes away. If that doesn't work, call for a recess, or even a postponement. (If keeping your temper in check is a problem for you, turn to Chapter 18 for useful tips and techniques.)

The Art of the Deal

When Leonardo da Vinci was working on his painting "The Last Supper," he became angry with a man and lashed out with bitter words and threats. Returning to his canvas, he attempted to work on the face of Jesus but was unable to do so. He was too upset. Finally, he sought out the man and asked for forgiveness. Only then could da Vinci return to his workshop and finish his painting.

If you lash out at your opponent, it will have an adverse effect on you. At some point, you'll sense deep down that you erred. And if you don't make things right, it'll act as a constant, low-grade irritant, like a pebble in your shoe. It'll be an invisible barrier between you and your opponent, making your task of persuading him to give you what you want much more difficult. Deep down, your opponent will resent you and will harbor that resentment throughout the bargaining unless you do something to remedy your ill treatment—and the sooner the better. If that means apologizing, then apologize.

Similarly, if your opponent uses threats and intimidation and you don't respond in kind, it confuses your opponent, making her stop and think about her own improper conduct and giving you an edge. Take that edge and run with it! It may be just the ticket to tip the bargaining scale in your favor.

The Least You Need to Know

➤ You have been negotiating since the moment you were born.

➤ Nearly every facet of your personal and professional life involves negotiation.

➤ Mastering the art of negotiation will help you make more money, perform better on the job, and form better relationships with the people closest to you.

➤ The Golden Rule of Negotiating is simple: Treat your opponent the way you want your opponent to treat you.

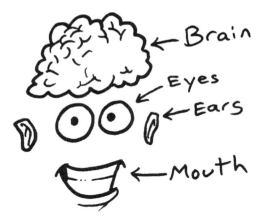

Chapter 2

Bargaining Essentials

In This Chapter

➤ Establishing the essentials

➤ The art of giving

➤ When they're just not listening!

➤ Attitude is everything

Maybe you're tired of getting the short end of the stick in your business and personal life. Maybe you just got burned trying to negotiate buying a new home. Or, maybe you want to ask your boss for a raise, or you're about to buy a new car, or you want a store manager to replace the defective computer for which you just plunked down $1,000 of your hard-earned money.

Most people aren't naturally good at demanding what they want—that's why classes in assertiveness training are so popular. That's also why the thought of negotiating may make you nervous. How can you get what you want without being a bully? What if you're faced with someone who doesn't want to help you? What if your offer is refused?

As in many other stressful situations, such as giving a speech or throwing a party, a large part of successful negotiation depends on careful preparation and a confident attitude. In this chapter, you will learn how to define your position, arm yourself with backup materials, and cloak yourself in confidence.

Prepare Your Position

You wouldn't deliver a speech without thinking about (or writing down) what you plan to say, would you? So why would you want to walk into a negotiation without knowing exactly what you want? It's not enough to think, "It's time I got a raise" or "I'd love to buy that car." Before you settle down to negotiate, you need to define your own position—what you really want, what you're willing to compromise on, and what you can—and *cannot*—afford to lose.

Talking Points

"Chance favors the prepared mind."
—Louis Pasteur

Your Ideal Deal

Say you've decided to ask for a raise. You won't succeed by storming into the boss's office and demanding more money (tempting though that sounds). First, you must determine your *primary base*: your objective; your goal. You have to decide your terms in advance: In this case, that means knowing exactly how much you'd like to see in your next paycheck. If you're currently making $35,000 a year, perhaps you're looking for a raise of $5,000, to bring your salary up to $40,000. That makes your primary base a $5,000 raise.

Let's take another example: You're in the market for a new car. First, you take a realistic look at your budget. After crunching numbers you decide you don't want to spend more than $200 a month for your car payment. That's your primary base.

Negotiable Terms

Your **primary base** is your objective or goal, for each of the important issue or issues that you are trying to negotiate.

Realize that the more realistic and reasonable your goal, the more likely it is that you reach it. But how do you decide what a "reasonable" goal is? You have to do some research before you head into the negotiation. The "Doing Your Homework" section in Chapter 9, "The Paper Chase," talks more about this topic.

To help you start charting your goals, take a look at the "Negotiating Your Goals" worksheet. Many of the issues that frequently crop up in business or personal negotiations are listed here.

Use the worksheet as a guideline to help you decide which issues will affect your negotiation. You can also rank each item numerically in order of its importance to you.

Negotiating Your Goals

Money: This is probably your biggest issue. How much of a raise do you want? How much would you like to sell your house for? How much will you pay an ad agency to develop a campaign for your widget company?

Your terms: _____

Rank:_____

Payment schedule: Determining when and how you pay for something is almost as important as determining how much you pay. Will you get a better deal if you promise cash up front? Or would you like to spread your payments out over a period of months?

Your terms: _____

Rank:_____

Time: Deadlines can be critical, particularly in business negotiations. How soon do you need to move into a new home? How quickly can the agency get your campaign done? If you are working on a deadline, think about how much you are willing to concede in terms of money to get the deal finished on time.

Your terms: _____

Rank:_____

Service: Think of any services you might want after you close the deal if the product you are negotiating for proves defective.

Your terms: _____

Rank:_____

Improvements: What kinds of add-ins will you need in the future? This consideration can be important when you buy high-tech items such as computers that must be constantly updated with new hardware and software.

Your terms: _____

Rank:_____

Returns: If you are negotiating for a product, how easily can you return it if you're not happy with it? What kind of return (replacement, exchange, or refund) will be available? How much of the original price will you expect to have refunded?

Your terms: _____

Rank:_____

Future business or consumer tie-ins: If you close this deal, what kinds of benefits or concessions will you get on future deals?

Your terms: _____

Rank:_____

Volume deals: Will you earn extra negotiating points if you suggest a large deal? If you're the buyer, can you negotiate for a price break on a larger order? If you're the seller, will you consider giving the buyer a better deal for a larger purchase?

Your terms: _____

Rank:_____

Other: Include any other terms that affect your negotiation here.

Your terms: _____

Rank:_____

Negotiable Terms

Alternative goals are compromise positions you're willing to accept if your primary base proves to be unattainable.

Keep in mind that your "ideal deal" may not be the opening offer that you present at the actual negotiation. (I'll talk more about offers in Chapter 19, "Offers and Counteroffers.") Your ideal is simply a yardstick against which you can measure all other offers you receive.

What's Your Alternative?

So you're almost ready to march into your boss's office and ask for a raise. Your clients love you, sales have been soaring since you've come on board, and—most importantly—the company Christmas party you organized last year was a smashing success.

You think you can't lose. But you're caught off-guard when your boss says, "Sure, you deserve a raise. But there's no money in the budget, and there's nothing I can do."

What should you do? Quit in disgust? Throw a tantrum? Mutter, "Maybe next year," and slink away? No way! Well-prepared negotiator that you are, you've decided in advance on some alternative goals you are willing to accept if your ideal deal can't be achieved.

Your alternative goals constitute a fallback position—the deal you are willing to settle for if your original position is turned down. So if the boss says no to a raise, follow up with something else: How about more vacation time? More flexible working hours? An agreement to reopen salary negotiations in six months' time? A marble fountain and crushed-velvet carpeting for your cubicle? (Just kidding.)

The beauty of preparing alternative goals in advance is that by arming yourself with alternatives, you can hear the word "no" and still achieve very good negotiating results. You might even be able to turn a "no" into a "yes" because your boss, when confronted with your alternatives, may decide it's easier to just give you your raise.

Look back over the worksheet of negotiables that you filled out earlier. Now use the "Terms and Alternatives Worksheet" to help you figure out the alternatives for each of the issues that you'll be negotiating.

Terms and Alternatives Worksheet

Ideal Terms	Possible Alternatives
_____	_____
_____	_____
_____	_____
_____	_____
_____	_____

Setting Your *True* Negotiating Goal

A lot has been written about whether a negotiator should set out to win the negotiation. Many advocate that you strive for what is often called a "win-win" situation, where both sides feel good about the outcome and, in essence, feel as if they prevailed. Is that realistic? Remember, in virtually every negotiation, both sides are seeking a basic objective—and their objectives may not be mutually compatible.

Dealmaker

Always set out to win a negotiation. Have definite objectives and work to accomplish them. If you can make your opponent feel good about the deal in the process, that's great—but it *isn't* your primary goal.

For example, say you have your eye on a used car but feel the maximum you're willing to pay is $5,000. Anything higher than that will stretch your resources and leave you financially vulnerable if you run into troubled waters. The seller, however, wants $7,000 to pay for his kids' college costs and pay off some pressing debts. If you settle for $6,000, neither you nor the seller accomplished your objective. You had to fork over $1,000 more than you intended, and the seller got $1,000 less than he needed. So, certainly the compromise wasn't a "win-win;" it was a "lose-lose."

If, on the other hand, you get the car for $5,000, you've accomplished your negotiating objective. Is the seller going to feel happy about the outcome? Probably not. He wanted $7,000 but got $2,000 less. Should you be concerned about the seller's unhappiness? Would the seller lose any sleep if you paid $7,000 for the car, $2,000 more than you intended? Again, probably not. In fact, the seller would undoubtedly sleep well that night knowing he accomplished his objective of getting you to fork over $7,000 for the car.

Set Out to Win

Your goal should be to win every negotiation. Obviously, you're not going to always do that. No one bats 1000. But with that as your goal, your chances of reaching it are far better than bargaining with no goal or with a negative attitude that you can't reach your goal.

If you can attain your negotiating objective and still make your opponent feel good about the outcome, that's fine and very admirable. But that's not part of your negotiating agenda. Focus on what you intend to get. It's like a game of chess: One side has to win. A tie, someone once said, is like kissing your sister or brother. The loser in a chess game may not like losing, but the winner can't let that dominate his game plan. His plan is to checkmate his opponent's king—to win. So should yours be when you negotiate.

Compromises Can Be Costly

To see how a failure to keep your eye on "winning" can be costly, consider this scenario. You've always had the urge to start your own business. You need about 1,500 square feet of retail space, and after diligently checking out what's available, you've settled on a site that you feel fits your new business to a "T." You (or your accountant) prepare a projected profit and loss statement and come to the inescapable conclusion that the most you can pay for the site is $10 a square foot.

The only problem is that the landlord wants $12 a square foot. If you accept the $12, or even compromise for $11 a square foot, that means you failed to accomplish your negotiating objective and that you clearly did not win the negotiation. On a more practical level, it also means that you must re-adjust your projected profit and loss statement to compensate for paying the additional $1 or $2 a square foot increase over the $10 you were willing to pay. The result could seriously hurt your new business: Most business start-ups need every penny they can muster, so that $1 or $2 per square foot you have to pay over your $10 per square foot goal can be a killer.

Setting a Goal Makes You a Better Negotiator

One of the benefits of setting negotiating goals is that you try harder to accomplish them. It's always easier to organize your energies and skills when you have a clear goal in mind—and it's easier to stay motivated, too. With clearly defined goals, you'll find yourself becoming a better and better negotiator.

The Art of the Deal

Imagine a football game with no goal lines, just an endless field on which both teams move back and forth. It won't be long before the teams lose their incentive. But put those goal lines in, and the picture changes dramatically. Come hell or high water, the teams are going to do everything within their power to reach that goal line. That's what drives them forward and makes them better players.

Dealing Yourself an Ace in the Hold

Before you negotiate, you should also consider the options you have if you cannot reach an agreement. These options make up your *BATNA—your Best Alternative to a Negotiated Agreement*. Developing a BATNA in advance of the negotiation will keep you from accepting poor terms—or turning down terms that you ought to accept.

In the case of asking for a raise, for example, you might say to yourself, "If my boss turns me down, I'll continue working at my job, but I'll approach Company Y and see if that manager position is still open." At this point, approaching Company Y is your BATNA.

You can always improve your BATNA before you even head into negotiations. Say you interview for the Company Y job *before* you negotiate for your raise. Let's say that Company Y is very impressed with you and makes you a handsome job offer.

That job offer now becomes your new BATNA. You can use it as a yardstick to measure any raise that your current boss offers you. Is your current boss offering you a better deal than Company Y? Or are you undervalued at your present company? That's how BATNA works—as a yardstick to measure any proposal.

Getting onto Second(ary) Bases

Once you've determined what you want, what you're willing to settle for, and what you can and cannot afford to lose, you must consider any and all forces that will work in your favor. Any factors that bolster your primary base are called your *secondary bases*.

Let's talk in terms of that car-buying example we used back at the beginning of this chapter. Your primary base was to spend no more than $200 a month for your car payment. Your secondary bases might be the following:

1. the car salesperson will be working on commission and anxious to make a deal with you, and

2. several other dealerships in the area are all offering special sales and deals.

In other words, it's a buyer's market, and that gives you the negotiating edge.

Negotiable Terms

Your **secondary bases** are any factors or considerations that will strengthen your case for achieving your primary base.

Knowledge Is Power

You may never have to state your secondary bases explicitly once you sit down to the bargaining table. But you should keep them in mind as you negotiate—they will boost your confidence and prevent you from settling for an unsatisfactory deal. Effectively using your secondary bases during the bargaining will get you your primary base.

Strategic Alliances

In most of the everyday negotiations discussed in this book, you can successfully and confidently represent yourself. But certain negotiations, such as buying or selling a home, or negotiating a labor issue, carry important financial or legal ramifications and therefore require professional help. In those cases, you might consider hiring one of the following:

➤ *Lawyer.* A lawyer is an individual who is knowledgeable about the law and licensed to assist people with their legal needs. Some lawyers have general practices and deal with a variety of legal issues; others limit their practices to particular areas (real-estate law, personal injury law, divorce law, and so on).

➤ *Broker or agent.* You may use a broker or agent when you buy or sell a home or real estate (see Part 7, "Real-Time, Real-World Negotiating").

➤ *Mediator.* If you can't reach an agreement with your opponent, you might call in a mediator. See Chapter 20, "Closing with Class," for more information about mediators.

➤ *Arbitrator.* An arbitrator is another party who can settle a dispute. See Chapter 20 for more information about arbitrators.

Dealbreaker

Watch your attitude! Going into a negotiation with the conviction that you're bound to fail is likely to become a self-fulfilling prophecy.

Be aware that the responsibilities and definitions of lawyers, brokers, agents, mediators, and arbitrators differ from state to state. If you consider hiring one of these experts, be sure to consult your local attorney or bar association to find out the rules and regulations in your state.

Psyching Up

So now you know your terms and you're loaded down with files and documents that bolster your case. There's one last crucial piece of ammunition that you need: confidence.

Before you can be successful in any negotiation, you must *believe* that you can be successful. Once you've settled your position, review the issue from all angles until you're fully convinced of the merits of your case. Your conviction and enthusiasm will be obvious when you negotiate.

One of the best ways to develop a positive mental attitude is to practice it every day, in everything you do. You can't expect to radiate optimism and competence during negotiation if you walk around feeling pessimistic and hopeless about everything else that happens in your life.

So try to maintain a positive mental attitude on small matters as well as large. (Not only will you be a better negotiator, but you'll be more fun to be around!) Believe that you can change a tire, win a game of tennis, bake a mouth-watering loaf of bread, snatch the last available seat on the subway, and conquer whatever challenges you face. That belief will foster the positive attitude that will help you win virtually any negotiation, large or small, simple or complex.

The Least You Need to Know

➤ Define your goals and alternative goals before you enter into any negotiation.

➤ If you accomplish your objective or goal and your opponent feels good about it, that's fine. But making your opponent feel good about the outcome is not your objective.

➤ Use your BATNA—Best Alternative to a Negotiated Agreement—as a guideline to evaluate all proposals and agreements.

➤ Don't hesitate to recruit professional allies (legal, financial, and the like) if your negotiations require such specialized skills.

➤ A positive mental attitude will boost your powers of persuasion and make you a better negotiator.

Scoping Out the Other Side

There's you, with your goals. And there's the other guy, who can give you what you want or refuse. In every negotiation, there's "the other side"—whether that's your boss, a store owner, a realtor, a friend, or a member of your family. Obviously, if you want to prevail in negotiating, it's not enough to know what *you* want: You've got to consider the other half of the dealmaking equation as well. That's what this chapter is all about. Here, you'll learn how to understand and predict your opponent's moves—before you reach the negotiating table.

A Rose by Any Other Name

Obviously, in many negotiating situations, the person you're dealing with will be a friend, colleague, or family member—someone whom you like and whose company you enjoy. But in the process of a negotiation, that person is on the opposing side from you. We've got to call him—or her—something, so the term "opponent" here is used to distinguish between the opposing sides in any negotiation. It is not meant to suggest that you have an antagonistic relationship with the person you negotiate with.

First Things First!

Before you begin negotiating, you need to figure out who to negotiate with. Who has the authority to make all final decisions involving the negotiation? That's the person who can say "yes" to you. In fact, let's call that person the "yes" person. If you don't deal with the "yes" person, negotiation will be difficult (or even impossible) for a number of reasons:

➤ You won't be displaying your finely honed negotiating skills to the person who most needs to see them.

➤ You won't be able to observe and influence the "yes" person during the hottest point of the negotiations. The "yes" person will be safely insulated from any argument or debate that arises.

➤ Your position might not be correctly relayed to the "yes" person.

Take Me to Your Leader

It's usually fairly easy to identify the "yes" person. If you're interested in buying something (a house, a car, a tea set), you can safely assume that the owner of the item is the "yes" person. If you're negotiating with a small business, you will generally negotiate with the store manager or company owner.

In some situations (for example, if you're dealing with a large corporation with a complex hierarchy), the "yes" person might not be immediately obvious. If you're in doubt, ask who has the authority to resolve the matter. Then arrange to meet with that person.

Negotiable Terms

The **"yes" person** in any negotiation is the person who has the authority to resolve the issue you are trying to negotiate.

On occasion, the "yes" person might not be a decisive individual, but one who prefers to think matters over or consult with others. Don't object to that. You don't want to push too hard and risk turning the "yes" person off.

On other occasions, you might bargain with someone who is not the "yes" person but who still acts decisively, as if he can agree to a deal. If that person is an agent of the "yes" person and is acting within the scope of his authority, then don't hesitate to close the deal. When you do, however, you run some risk because the person you are dealing with may *not* have the authority to bind the "yes" person to a deal.

In the final analysis, try to bargain with the "yes" person whenever possible. It's the surest way to get results.

When Three's a Crowd

As you plan your negotiating strategy, always direct your argument to the "yes" person—even if there will be other people present, and even if the "yes" person is not present. You want to be tactful and subtle when you do this because you want to treat everyone with whom you bargain with respect and courtesy. The "yes" person's colleagues will undoubtedly tell her about your behavior and advise her whether or not to deal with you.

Say you bought a new boat, which started to sink every time you tried to sail. Each time, the dealer sent a repair person to fix your boat's problems. But when the engine finally spluttered out and almost moored you on the high seas, you decided to ask for your money back.

Dealmaker

Lawyers are not obligated to have their clients present during negotiations—which means you don't get to deal directly with the "yes" person. Ask if the lawyer will bring her client to the bargaining table anyway. An inexperienced lawyer might agree, which gives you an excellent chance to influence the "yes" person directly.

The dealer's employees tell you they don't want to give you a refund—instead, they offer to continue to repair the defects or to get you another boat. You advise the employees that you want to deal with the owner of the dealership—the "yes" person. He is the one who has the most to gain or lose if you are a happy or dissatisfied customer.

The Art of the Deal

When, no matter what I've tried, I still find that I must negotiate with someone other than the "yes" person, I don't despair. I just make especially sure to keep my speech short and simple. I know that my opponent will have to pass along everything I say to the true "yes" person, and if I make a complicated argument, it is likely to get garbled in the transmission.

The owner avoids you (not surprising, considering the quality of his product), and you find that you must instead continue to talk to his employees. You should still direct the brunt of what you're saying toward the owner. Mention how much you would like to continue to do business with the owner, or any other legitimate issue that will influence the owner directly. This is the way to ensure smooth negotiating sailing. (Sorry about the pun—I couldn't help myself!)

Researching Your Opponent

The more you can learn about your opponent before you negotiate, the more effective and successful you'll be at the bargaining table. Depending on the type of negotiating you'll be doing, you should check out some of the following sources of information:

➤ *Ask others in the business.* Most people know a lot about their colleagues and competitors. For example, if you're about to negotiate with a mechanic who botched your car repair, you could ask other mechanics for more information on what kind of repair needed to be done, how your mechanic operates, and so on. Business people routinely do this type of checking.

➤ *Check with your local library.* This is a fertile source of information. You can check *Who's Who* directories, business listings, and the *Encyclopedia of Associations* (see next point) for information. Ask your librarian for help as well.

➤ *Log onto the Internet.* The World Wide Web is a rich resource of information on just about everything—and every business—you can imagine. From looking up comparative product pricing to checking out a company's financial standing, odds are you can find most of the information you'll need with a few well-chosen searches on the Internet.

➤ *Check with associations.* The *Encyclopedia of Associations* will give you a listing of all the trade associations to which your opponent may belong (for example, the Bar Association, real estate associations, medical associations, and more). Many trade organizations provide biographies and directories of their members. These materials can be a good source of information.

➤ *Check with a stockbroker.* If you are involved in a business negotiation, a stockbroker can get you a wealth of information (annual reports, changes in executive personnel, and so on) on any company whose stock is publicly traded.

Your goal is to learn as much about your opponent as you can *before* you begin negotiating. That will give you a much greater chance of finding common ground, developing rapport, and influencing your opponent to agree to a deal. Let's say you're being wooed by a company for a sales position. You've researched the company thoroughly by scouring its annual reports, reading industry newsletters, and talking to friends in the business. You find that the company is getting trounced by its chief competitor and that earnings have decreased over the last three years.

Now when you sit down to discuss the position, you've got the upper hand. You know that even though your new job will be difficult (and possibly short-lived, if the company's finances don't improve), you can bargain for a better salary and benefits package because the company badly needs your services.

Making Your Opponent Happy

In the previous chapter, you learned that you should always strive for a "win" in negotiations. That's your primary goal. But you can maximize your chances for a win if you try to figure out what your opponent's goals and motivators are. (Anything that influences someone to act is a *motivator*.) If you can find something in your proposal that is attractive or beneficial to the person you're negotiating with, you'll have a much better chance of conducting a successful negotiation.

For example, most salespeople work on a straight commission (the money they earn is based on the sales they make rather than a fixed salary or hourly wage). If you're in the market to buy something, you can aim for a bargain while the salesperson aims to make a sale and thus earn his commission. Remember, your opponent wants to feel good about any agreement reached with you, so always point out any benefits that your proposal offers to your opponent.

Or, let's say you're eyeing a new home and the broker reveals that the seller is anxious to make a quick sale because she's transferring to a new job. Now you can assume that the seller will accept any reasonable offer you make. The seller thus gets a quick sale and can transfer to the new job with one less worry.

Negotiable Terms

A **motivator** is anything that influences your opponent—or you, for that matter—to act.

The following worksheet helps you identify the goals of both parties. For every one of your goals, think of what your opponent will want. Then brainstorm a compromise that lets you both get what you want.

Your Goals	Your Opponent's Goals	Terms That Satisfy Both Sides
_____	_____	_____
_____	_____	_____
_____	_____	_____

Dealmaker

When it comes to selling a home, brokers are prone to giving away information about the seller because they want to make the sale. If you are negotiating with a broker, find out as much as you can about the seller's situation. If a broker is representing you, be careful not to give him information that you don't want a potential buyer to hear.

What If You Both Can't Win?

Unfortunately, in certain negotiations there's just no way for parties to walk away from the bargaining table feeling good about the outcome. This is especially true for negotiations that involve settling disputes. In fact, a majority of court cases that involve disputes stem from negotiations that could not be settled at the bargaining table.

What's your approach when it's obvious that your opponent is not going to feel good about the outcome? Think back to Chapter 2, "Bargaining Essentials," and your answer will be clear: You strive to accomplish your negotiating objectives. Don't cave in on your bargaining goals just to make your opponent feel good about the outcome. That may seem harsh, but it's not: Your opponent has the same goal—to accomplish her bargaining objectives.

Becoming the Equalizer

Once you've established your opponent's motives, you'll be able to predict how he will act at the bargaining table. When you know in advance what arguments he will raise, you'll be able to answer each one of them.

Negotiable Terms

Equalization is answering your opponent's position. This can be done by raising counterarguments or by offering a consideration (financial or otherwise) that addresses or offsets your opponent's concerns.

Equalization is the ability to answer your opponent's positions or arguments with equally compelling positions of your own. Equalization is absolutely essential. If your opponent raises an issue that you can't equalize, his argument will remain hanging in the air with no response. Then you'll never convince him to meet your terms.

One way you can anticipate and understand your opponent's moves is to think about what *you* will do at the bargaining table. Whatever arguments you plan to use, assume that he will be thinking along the same lines—only from the opposite side.

For example, say you're preparing to buy a new home. The one you're interested in is in a great location and has a lot of potential, but there are also quite a few flaws with the place. The sellers, Joe and Jane Jones, are asking for a lot more money than you are willing to pay. You want the place, but at a better price.

One of your strategies is to point out the defects in the property—the leaky roof, the old siding, the cracks in the driveway, the ancient wheezing furnace. Then you think: How will the Joneses counteract my arguments? They'll probably point out all the pluses of their house and possibly will soft-pedal the defects.

Four Ways to Equalize Your Opponent's Position

Here are four good ways you can equalize your opponent's positions:

➤ *Show that your opponent's position is not well-founded.* Let's say that you think the Joneses will point out the house's virtues—the new avocado living-room carpet, the lush lawn, and the large backyard shed. If you can prove that these wonders do not offset the costs of necessary repairs to the roof, the siding, the driveway, and the furnace, then you've equalized their position.

➤ *Distinguish your opponent's position.* Let's say you're pretty sure the Joneses will claim that the price they are asking is in line with the prices for similar houses in the neighborhood. You can check around and learn that the other homes are substantially newer and better-maintained. That information would prepare you to distinguish the Joneses' older, less well-maintained home from the others.

➤ *Advance your own position, which is equal to or greater than your opponent's position.* You did this when you asserted that the repair work you will have to put into the house (fix the roof, the siding, the driveway, and the furnace) more than equals the worth of the work the Joneses have already done.

➤ *Show that your opponent's position is not relevant or material.* The Joneses tell you that they have a close friend who thinks their asking price is actually too low. Unless their friend is in the real estate business, though, her opinion isn't really relevant to your negotiation. You can point that out to equalize the Joneses' position.

Equalization in Action

To give you an example of a well-prepared negotiation strategy, say you must complete a report for your boss by early next week. You need some figures from Monica, a colleague of yours in the marketing department. But Monica says she's swamped and won't have time to run the numbers until next Thursday, at the earliest. What can you do?

You have to equalize Monica's assertion that she's "swamped." You can do this in a variety of ways:

➤ By showing her that the information you need won't take a lot of time to prepare

➤ By offering to help her with preparing the information you need

➤ By offering to take some other project or chore off her hands so that she's got some free time

➤ By advancing your own position by emphasizing how important this project is to your boss and how much credit both you and Monica will reap if the project is well-received

Any of these suggestions should be enough to equalize Monica's position. And all of them can have the added benefit of making Monica more open to helping you out in the future.

Your Equalization Worksheet

It's always best to go into negotiations well prepared and with a clear idea of any obstacles that may stand in the way of securing your goals. Fill in the "Argument and Counterargument Worksheet" as you prepare for your negotiation. By preparing some key points in advance, you'll be much more eloquent—and persuasive—when you reach the actual negotiation.

Argument and Counterargument Worksheet

Your Argument	Your Opponent's Argument	Your Counter Argument
_____	_____	_____
_____	_____	_____
_____	_____	_____

The Least You Need to Know

➤ Before you begin negotiating, you must identify the "yes" person—the person who has the power to give you what you want.

➤ All your arguments should be targeted toward the "yes" person, whether or not that person will actually be present during the negotiation.

➤ Find out as much information as you can about your opponent before you reach the bargaining table.

➤ You will have the best chance of succeeding if you can meet at least some of your opponent's goals.

➤ As you prepare for negotiation, examine your moves to discover your opponent's countermoves.

➤ You must equalize every position your opponent advances, even if you consider a position ridiculous.

Chapter 4

On Your Mark . . . , Get Set . . . , Negotiate!

In This Chapter

➤ Setting up for the big deal

➤ Appearances count!

➤ Coping with surprises

➤ Opening gambits

➤ Salvaging a negotiation gone sour

I once had a client who liked to swing all his big business deals in his office conference room during his lunch hour. His negotiations were sumptuous affairs, with catering provided by a swank nearby hotel. His opponents were dazzled by the colorful trays of food laid out on the conference room table. They feasted on platefuls of food, while he only nibbled.

My client wasn't just being a generous, hospitable guy. Controlling the place and time of his meetings was one way that he secured his hold over the negotiations. Lulling his opponents with rich food (thus dulling their minds from overeating)—while he himself did not indulge—was another way he maintained his mental edge.

In this chapter, you learn how to arrange and open negotiations so that you gain—and maintain—the negotiating edge.

Dealbreaker

Your smooth, logical, carefully prepared presentation can be demolished if you're stuck making it amid constant interruptions in your opponent's office. Even if he's fundamentally receptive to your position, he won't have the freedom to concentrate and could well end up refusing you.

Setting the Stage

Once you've worked through the previous chapters and planned your arguments and counterarguments, you're ready to begin negotiating. All you need to do is arrange a meeting. But wait! There are subtle nuances of time and place that can work for you—or against you—before you even open your mouth to begin negotiating. Read on.

The Home-Team Advantage

Ask any sports team where they'd prefer to play the big game, and without exception they'll say on their home field. That's the place where they are most comfortable and where they won't have to deal with unfamiliar territory. That's also where their opponents are the most uncomfortable.

That's where you want to play the negotiating game—on your *home field*. Your home field is any place that you are familiar with and where you feel completely comfortable. Depending on the negotiation, you might use your office, home, car, or even a restaurant or club that you visit regularly as your home field.

Why is negotiating on home base so important? When you negotiate on your home field, your concentration won't be broken by trying to adjust to unfamiliar (and possibly uncomfortable) surroundings—but your opponent's will. That gives you the edge.

Neutralizing the Negative

If you are not in a position to select your home field, the next best place is a neutral place. Here, at least, you'll be on an equal footing with your opponent because you both will be unfamiliar with the selected spot. Some neutral places include a conference room, or a restaurant or coffee shop that neither you nor your opponent regularly frequent. Any place that's not home field for either you or your opponent is a neutral place.

The last place you want to negotiate? You guessed it: Avoid your opponent's home field like the plague.

In some negotiations, this is easier said than done. When you buy a new car, for example, your early negotiations will take place at the dealer's showroom, which is your opponent's home field. That's unavoidable. However, you can take some action to help neutralize the situation.

For instance, don't go into the salesperson's office to discuss the deal. Try to avoid the showroom, too—it's still pretty much the territory of the salesperson. If it's a nice day, walk outside and discuss the deal there. Now you're luring the salesperson away from his usual home turf—his office, where he's completely comfortable.

Stuck Behind Enemy Lines . . .

On occasion you'll get trapped into negotiating on your opponent's home field. Your boss, for example, might collar you in the hallway and ask you to come back to her office to discuss an important project she wants you to take on (one that you have no extra time for). What do you do then?

➤ Try to move the negotiation to your home field. You might suggest that your office would be more comfortable, or that you have to return there anyway to get some relevant papers or materials from your desk.

➤ If you can't get away from your opponent's home field, you can still shift the dynamic of the negotiation. Try to assert yourself by standing up or moving around. This will put your boss a little off balance and give you a little more control.

➤ Don't be the first person to speak. Let your opponent open the negotiation so that you have an extra chance to understand what her position is and what your own approach should be.

Dealmaker

If at all possible, try to lure your boss into your office. Not only will you be on home turf, but your massive files and humming computer will prove your productivity. If that isn't possible, try for a neutral conference room or nearby restaurant.

Timing Is Everything

The importance of selecting a good place to have your negotiation may be obvious—but that's not the only factor you should keep in mind as you make your plans. It's important that you negotiate when you are at your mental and physical peak. Whenever possible, choose the time that works best with your own personal makeup.

Each of us has a metabolism that, together with our personal traits and habits, governs our actions. If you're a late riser and don't get rolling until after lunch, try to do all your negotiating later in the day. On the other hand, if you're alert the moment you open your eyes in the morning, do your negotiating then.

Remember my client who lulled his opponents into a stupor with food? Eating a heavy meal will dull your mind and slow your responses. Eat lightly before you negotiate— just enough to keep you mentally alert, no more. Also avoid alcoholic beverages. If you overindulge before a negotiation, you're penalizing yourself and giving the mental edge to your opponent.

Finessing the First Impression

If you had a serious problem and you walked into a lawyer's office to get some help, you'd be shocked if the lawyer wore rumpled, smelly clothes and badly needed a haircut. In negotiation, as in almost everything else, you will be judged by how you look, and the first impression you create is the most lasting one. If you look competent and professional, your opponent is more likely to believe that you are.

But don't go too far overboard worrying about what you wear. Any number of books and articles have been written about how to "power-dress" when you negotiate. Some, for example, recommend that you wear red (a "power" color) when you go in to ask your boss for a raise. Dress to look competent and professional—so that you make a good impression. But don't be lulled into thinking that what you wear will be the deciding factor in your negotiation.

Your objective is to get your opponent to focus on what you're saying and doing, not on what you're wearing. The key is to be natural. Wear clothes that you are comfortable in. Wear conservative colors such as browns, blues, and grays, and avoid flashy styles and clunky accessories. They'll focus your attention on what you're wearing, not on what you're saying or doing.

How you dress has one other important impact: It affects not only how well your opponent hears your argument, but also how your opponent sees you as a person. If you dress in expensive Armani, for example, your opponent will see you as a person with deep pockets, not the image you want to project if you are hunting for a bargain. Make sure your clothing projects an image appropriate to your negotiation.

The Art of the Deal

What if someone approaches you with a negotiation and you simply aren't ready? If you're wise, you'll decline—or at least devise some kind of stalling tactic. If you have a more pressing meeting or project on your hands, use this to postpone—otherwise you'll be unprepared to negotiate effectively. Or, you can simply admit, "I really want to discuss this with you, but I haven't had a chance to think about it yet." Then set up a meeting for a later date.

Your Opening Moves

As the saying goes, "You never get a second chance to make a good first impression." How you start a negotiation will have an important—even crucial—impact on its final outcome. A good first impression makes your opponent more receptive to your entire presentation and may take you one step closer to getting what you want. Making the right opening moves sets the tone for the remainder of your negotiating game.

You want to win the respect of your opponent as early as possible—and that won't happen if you're flustered, haggard, or unforgivably late. Make sure you've got precise instructions as to where and when the meeting will happen, and then make a point to get there early.

Never start a negotiation until you are comfortably settled. Stash your coat, purse, and any other items you won't need during the negotiation. Take a minute to flip through your materials, if you have any, and make sure everything is in order. Review any notes you've made that you think you might use during the bargaining.

Even if you can't function without coffee (I know the feeling), you should set aside any cups before you sit down. You don't want a container to shield you from your opponent just at the point when you want to make an impression. Get a refill only after the discussions have started and after you've already made your first impression.

Setting the Mood

When you meet your opponent for the first time, do so with a warm, genuine smile, even if you're nervous about the upcoming negotiation. A smile says that you are prepared to approach the negotiation on an objective basis, even if it might turn difficult or controversial. Your smile is also a sign of confidence.

Once you've smiled and introduced yourself to your opponent (if he is a new one), you want to find some kind of common ground. This not only helps break the ice, but it also helps to convince your opponent that you are a capable person.

There's another reason for a little preliminary small talk as well: If you rush into business too quickly, before you've had the chance to cultivate a positive negotiating environment, you may end up putting your opponent prematurely on the defensive. Then he'll be resistant to giving you what you want, even if your position is a solid one.

Many people are uneasy making small talk, but it isn't difficult. You can take a variety of

Dealbreaker

Unless you're one of the rare few who are never at a loss for just the right words, don't enter a negotiation planning to just "wing it" during the initial stage. You'll probably end up stammering or flailing around for something to say, which will do nothing for your image.

approaches, and any one will do, as long as you remember one thing: Be genuine. You don't want to appear insincere at this crucial stage, when you're trying to make a good first impression.

Turning Little "Yesses" into the Big One

Think of successful negotiating as a series of steps. Getting your opponent to say "yes" to just about anything should be one of your early objectives. You want to create a bond between the two of you, one based on an agreeable, friendly state of mind. One way to do this is to discuss a common interest, concern, or viewpoint that you and your opponent share.

If you took my advice back in Chapter 3, "Scoping Out the Other Side," and researched your opponent, you should already know a little bit about his work experiences or personal interests. If you're familiar with your opponent's work, for example, you might want to talk about the projects he's handling or the state of the industry. If you've negotiated similar matters before, don't be reluctant to (tactfully) point this out as well. ("I've handled deals with several other store accounts, and they've all been happy with Acme Widgets. I'm sure you and I will work well together too.")

You don't need to restrict yourself to industry issues and interests, either. Other reliable small-talk subjects include these:

➤ Weather. Sure, it's a cliché, but it can form a springboard to many other subjects. ("It's so beautiful outside. Perfect weather for sailing." "Isn't this rain awful? I feel like holing up at home with this great new book I've got.")

➤ Common hobbies, such as camping, gardening, sports, cooking, reading, music, and so on. Stay alert and look for cues as to what hobbies your opponent is interested in.

➤ Travel and places you've both visited.

➤ The trials and tribulations of raising kids (if both you and your opponent have them) or pets (ditto).

Talking Points

"Well begun is half done."
—Aristotle

Do whatever you can to put your opponent in a positive frame of mind before you get into the brunt of your case. If you show up at your local auto dealer to complain about the lemon you've bought, don't launch into a litany of complaints. You might start off by saying instead that you and your family are good customers of the dealership. That flatters your opponent, breaks the ice, and makes the dealer anxious not to alienate you—he could lose many customers if he doesn't treat you right.

If you're talking with your boss about a raise, you can set an upbeat mood by first mentioning your latest office success or an important project you've recently completed. ("Here are the monthly sales figures on the new line of widgets. They've been flying out of the stores.") Now you've got your boss in the proper frame of mind and have paved your way into the next phase—dazzling her with your excellent track record and capping that off with your request for a raise.

> **Dealmaker**
>
> Whenever your opponent raises a valid point, say so. This promotes progress and works to your advantage by making him see that you're approaching the negotiation as a fair, reasonable, and cooperative person.

Taking the Plunge

When you've finished with the small talk, you should explain why you're there. Be concise and polite. Don't say, "The car is a piece of trash." Say, "I'm disappointed in the car I bought here," and then list specifically what's going wrong with it.

You want to start mild so that you can test your opponent's reaction. If your opponent doesn't seem particularly concerned or upset, that's a good sign that he's in a receptive mood.

Negotiating Speed Bumps and Roadblocks

But maybe things don't go so smoothly. Perhaps when you start to state your case, your opponent winces or reacts with disbelief. You should acknowledge his reaction and ask why he's reacting that way. Maybe it has nothing to do with you—he's just having a bad day and his problems are affecting your meeting. If that's the case, ask if he wants to reschedule. Better to postpone negotiations than to deal with an opponent who is in a bad mood at the outset.

But what if *you* are the cause of your opponent's mood? What if he says, "There's nothing wrong with my cars. Maybe if you weren't such a lousy driver you wouldn't have so many problems."

I'll talk more about keeping emotions out of negotiation in Part 5, "Problem Solving." For now, you've got to tactfully convince your opponent that his bad attitude is unjustified. You want to coax him back into a receptive mood, not convince him of the merits of your position.

In the auto dealer's case, no one likes to be confronted with his own poor workmanship or defective products. You might try to clear the air by simply pointing out that the discussion is not pleasant for either of you, that you would like to continue to shop at his dealership, and that you know you both want to work out a "fair and reasonable" solution. The words "fair and reasonable" usually work like magic because everyone wants to believe that they are fair and reasonable people. Make the frequent statement that you are looking for a "fair and reasonable" solution.

By suggesting that you both have the same goals—a desire to be fair, to solve the problem, and to maintain a business relationship—you make it seem as though both of you are on the same side. Usually, this approach will calm your opponent and will also boost your confidence in your negotiating powers.

Once you've established a genial mood and common ground, plunge into the substance of your position. Refer to your documentation, if you've brought any. Be bold!

Talking Points

"One of the best ways to persuade others is with your ears—by listening to them."

—Dean Rusk

What if I'm Rebuffed?

Very few people will turn you away if you open negotiations in a friendly, professional manner. Still, on occasion you may run into an opponent who refuses to deal with you. (For example, a salesperson who says, "Sorry—absolutely no refunds, ever.") What do you do if you are snubbed? Take a deep breath and try the following tips:

➤ Stay pleasant and smile—it's disarming.

➤ Immediately come back with a reasonable response. Say, for example, that it would be in the best interests of both of you to settle the issue in a professional, cordial manner.

➤ Don't get angry. (The problem of anger in negotiation is discussed in Chapter 16, "Don't Get Your Dander Up!")

➤ Even if all else fails, don't quit. Tell your opponent that you'll come back to discuss the issue at a later time. (Set an actual time, if possible.) That gives your opponent time to cool off.

Above all, keep in mind that a rebuff does not have to mean failure. If you leave the scene on a positive note, you can take a little time to review any new information you've gathered during this first negotiation attempt (especially information from your opponent's perspective). This will come in handy when you're planning a new strategy.

The Least You Need to Know

➤ Always try to negotiate on your home field, the place you are most comfortable.

➤ Choose the time of day when you're at your mental peak to negotiate.

➤ Wear comfortable clothes when negotiating, and choose your clothes to suit the situation—your clothing should be understated enough that your opponent can focus on what you're saying, not on what you're wearing.

➤ If you are caught off-guard by a negotiation, reschedule it for a better time.

➤ Try to establish your credibility and discover common ground with your opponent before you launch into your bargaining position.

➤ Open negotiations with confidence. If your opponent seems reluctant to deal with you, suggest that you both have a common interest in resolving the issue.

Part 2
Bargaining Table Techniques

Any art that is worth mastering requires the mastery of a series of techniques. There are cooking techniques, gardening techniques, driving techniques, and even breathing techniques.

The same can be said of negotiating. These negotiating techniques are your means of carrying out your plan of action, no matter what opposition you might be facing. These techniques are designed to motivate your opponent to reach an agreement with you.

When your negotiating arsenal contains a variety of bargaining techniques, you're equipped with many different ways to reach your goal. You can pick and choose the right technique to get the best results. This part takes you through the basic techniques

Chapter 5

Increasing Your Word Power

In This Chapter

➤ The virtues of simplicity

➤ Those amazing adjectives

➤ Learning the language of the opposition

➤ The other side of talking

➤ Boosting your power of communication

I once negotiated the purchase of a large building for which the seller wanted more than a million dollars. I raised the issue of the high costs of replacing the plumbing and electrical wiring. My opponent said the wiring problem was "curable functional obsolescence." Huh? Couldn't he just say that the outdated wiring could be replaced?

Words, wrote Rudyard Kipling, are "the most powerful drug used by mankind." The words you use are the most powerful weapons in your negotiating arsenal. In this chapter, you learn how—and when—to use the right words, and you'll learn the importance of attending to your opponent's words as well.

Keep It Simple

At all stages of negotiation, it's important to speak clearly so there is no danger of misinterpretation. Avoid strange words or general, catch-all phrases that may not convey the message you are trying to send and that often will call for additional explanations. The following table, "Simplifying Your Argument," shows some examples of what I mean.

Simplifying Your Argument

Hard to Understand	Easier to Understand
Execution of documents	Signing the papers
Remuneration	Salary, wages, or any financial benefit
To wit	Namely
Tendering possession	Moving out
Warrants	Promises

Try to avoid words, terms, or phrases that have multiple meanings. If they must be used, be sure to define them early in the negotiation to avoid any later misunderstandings.

Make It Vivid

Here's a true story that clearly illustrates the power of descriptive language. A lawyer represented a boy who had lost both arms in a train accident. When the lawyer made his final argument to the jury, he simply said, "Ladies and gentlemen, I just had lunch with this boy. He eats just like a dog." The lawyer used attention-grabbing language at its finest—every member of the jury could imagine the poor boy at mealtime. Not surprisingly, the jury ruled for the injured boy.

Before you negotiate, think about the most persuasive words and phrases you can use to give your presentation impact. You want your language to get your opponent's attention. Remember that your words are the vehicles that drive thoughts from your mind to your opponent's mind. Would you rather send your thoughts in a Lexus or a car ready for the junk heap?

Talking Points

"To get your ideas across, use small words, big ideas, and short sentences."

—J. H. Patterson

Your goal is to present your argument colorfully—but clearly. Whenever possible, use concrete details to describe a situation rather than a general statement. The more you can bring the matter alive with vivid mental pictures, the more persuasive you will be.

Another way to make your argument more powerful is to avoid catch-all phrases—they're too broad to have any meaningful impact. Don't close a negotiation by saying, "That takes in the whole ball of wax." You'd be better off saying: "So we're in agreement on the sales price, the quantity, the shipping date, and the terms of payment." The table, "Specific Speech," shows some more examples of phrases to avoid.

Specific Speech

Catch-All Phrase	Specific Terms
"We've settled everything." (commonly used when closing a bargaining session)	"We've settled the following points . . . ."
"Financial package." (commonly used in business negotiations and salary discussions)	"We've agreed upon these finances: terms . . . ."
"Settlement package."	"The settlement terms are as follows . . . ."
"Under warranty."	"The warranty for (list specific product) includes (list specific terms of warranty) . . . ."
"Repair job" or "Remodel job."	"The repair (or remodelling) of Item X will include the following: (list specific repairs to be performed) at (list the agreed-upon, itemized, price)."

The Art of the Deal

Two priests were so addicted to smoking that they desperately puffed away on cigarettes even while they prayed. Both developed guilty consciences and decided to ask their superior for permission to smoke. The first asked if it was okay to smoke while he was praying. Permission was denied. The second priest asked if it was okay to pray while he was smoking. His superior found his dedication admirable and immediately granted his request. Both had the same goal, but only the one who used careful language succeeded in achieving it.

Say you're selling your car and you want to emphasize how well it has been maintained. You can say that the car is in very good condition—or you can relate all the tune-ups, oil changes, and washing and waxing you've done. Your detailed description (supported, if possible, with receipts) will make a much greater impact on your opponent.

Speak Your Opponent's Language

There's one exception to the "keep it simple" rule: That's when you're negotiating in a field that relies on its own specialized language, or *jargon*. If you're going to be negotiating a deal that involves technical knowledge—such as a complex real estate deal, the purchase of or service for a computer, or a complicated car repair—you'll need to be familiar with the lingo.

The Case for Clarity Through Jargon

Let's say you just installed some new software on your computer. Suddenly, your PC just up and dies—you don't know why, but it just won't do anything anymore. You need it working again, and fast, so you call the computer company's service representative.

The service rep might do one of several things—it all depends on what caused your machine to give up the ghost. If your hard drive crashed, you'll need a replacement, and that might cost you—big, unless you've got warranty coverage. If, on the other hand, it's a problem with one of your newly installed programs, you might just have to make a few adjustments that the rep can talk you through over the phone.

Negotiable Terms

Jargon is the specialized language of a particular organization, occupation, or group.

But computers are pretty complicated—you're going to get the best and most appropriate service only if you can help the representative figure out what's gone wrong. That's where jargon helps. If you can specify, "My XYZ system has a Pentium processor, 32 megabytes memory, a 3.2 gigabyte hard drive, and a 256 kilobyte internal cache," the rep can quickly discover that it doesn't meet the requirements of one of your new software programs and can tell you how to clear up the problem with a few keystrokes.

If you can't give the rep the info she needs to diagnose the problem, she may say you have to pack it up and send it to the shop, leaving you PC-less for at least a day (not good for those of us who use these machines for our work) and with a potentially high repair bill.

Jargon Makes the Business World Go 'Round

It's not just high-tech industries that rely on jargon. The following table, "A Jargon Sampler," shows some examples of jargon you may encounter in particular negotiating situations.

A Jargon Sampler

Buying a Home	Leasing a Car	Appraising Property
Warranty deed	Closed lease	Appraiser
Lien	Lessor	Fair market value
Escrow	Lessee	Highest and best use
Fixtures	Leasing agreement	Depreciation
Special assessments	Security deposit	Cost approach
Survey approach	Trade-in allowance	Income capitalization
Mortgage	Standards for wear and use	Comparable sales approach
Mortgagor	Wholesale value at end of lease	
Mortgagee		
Title policy		

Boosting Your Bargaining Power

Speaking your opponent's language boosts your negotiating power for a number of reasons:

➤ Your opponent will immediately understand and relate to what you're saying.

➤ Your opponent will be much more likely to be influenced by what you're saying.

➤ Your opponent will recognize you as an equal.

Think about all the ads for car leasing you've seen these days—they're hotbeds of jargon and specialized terminology. If you're in the market to lease a car, the agent might mention a "closed lease." At the outset, you'd want the leasing agent to define the term. (For the record, it means that at the end of the lease you can return the car with no further obligations.)

Or, if you're negotiating a real estate deal, it's important that you understand the difference between a "net lease," a "net, net lease," or even a "net, net, net lease." (Imagine how confusing it must be to use them in conversation—they even look puzzling on paper!)

So make it clear at the outset that when you say "net, net, net lease," you are talking about a lease in which the tenant pays all taxes,

Dealmaker

If your opponent is using language you don't understand, don't hesitate to ask her to repeat or clarify a statement.

insurance, repairs and maintenance, and other charges and expenses of operating and maintaining the property; the rent the property owner receives is free of all those charges and expenses.

Once you know what the term means and are comfortable with it, you can freely use it during the discussions to communicate more effectively with your opponent.

The Sound of Silence

Silence, as Winston Churchill once observed, "enhances one's authority." Don't assume that you have to out-talk your opponent to win at negotiation. You have too much to lose by mouthing off indiscriminately:

➤ You lose the opportunity to think about what you should be saying and when you should be saying it.

➤ You lose the chance to hear your opponent's positions and formulate the best response to them.

➤ You may inadvertently blurt out information that damages your negotiating position.

If you're in doubt as to whether to speak—or what you want to say—the best approach is to remain silent. If you reveal or blurt out information harmful to your position, you've made yourself fair game for your opponent. Keep in mind the wisdom of the old adage: "Even the swiftest horse can't overtake the word, once spoken."

At a Loss—Because of Words

I once represented a widow whose husband's poorly drafted will caused her a great deal of financial confusion. Her tax statements were audited, and the revenue agent who reviewed the case started claiming that she owed a lot of money. I tried to convince him that she didn't, but he wouldn't let up.

After several arduous conversations, he finally blurted out the real reason he was pursuing her so doggedly: She was a "test case." The government sometimes tries these cases to set future tax policy. My client, in other words, was being used as sort of a legal guinea pig. Once I knew that, I figured out how to remove her situation from the "test case" category, and the issue was settled.

Strategic Silences

Use silence strategically after you've made a solid point. This gives your opponent time to fully absorb your meaning and encourages him to draw his own conclusions. Since we're all powerfully influenced by our own conclusions—rather than what someone else tells us to believe—silence is a powerful negotiating tool.

Remain silent after your opponent has made a proposal; your silence suggests disappointment or disapproval. Your opponent may rush in, offering concessions that will sweeten the deal. Whenever an opponent makes a proposal—whether it's a good one or not—always consider giving it the silent treatment.

What if you're a constant chatterbox who finds it difficult to remain silent? If you are uncomfortable with silence (many people are), you can use some easy techniques to keep from mouthing off:

Talking Points

"Even a fool, when he holdeth his peace, is counted wise; and he that shutteth his lips is esteemed a man of understanding."

—Proverbs 17:28

➤ Calm yourself by taking a deep, long breath. Don't speak while you do this.

➤ Gently grit your teeth (don't hurt yourself!). This will provide you with a potent physical reminder to stay silent.

➤ If you have a drink with you, take a long, slow sip. This will physically prevent you from saying anything until you've finished.

During some of your silence, you should, of course, be listening.

The Advantages of Being a Good Listener

When people think about negotiating, they usually think about talking—their *own* talking. But both sides have to inform the other of their bargaining positions. Any skilled negotiator, therefore, will confess that listening is an important part of their negotiating arsenal and that it is often more persuasive than chattering on and on. A good listener gains a number of bargaining edges.

Listening Makes Your Opponent Feel Involved

It's important that your opponent has a full and complete opportunity to express his or her views. If a person doesn't have that opportunity, he's not going to agree with your bargaining position because he'll feel he still has unused ammunition. You must, therefore, fully allow your opponent to make his pitch.

By being a good listener while your opponent is talking, you make him feel like a full participant in the bargaining process and convey that you're sincerely interested in learning what's on his mind. It also warms up your opponent, whereas if you constantly interrupt, he'll feel that you're trying to ram your viewpoints down his throat. By listening, you create a bond that makes your task of persuading your opponent to go along with your position much easier.

Dealbreaker

If there's even the slightest hint that you're listening just to bide your time until you can break in to speak again, you'll have severely damaged your credibility and perhaps even killed your chances of getting your opponent to give you the deal you want.

Listening for Clues

When your opponent is talking and you're listening, your opponent is giving you an excellent opportunity to gain valuable information, especially about the pros and cons of his or her bargaining position. This can be critical because it allows you to come up with good responses and thus equalize your opponent's bargaining position (you learned about equalizing in Chapter 3, "Scoping Out the Other Side").

Some people you'll negotiate with will start talking and get on a roll until they've blurted out all sorts of information useful to your position. Let them ramble on. Store up the useful information they're giving you, and after they've fully expressed themselves, hit them with your side of the case, using those bits of information they gave you that you feel support your own position. Do it tactfully, of course—if you throw it in their faces, they'll resent it and you'll have made your job a lot tougher.

The beauty of this is that when you're a good listener and employ the useful information your own opponent has provided you, it's virtually impossible for your opponent to then contest or question that information. After all, you're supporting your bargaining position on information that they, themselves, have provided.

They'll Fire All Their Ammo

It's critical that you allow your opponent to say everything that's on his mind regarding his bargaining position. If you don't, you really have very little chance of persuading him to go along with *yours*.

But the only way to let your opponent have his say is to be a good listener. Give him your undivided attention. When you do, you're telling him that you're interested in his position and that you will give it due and fair consideration.

Usually what happens is that, once your opponent has fully talked himself out, he'll say something like, "Well, that's the way I see it," or maybe something stronger like, "I think my price is fair." When that occurs, you know you've given your opponent a full and complete opportunity to fire all his ammunition. You've been a good listener, and your opponent will know it.

Now you can begin firing your *own* ammunition, and you're likely to have a very receptive opponent. If he interrupts, let him. If he asks questions, that's okay, too—it's a good sign that he's receptive to what you're saying. And if he tries to counter your argument with something he has already said, you can politely inform him that you're fully aware of that factor and explain why, in your view, your position should prevail.

Listening Buys You Time

While you're listening, devote a part of your thoughts to countering strategies. Certainly, before you began negotiations you thought out your bargaining strategies. But the information you're getting while listening to your opponent may be new and may lead you to alter your original bargaining plan. You can do that while you're listening.

Dealmaker

If your opponent constantly interrupts you during your argument, that's a sign that he or she wants to do some more talking. Put your listening cap back on and let your opponent fire away.

In fact, this is not difficult to do. We all tend to divide our concentration when someone is talking to us. Perhaps we're thinking of a response, formulating a question, or even daydreaming about an entirely different matter. When you're bargaining, you want to keep most of your attention focused on your opponent's information, but use your divided concentration to re-examine your strategies to see if they need any fine-tuning. Just make sure that your main attention is focused on your opponent—you don't want to give the impression that you're not sincere.

The new information you've gathered can give your negotiating momentum and put your opponent on the defensive. That's where you want your opponent to be, because defense doesn't score points. You, on the other hand, will take the offense, and can then score as many points as you need to prevail.

The Art of the Deal

Even in a football game, defense doesn't score. Once the defense recovers a fumble and heads down the field toward the opponent's goal, the defensive player becomes an offensive player. When you're negotiating, always remember: "The best defense is a good offense."

Motivator Madness

Whenever any of us does something, we have a motive—but sometimes that motive isn't obvious. For example, if you shine your shoes, your motive may be to impress your boss or your date, or you might just be satisfying your personal need to be neat. When you take a walk, your motive might be to get some exercise, enjoy the sunshine, or get off by yourself to do some heavy thinking.

Your opponent has motives, too, and by listening to him you can often figure out what those motives are. That puts you in a more secure bargaining position because you can come up with a strategy to satisfy that motive and thus influence your opponent to go along with you.

Here's how it works. Say you're negotiating to buy that dream house, and the seller says she wants to take along that beautiful birdbath in the front yard. What's her motive for wanting the birdbath? You can reasonably assume she's got another house for that birdbath, or plans to give it to someone else as a gift.

Sure enough, when you inquire, you discover that she's finishing up a new home and had the landscaper design a nice spot for the birdbath. Now you know an important motivator: Your opponent is undoubtedly anxious to sell so she can move into her new home, and understandably doesn't want to carry two mortgages at the same time. Knowing her motive for keeping the birdbath has thus greatly improved your bargaining leverage.

The Art of Extrapolation

Say you're thinking of doing some fishing, but you want to be sure you'll catch more than the sun's rays. So you approach a stranger fishing off a dock and ask, "Having any luck?"

The stranger might merely say "Yes." But that's *his* conclusion, not yours. Instead, however, he might respond by saying: "I'm on my third carton of bait, and I've been here only a half hour."

So what do you think about fishing now? Just by considering the facts, *you were able to draw your own conclusion* that the fishing is fine. And you'll be much more strongly influenced in your opinion of that fishing hole because it is the result of drawing your own conclusions. That's called *extrapolation*—using facts to come to a conclusion on your own.

Negotiable Terms

To **extrapolate** is to infer a conclusion from already available information.

Extrapolation is a powerful bargaining tool because we are always more influenced by our own conclusions than anyone else's. If you can state the facts in a way that forces your opponent to draw her own conclusion—the conclusion you want her to reach—you stand a much better chance of winning the negotiation.

Most of the time, when we reach a decision, we act on it. That's what happens when you permit your opponent to reach her own conclusion on what *you* want. Your opponent will quickly act on it.

Extrapolation in Action

Say you want to sell your business. You have a potential buyer who asks, "What kind of profit can this business make?"

You can offer your opinion, or the opinions of other knowledgeable people. But why not let the buyer draw her own conclusion? Why not lead your opponent to extrapolate? Here's what you might say:

"Sales have increased an average of 10 percent over the last three years, and net profits have grown 15 percent over that same period. The company has two new products that are hot sellers and another product in the development stage that looks very promising."

By stating facts about the performance of the business, you allow the buyer to form her own conclusions about the future profit potential—conclusions that are favorable to your cause.

A Final Word on Language

As with anything else, your command of language will increase only with practice, practice, practice. Read a wide variety of books, magazines, and newspapers so that you harvest a wide vocabulary. And work crossword puzzles—they're great vocabulary builders, too. (That way you won't be thrown when someone whispers "curable functional obsolescence" in your ear.)

Practice speaking plainly in all situations. Strive to communicate, not to impress. Learn to stay silent when you have nothing to say. You will be a more valued conversationalist and a ferocious negotiator.

The Least You Need to Know

➤ Use simple language instead of complex terminology.

➤ If your opponent uses terms you don't understand, ask for clarification.

➤ Be as descriptive as possible; avoid generalities.

➤ Learn to remain silent when you aren't sure what to say or when you've made a strong point.

➤ Your opponent's words are important, too—by becoming a good listener, you can gain some significant bargaining advantages.

➤ Use extrapolation to let your opponent draw her own conclusions. This is more likely to motivate your opponent than anything you say.

➤ Cultivate a wide vocabulary at every opportunity.

Chapter 6

Getting Physical

In This Chapter

➤ Body-talking

➤ Reading the language of gestures

➤ "Propping up" your negotiation

When all is said and done, negotiation is really just a specialized form of communication. This means that everything that can be used to communicate can be used in negotiating. Sure, you're aware of the importance of words, but do you realize that even when you're not talking, you're still communicating volumes? A raised eyebrow. A satisfied smile. A clenched jaw. All these, and more, can give away your reaction to your opponent, even if you don't say a word.

In this chapter, you'll learn how to monitor body language—yours and your opponent's—to improve your bargaining position. Then you'll learn about another nonverbal way to bolster your negotiating: by using props.

The $30-Million Poker Face

When James Ling decided to sell a company called Computer Technology, he expected an offer in the range of $60 million to $65 million. He arranged a meeting with interested buyers at Prudential Insurance. He and his associates took their seats across the bargaining table from the Prudential reps. The atmosphere was tense. Then the reps announced Prudential's opening bid: $90 million. The book *Ling*, by Stanley H. Brown (Atheneum, New York, 1972) records Ling's reaction:

"I sat there trying to organize my thoughts, because here I am with an opening bid $30 million higher than I had expected. . . . My face was a complete mask, it showed no expression of any kind. . . . I suggested that (my associates) and I should caucus. . . . I did not smile as we (left the conference room)."

Had Ling or any of his associates smiled, they could have completely blown the deal. A smile would have spoken as loudly as words: "Whoopee! Your offer is much higher than we expected."

Negotiable Terms

Body language is a constellation of gestures, postures, and movements that communicate what a person is thinking or feeling. They may be purposefully performed, or they may be wholly subconscious.

Maximizing Your Movements

Even if you're not negotiating a $90 million takeover deal, your body language is extremely important. You need to learn how to control your body language so that it conveys a message consistent with your negotiating goals, and you need to learn to read your opponent's body language to pick up useful cues to use in your own bargaining process.

The Eyes Have It

The most important gesture to include in your body language repertoire is good eye contact. No other movement conveys your honesty, sincerity, and confidence more accurately. From the minute you meet your opponent to the handshake that seals the deal, you must make and maintain eye contact. Whenever you're making a point, look directly at your opponent. If you look away, you give the impression that you don't believe in what you're saying.

Common Gestures

You can add polish to your negotiating by pairing up key phrases and ideas with a few other common but powerful physical gestures. Here, I've translated five phrases into their body language equivalents. You might want to incorporate some of them into your next negotiation:

➤ "What do you think about this?" To introduce a new idea or suggestion, place your hand out with your palm turned upward.

➤ "I'm passionate about this!" If you really want to convey determination to stick to a point, use a raised fist. This is a powerful gesture, so use it sparingly.

➤ "This is important." Point your index finger to call attention to an important issue.

➤ "Uh-uh." If you want to say "No way" to a suggestion or concession, make a sweeping gesture with your hand, palm facing downward.

➤ "Let's not get into this." To convey a warning or caution, place your hand straight up, palm out, like a traffic cop.

When it comes to your physical gestures, the most important point is to act naturally and appear relaxed. People are quick to sense artificiality, and your opponent will not respond or be influenced by you if she feels she is being "put on."

Your movements, like your words, should fit the subject matter. You don't pound the desk or swing your arms when you're talking about a trivial issue. Exaggerated gestures will create an artificial impression and will also lose their impact when it comes time to use them on a larger issue.

If you're not comfortable with the technique of using your body for emphasis, practice before a mirror. Keep working on your moves until they look smooth, natural, and believable.

Dealmaker

Maintaining good eye contact is so powerful that it can actually make a weak bargaining position appear stronger. Catching and holding your opponent's gaze and adding a sincere smile, can materially increase your chances of success.

The Great Stone Face

When you're negotiating, the gestures you *don't* make can be as telling as those you *do* make (remember James Ling's $30 million poker face). A gasp, a flinch, or a smile can speak volumes about your position—volumes you just may prefer that your opponent *not* be able to read. Remember, your opponent may be reading *your* attitude, *your* facial expressions, and *your* tone of voice just as sharply as you are watching his.

If you find it difficult to control your facial expressions and gestures, here are a few simple techniques you can use to rein yourself in:

➤ Gently grit your teeth (not too hard—it'll hurt and it'll show) to keep your face immovable.

➤ Think of something sad. This is a trick actors use when they need to shed tears during an emotional scene.

➤ Slowly take a deep breath.

➤ Make hard fists or grab the seat of your chair to tense your body and remind yourself to remain impassive. Just make sure your opponent can't see you doing this—she may misinterpret your gestures.

➤ Practice controlling your reactions in everyday life. You will find it easier to do later when you negotiate.

If harsh words are exchanged during the negotiation, don't glower for the remainder of the meeting. Express your displeasure however you have to—then move on. That's a good way to let your opponent know that you're not going to let one bad exchange stifle the entire discussion.

At the other extreme, don't go through the negotiation with a smile fixed rigidly on your face—that's unrealistic. Let your facial expressions flow naturally.

Dealbreaker

You storm into your opponent's place of business, slam your fist on his desk, and bellow: "This $2.75 wdget doesn't work! I demand satisfaction, or I'll sue!" Given the triviality of your claim and the overkill of your body language, don't be surprised if your opponent thinks you've lost a marble or two.

When the negotiating session is over, depart with a friendly, genuine smile and a warm handshake—even if the negotiation has been tough. Don't show displeasure. A warm smile will prove your objectivity and can help smooth your way in later meetings or discussions.

Reading Your Opponent's Body Language

During negotiation, it's just as important to observe what your opponent does as it is to listen to what he says. Fix your attention on your opponent's body language—you can often pick up significant information.

Watch your opponent during discussions. Don't spend your time taking notes—only jot down the terms of agreements you've reached or information you don't want to forget. Don't look at other distractions in the office. Your opponent's facial and body expressions will be sending out all kinds of signals, and you want to be certain you're in a position to catch as many of those signals as possible and make use of them during the negotiation.

Use use the following table, "A Body Language Primer," to translate common gestures into their verbal equivalents. Just keep in mind that this is by no means infallible: people from different cultural backgrounds may use similar gestures to mean very different things.

A Body Language Primer

Body Language	What It Could Mean
Avoiding eye contact	Lack of confidence in bargaining position
Hunched-over posture	Lack of confidence in bargaining position
Touching tips of fingers and thumbs together (commonly called "steepling")	Confidence
Making excessive eye contact	Trying to bully or intimidate
Moving too close to opponent	Trying to bully or intimidate
Shifting eyes	Trying to deceive

Body Language	What It Could Mean
Fiddling with objects, such as hair, pencils, or papers	Lack of confidence
Drumming fingers on desk, tapping pencil	Displeasure at your presence
Crossing and uncrossing legs	Impatient; wants to cut a deal quickly
Keeping legs or arms crossed	Not receptive to your bargaining position

Propping Yourself Up

I once had a client who wanted to entice a well-known celebrity to endorse his business venture. I had an eye-catching mock-up of the proposed business name and logo made, which I kept under wraps during the early bargaining. Then when my instincts told me to go for it, I unveiled the design and set it on the table for my opponent to see. Its impact was immediate. He eyed the replica closely and slowly nodded his approval. After that, we quickly reached an agreement.

Chapter 9, "The Paper Chase," discusses the different kinds of documents that you might want to bring to the bargaining table. Any and all of the materials that you bring along with you—files, reports, pictures, diagrams, slides, artwork, videos, and documents—can be used effectively as props.

Negotiable Terms

Props are any materials, documents, or accessories that help you demonstrate and strengthen your bargaining position.

The Proper Use of Props

You've heard the phrase, "A picture is worth a thousand words." That's certainly true in negotiation. A single photograph or document can make or break your case more effectively than anything you could possibly say. There are many benefits to using props:

➤ *Props legitimize and document your position.* If you're asking for a raise, for example, and one of your key arguments is the phenomenal sales you're responsible for, bring in a sales report and go over it with your boss. Then leave the report with the soaring company profit figures in plain view while you negotiate. Throughout your negotiation, this will serve as a constant, silent testament to your contributions to the company.

➤ *Props dramatize your bargaining position.* That's why lawyers who prosecute murder trials always try to get graphic photographs of the victims and crime scene admitted into evidence. Those pictures convey the viciousness of the crime to the jury more effectively than anything anyone can say. You can get the same result when you use props when you negotiate.

➤ *Props allow you to concentrate on something else.* In the heat of negotiation, you can't keep track of myriad financial figures or complex legalese. Props can communicate and exhibit that information for you. They free you to focus on other aspects of the bargaining.

➤ *Props break your opponent's negotiating momentum.* When you display a prop, your opponent will react immediately. She'll focus on it and will lose concentration on her own position.

Dealmaker

When you've got an exceptionally complex or highly disputed negotiation to handle, well-chosen props can clarify your points more powerfully than any other item in your bargaining arsenal.

Becoming a Visual Aid Virtuoso

Because they wield so much power, props must be used carefully and delicately. Here are a few pointers:

➤ Be intimately familiar with any props you bring. You don't want a prop to backfire. For example, if you're bringing a contract or warranty, read the entire document thoroughly, not just the sections that bolster your side. A skillful opponent might discover a clause or condition lurking in the small print that works against you. Similarly, check all video and audio tapes, brochures, and so on before displaying them at the bargaining table.

➤ If you're unsure about using a prop, put yourself in your opponent's shoes and ask yourself whether the exhibit would have a dramatic, favorable influence on you. If the answer is "Yes," then use it.

➤ Similarly, always have a definite objective when you use props. Be sure your props will boost your bargaining position. If you're not sure, don't use them because their impact on your opponent can be strong.

➤ If you use props, make sure they are top-quality. Your opponent won't take you seriously if your case relies on miscollated photocopies or a fuzzy videotape.

Picking Your Prop Moments

You want to produce your props at that point in the bargaining when they will have the greatest impact and influence on your opponent. The more bargaining experience you gain, the easier it'll be for you to decide the best time to use your exhibits. Until you develop that sense for yourself, however, here are a few warnings to keep in mind:

➤ When your prop is a key part of your bargaining position—like those impressive sales figures—display it throughout the entire negotiation. Refer to it frequently. The prop's presence will reinforce your position, and the longer your opponent looks at it, the more convincing and formidable it becomes.

➤ If your prop is only a small part of your bargaining position, display it for only that part. Then tuck it away out of your opponent's view. You don't want your opponent distracted by your prop once it has served its purpose.

➤ If your prop makes a powerful summation of your overall case, it's sometimes most effective to hold it in reserve until you begin your closing remarks.

In every case, before you begin negotiations, make sure you've taken the time to practice working with your props so that when you do bring them out, you can do so smoothly and comfortably.

When You Negotiate over a Prop

When you are negotiating to buy or sell something—property, a house, or a car, for example—the object itself can serve as a prop.

The Art of the Deal

In negotiating the price of a piece of land, I had a written appraisal—my first prop. At our meeting in my office, I gave my opponent a copy of the document and explained it in detail, page by page. We then left the office and visited the property—my second prop— where I once again listed the highlights of the appraisal. I was able to drive my point home through three separate channels: my words, the appraisal, and the view of the property itself. By using props so powerfully, I convinced my opponent to accept my value of the property.

In some cases, props are the only way to win your case. I once negotiated a controversy over the quality of food that was being created for a proposed large restaurant chain. One side claimed the food was fine—the other side said it simply wasn't good enough. A food expert, who was called in to make taste samplings, concluded that the food was indeed okay. In this case, the food expert was the prop, and taste tests were worth a thousand words.

The Least You Need to Know

➤ Use body language to emphasize your arguments when you negotiate.

➤ Your body language should be relaxed and appropriate.

➤ Control your facial expressions so you don't give any extra information to your opponent.

➤ Watch your opponent for telltale gestures and expressions that may reveal his position.

➤ Use props such as documents or videos to legitimize, dramatize, and emphasize your bargaining position.

➤ Only use props that are professional-looking and that you are entirely familiar with.

➤ If your prop is an important part of your bargaining position, display it throughout the entire negotiation. If not, put it away once you've used it to make your point.

Chapter 7

Timing Is Everything

In This Chapter

➤ The virtues of patience

➤ Critical timing: placing your offer (or counteroffer) on the table

➤ Getting your timing back

➤ Devastating deadlines

➤ Negotiating the timing that works for you

I once spent several heated sessions negotiating with a business competitor. After our third meeting, he promised to call within the week to set up yet another conference. I didn't hear from him for three weeks. When he finally did call, he said he wanted to meet that very day.

In my experience, people who are anxious to meet right away are usually prepared to the hilt and raring to negotiate. All my instincts said, "Stall him!" So I did. I begged off and suggested that we meet the following week. This took the edge off my opponent, bought me a little time to prepare, and put the negotiation back in balance.

Timing has a crucial impact on your negotiating position. Appear too eager, and you may get taken for a ride. Let a negotiation slide, and your opponent may find a better deal elsewhere. While it's impossible to teach a good sense of timing, it does gets better with experience. This chapter shows you how good timing can help you achieve your bargaining objectives.

Perfecting Your Patience

Most cats, when they want to go outside, pick a good spot near the door and patiently wait. When someone happens to open the door, out the cat goes, quickly seizing the opportunity to accomplish its objective. As you can see, cats have an innate sense of good timing.

Too many people, on the other hand, think successful bargaining means meeting, talking, and cutting a deal. But that's the exception, not the rule. Most negotiations—especially those that involve important matters—occur over a period of time, with more than one face-to-face meeting, telephone calls, e-mail, and even some correspondence such as letters. I recently finished a real estate negotiation that required about six meetings and a substantial number of telephone conferences and written correspondence. Patience, therefore, is not a luxury—it's a necessity.

Talking Points

"Patience accomplishes wonders. There is little done in this world worth doing without patience."

—Ida Scott Taylor

Patience in Practice: Going for a Raise

Picture this: You've been doing a great job for your company, and you're thoroughly convinced that you've earned a good raise. You're a little fearful about approaching your boss (most people are), but you know if you don't that it's highly unlikely your boss is going to take the initiative and hand you the additional money (most bosses won't).

A major mistake most employees make is rushing the process. They think one meeting with the boss will do the trick. Actually, the opposite is true. To get the raise you want may take several meetings with your boss. That's how you should plan your negotiating strategy.

The First Meeting

At the first meeting, your goal is to lay your groundwork as to why you're entitled to a raise. Be tactful and positive. Inform your boss of your good performance with the company, your loyalty, and other positive factors that build up your credibility for a raise. Your major goals at this first meeting are listed here:

➤ Lay the foundation for your boss to give you the raise at some point during a bargaining process that may take more than one meeting.

➤ Get some feedback from your boss on your prospects of getting the raise. You'll know if your boss is receptive to the idea both by his words and his attitude. If, for example, he smiles and keeps the conversation light, you're on your way to getting that raise. If he gets a sour look on his face, you've got to go back to the drawing board and rethink your strategy. But don't give up—stay at it! Rome wasn't built in a day, and neither are most raises.

Your boss is probably going to want some time to digest your request, to roll it over in his or her mind, and even to do some thinking about how much of a raise is fair. You want to give him or her a reasonable amount of time for all this thinking.

Holding Back Helps

Notice here that although your primary base for your overall negotiation is to get a raise, it is *not* your goal at this first meeting—not yet.

Your boss may even ask you how much you think your increase should be. That's a trap you try to avoid. (Chapter 19, "Offers and Counteroffers," explains in detail why you should try to get your boss to throw out the first figure on the table.) In a nutshell, here's why you generally don't want to be the first to name a figure:

Dealmaker

In most negotiations, it doesn't matter at what point in the process you reach agreement—all that matters in the end is that you attain your goal. So don't rush things. Let the bargaining proceed gradually, like fruit ripening on the tree.

➤ If you lead out with a figure, that sets your upper limit, and your boss may work from there to decrease that figure.

➤ When your boss leads off with a figure, it sets the lowest amount you can expect, and you can work from there to increase that amount.

There is an exception, however, when you may want to lead out with a figure. This is called the "Vinegar and Honey" technique and is explained in Chapter 10, "Top Negotiating Techniques."

Letting the Story Unfold Naturally

If you approach your boss about a raise and expect to accomplish your objective in only one meeting, you run a great risk of pushing your boss into a decision before he has time to think the matter over. If you persist, your boss may turn you down even though you've earned the raise and even if, deep down, your boss wants to give you more money.

Good negotiating takes time. For one multi-million dollar deal I won, successful negotiations required six meetings. If I had pushed during the earlier meetings to reach an agreement, the deal would have fallen through.

Learning from the Pros

The main reason why skillful negotiators have learned to develop patience is that they've experienced past failures by trying to push things, to bully through a deal when the other side wasn't ready.

Talking Points

"Too great haste leads us to error."

—Moliere

There could be numerous reasons why your opponent is not ready to make the deal. Here are some common ones:

➤ *More information.* Most people want to be sure they have all the information they need to make an intelligent decision and will resist making a deal until they do.

➤ *More time to think the matter over.* This is a common reason why delays occur and why you have to be patient. If you try to push through a deal when your opponent wants more time to think the matter over, it could cost you the deal.

➤ *Consultations with others.* Business people are especially prone to wanting to consult with their lawyer or accountant or associates. Give them that time. If the deal you're proposing is a fair one, the people they consult with will concur, which is to your advantage.

➤ *Intervening factors, such as an illness or death in the family.* Never push for a deal when your opponent is experiencing personal or family problems. It's the quickest and surest way to fail.

Let's take a real-world example to show how a well-paced, patiently conducted negotiation might play out. Say you've had your eye on that dream house, so you decide to take the plunge. It's a large purchase, so you inspect the property and you're tempted to either accept the listing price or make a lower offer right on the spot.

Pros rarely do that. They know that the seller wants to make a deal—that's why the property is listed for sale. They also know the seller's broker wants a deal because the broker is probably working on a straight commission. No sale, no commission. Therefore, a pro will take time to fully assess the situation, considering such factors as these:

➤ How long the property has been on the market. Usually, the longer it's been listed, the more anxious both the seller and broker are to cut a deal.

➤ Other overriding considerations that may influence the seller to accept a lower price. Perhaps the seller has been transferred. Maybe the seller has built a new home and can't afford to carry two mortgages.

➤ High interest rates. Figures alone may make it unlikely there will be much competition to buy the house.

Once a pro has fully analyzed all the relevant factors, he or she will then make an offer that is almost universally lower than the listing price, with a short deadline for acceptance. That puts the pressure on the seller and broker (both fear losing the deal) and increases the odds the offer will be accepted or the seller will come back with a counteroffer that's lower than the listing price.

Patience, Persistence, and Negotiating Success

Being patiently persistent unquestionably results in bargaining success. If you're patient, you'll have to be persistent; if you're persistent, you'll have to develop patience. The two are inseparable.

Dealbreaker

Emotion has no place in negotiating—it can prompt you to act too quickly, out of anger or desire. Keep your personal feelings as far from the negotiating process as you possibly can, or you'll hurt your own bargaining position.

Phase One: Your Opening Gambit

Let's go back to that well-deserved raise you're after. Usually, there's no overriding reason why you need the raise at the first meeting with your boss. Sure, you want the money as soon as you can get it. But the bottom line is that a little time won't be disastrous to you. Your goal is to get the raise, and if that requires patience on your part, so be it. But you want to persevere, to stay at it tactfully so you don't irritate your boss.

Phase Two: We'll Meet Again

If your boss wants time to mull the matter over or do some checking, that's fine. If at all possible, however, tactfully ask when your boss wants to meet again. If your boss says he'll get back to you on the next meeting date, that's fine—don't push it.

The Art of the Deal

Consider the story about the manager who told the salesman that the salesman was lucky to get in to see the manager. The man said the manager's secretary had turned away seven salesmen already that day. "Those seven were me," the salesman replied.

When your boss sets the next meeting, that eliminates any hint that you're pressing for an answer, even though you are.

Getting Time on Your Side

In any negotiation, the first question of timing is raised when you decide when to meet (see Chapter 4: "On Your Mark. . ., Get Set. . ., Negotiate!"). If your opponent is anxious to negotiate, you can assume that she is very confident of her ability to win. If that's the case, delay the bargaining because the timing is not favorable for you. Give your opponent a plausible reason for postponing—say you need more time to prepare or that you have another meeting. That throws off her timing and increases your bargaining power.

Dealmaker

Always explain to your opponent why you need more time. The more you can justify your request for an extension, the more likely you'll be to get one.

On the other hand, if your opponent sounds reluctant to meet, press as hard as you can (without getting offensive) to meet sooner rather than later. You want to use your opponent's unpreparedness to your advantage.

Once you are at the bargaining table, you'll have to ask yourself, "Is this the best time to say or do what I want to?" If your instincts are saying, "Yes," then go for it. In most cases, your timing will be right.

One of the best ways you can sharpen your sense of timing is to think over every one of your negotiations. Ask yourself if what you said and did had the maximum impact and influence on your opponent. If you're candid with yourself, this analysis process will help you hone your sense of timing.

Good Timing for Offers or Counteroffers

An *offer* is the first proposal made, either by you to your opponent, or by your opponent to you. A *counteroffer* is a reply to the initial offer or to another counteroffer.

Chapter 19 gets into offers and counteroffers in more detail. For now, it's only important that you understand the role of timing: You should know that *when* you make an offer or counteroffer will affect how your opponent receives it. If you make an offer (or counteroffer) prematurely, you'll get a rejection even if your proposal is reasonable because your opponent won't be mentally ready to accept it.

There's no set formula you can use to determine the best time to make an offer or counteroffer. You've just got to trust your instincts. But, until you've got a little experience under your belt, here are a few basic tips:

➤ Never make an offer (or counteroffer) you're unprepared to follow through on.

➤ Never make an offer (or counteroffer) in desperation.

➤ Never make an offer (or counteroffer) when your opponent appears harassed or angry.

You'll immediately know from your opponent's reaction if your timing was right. If your opponent is receptive, great! Press on with the bargaining. If you get a negative reaction, back off and continue to make or strengthen your general case. You may have to throw in some concessions or scale back your expectations—that's okay. Don't quit, be patient, and don't get rattled. As long as you're still bargaining, you have a chance to win.

Experience, ultimately, is your best teacher. The more you negotiate and review your negotiating experiences, the better your timing will become.

Help! I've Lost My Timing!

When you lose your timing, you'll know it. Nothing you say is well received, and nothing you suggest is accepted. You're on the defensive. A little voice in your mind asks, "How did I get into this—and how can I get out?"

The best way to salvage such a situation is to stop negotiating. Ask for a break: a short one if you can pull yourself together quickly, a long one if you feel you need more time. Use the break time to think about what you said and did and why it's not working. Prepare some new suggestions that may get the negotiating ball rolling again. In most cases, you'll be able to figure out your mistakes and how to correct them.

Negotiating on a Deadline

Nobody likes deadlines. But they're powerful tools in negotiation—that's when most issues are resolved. Setting a deadline is like sticking a ticking time bomb under your opponent. Deadlines are powerful motivators, and if you've been a sharp negotiator, your opponent will be motivated to act in your favor.

The trick, of course, is to be the one who controls the deadlines. Use deadlines liberally when you negotiate—but only if you're prepared to live with the consequences should you receive no response by the deadline. If you're not, don't set a deadline until you're confident you can live without the deal.

Art of the Deal

When negotiating real estate deals, I rarely give my opponents more than three to five days to accept an offer or counteroffer. That makes my opponent come to a decision quickly and limits the amount of time she has to shop around for a better deal.

Putting Your Opponent on a Deadline

When you set deadlines, fear becomes your bargaining ally. Your opponent is afraid of losing the deal, losing the money, and losing your business. Deadlines play on that fear in two ways:

➤ *Deadlines reduce your opponent's options.* If you don't set a deadline, you're giving your opponent an opportunity to shop around for a better deal. If he finds one, you're out.

➤ *Deadlines give you greater bargaining flexibility.* Say a number of buyers are interested in buying your home. You receive a firm offer from one buyer, but you want to hear some other offers before you seal a deal. So you make a counteroffer with a five-day deadline. Your deadline allows you to plan a definite course of action if the five-day period expires with no acceptance. You can immediately look for other buyers, or you can accept offers from other buyers you're already dealing with. You then wait for the five-day period to expire before you act on any other offers.

Determining the Deadline Period

Set the shortest deadline you can reasonably justify. True, no one likes tight deadlines—if your deadline is too short, you can make your opponent angry. But a deadline that seems too remote won't motivate your opponent to act quickly. You have to strike a balance.

You may have to adjust the length of your deadline in light of the particular circumstances of your negotiation. Factor in the personality, experience, and competence of your opponent. Usually, the more experienced and competent he is, the shorter your deadline can be. Your opponent may protest, but that will probably be for form's sake. In reality, he will expect a short deadline.

Always be prepared to offer a legitimate reason why you set your deadline. You can say you need time to deal with other interested parties (that's a good approach because it creates fear of loss in your opponent), or you have other business to handle and want to settle the issue as soon as possible. The important point is that you provide a plausible explanation for your deadline—that way, you diminish the risk that your opponent will be irritated by it.

Dealbreaker

The laws in most states say that an offer or counteroffer is open for a reasonable time if no deadline is set at the time the proposal is made. What "a reasonable time" is depends on the facts and circumstances of the particular case. Making offers or counteroffers without fixing a definite deadline for acceptance, then, is a risky business.

Should You Grant an Extension?

On occasion, you're bound to run into a situation where a deadline (set by you or by your opponent) must be extended. There are two very important rules you should follow when it comes to extending deadlines:

1. When you set a deadline, be absolutely certain that you can live with it.

2. Do not extend your deadline unless there is a legitimate reason to do so.

The two rules work together. If you set a deadline you can't live with, you'll have to extend it for no good reason. If you do that, your opponent won't take any of your deadlines seriously, which means that you'll lose substantial bargaining power.

If you've set a reasonable deadline and it expires, you must be fully prepared to walk away from the negotiation. If your opponent gives you a legitimate reason for needing an extension (such as personal issues, the need for more information, or the need to firm up financing), you're safe to extend your deadline. In that case, your new deadline will still be taken seriously.

Dealing with Deadlines Placed on You

If your opponent sets a deadline and you can meet it, meet it. If you can't, ask for an extension well in advance of the deadline. If you wait until the last minute, you'll have a lot of anxiety wondering if you are going to get the extra time you need.

If your opponent does agree to give you more time, ask for more time than you need. That way, if your opponent gives you less time than you've asked for, you're still ahead of the game.

If your opponent flatly refuses to give you more time and you can't make a decision without it, *insist* that you need an extension. Make it clear that the deal can't be settled unless you have more time. In most cases, you'll get what you're asking for.

Manipulating Time

Be very careful not to hurt your bargaining position by setting deadlines on yourself. Even a casual, innocent remark about your future plans may bind you into a deadline.

For example, if you tip off your opponent that you have another appointment or that you must catch a flight, you're setting a deadline on yourself. A skillful opponent will use anything that puts a time constraint on you. I have often dragged out a meeting until my opponent's

Dealmaker

It's human nature to prefer to procrastinate, to put off doing something until we absolutely must. That's why negotiating deadlines are so useful—they force you and your opponent to make a decision and take action by a specified time.

self-imposed deadline approached, knowing that time would motivate my opponent to cave in and give me what I wanted.

Avoiding Self-Imposed Deadlines

Home sales are a fertile area for self-imposed deadlines. Many times, the homeowners will reveal that they need to move right away, either because their new home is finished or because they have to relocate for their jobs. If you're the buyer in that situation, time is on your side. If you're the seller, don't admit to the buyers or to your agent that you have pressing deadlines: It will make you vulnerable to a less-than-ideal deal.

If your opponent is a skilled negotiator, he will probe to see if you have any self-imposed deadlines. He'll usually ask questions like, "How's business?" or "Are you making any money?" They may seem like innocent questions, but don't be caught off-guard.

He may be fishing to see if you have any travel, personal, or business commitments that impose a deadline on you. When you answer those questions, be brief. Short responses don't disclose any of your plans or commitments and thus don't reveal any deadlines that you have to meet.

I probe for self-imposed deadlines every time I negotiate. Sometimes I come up empty-handed, but many times I hit the jackpot and use my opponent's self-imposed deadline to my advantage.

The Least You Need to Know

➤ Don't expect to get what you want at the first bargaining session, especially if the negotiation is an important one: Patience and persistence are key.

➤ Always think about *when* you should say and do what you intend to say and do when you're bargaining. If you time it right, your odds of succeeding will substantially increase.

➤ If you feel you've lost your timing, ask for an immediate recess in which you can pull yourself together.

➤ Deadlines reduce your opponent's options and increase your options: Set the shortest deadlines you can reasonably justify, and probe your opponent to discover any self-imposed deadlines he or she may face.

➤ Don't extend your deadlines unless there's a legitimate reason to do so.

➤ If you can meet deadlines imposed on you by your opponent, do it. If not, ask for an extension as soon as possible and always ask for more time than you need.

➤ Be careful not to impose deadlines on yourself, and don't admit to any self-imposed deadlines.

Chapter 8

Questions, Questions, and More Questions

In This Chapter

➤ Why ask why?

➤ Using questions to your best advantage

➤ All queries are not created equal: the different types of questions

➤ Different questions do different things

How do experienced political or social personalities fend off media questions during a scandal? Usually, with two simple yet suggestive words: "No comment."

Most people do the opposite. They frequently answer questions even when they shouldn't, or when you don't want to.

The same thing happens to your opponent when you negotiate. Most inexperienced negotiators will answer questions even when they shouldn't. By asking questions liberally, you can boost your negotiating position. In this chapter, I show you how to ask all the right questions when you negotiate.

You're Asking Me?!

We all like to think we're interesting. That's why, when you ask questions, you're likely to get answers—people are flattered that you're asking for their opinion and expertise. When it comes to negotiations, therefore, questions are excellent probing tools for two reasons:

➤ They help you discover information that only your opponent knows or that is otherwise very difficult for you to get.

➤ They give you more control over the tone and flow of the negotiation.

There are several kinds of special-purpose questions, and each has a different purpose and place in negotiation. These different types of questions include the following:

➤ General questions

➤ Specific questions

➤ Leading questions

➤ Suggestive questions

➤ Obvious questions

➤ Questions that imply a choice

➤ Successive questions

Over the following pages, I'll describe each one, and how they can boost your negotiating skills. Before we begin: Any questions?

Dealmaker

Ask questions frequently throughout your negotiation. If you feel that certain questions are crucial to your position, write them out beforehand so that you can be sure to phrase them appropriately to achieve the greatest possible impact and get the best results.

Sizing Up the Situation

General questions are useful for probing for new facts and information. The best time to use these types of questions is during the early stages of the bargaining, while you and your opponent are still getting to know each other and before the terms have been laid out on the bargaining table. Your opponent will answer most, if not all, of your general questions with no suspicions at this point, so ask general questions freely.

If you've been careful in doing your pre-negotiation homework (reread Chapter 2, "Bargaining Essentials," and Chapter 3, "Scoping Out the Other Side," on researching before you negotiate), you may be so well prepared for the negotiation that you don't have any general questions to ask. But it's wise to come up with a few to ask anyway! Even if you already know the answers, the *way* your opponent responds may give you new insights into her personality and negotiating style.

For example, if your opponent withholds—or misrepresents—certain information, you know you're dealing with a cagey character who doesn't want to put all her cards on the table. This may be important to know when, later in the bargaining process, you need to rely on your opponent for less generally available information.

Questioning, in General Terms

The possibilities of general questions are endless and will vary depending upon the kind of negotiation you're conducting. No one can give you an exhaustive list of everything you might ask, but here are some examples of questions, keyed to specific types of negotiations:

During a business negotiation:

➤ "So, Company Z used to handle this account for you. What did you think of them?"

➤ "How long have you been in this business? With this company?"

When buying a home:

➤ "What's the neighborhood like? How are the schools? How's the recreation?"

➤ "What kind of condition is the house in?"

➤ "Why are the owners selling?"

When selling a home:

➤ "What are you looking for in a home?"

➤ "Are you interested in this neighborhood because it's near such good schools?"

To Every Question There Is a Season

As the bargaining unfolds, you should abandon general questions. For one thing, by continuing to ask more general questions, you run the risk of reopening issues that were already agreed upon.

More importantly, if you keep asking general questions as the negotiation gets specific, your opponent will begin to wonder about your preparedness. You don't want to give her the impression that you don't know anything about the subject at hand. She won't go along with you on anything if she feels you don't know what you're talking about.

And, in the worst case, your opponent might see a more sinister motive in your general questions. She may conclude that your bargaining position is weak and that you're trying to strengthen it by pumping her for more information. This is likely to seriously reduce her receptiveness to your position as the bargaining continues.

Dealbreaker

If you haven't done your homework about appropriate jargon (see Chapter 5, "Increasing Your Word Power"), it's may hurt your bargaining position once you move from general to specific questions. If you can't use the proper terms, you'll seem careless and uninformed.

Getting to the Heart of the Matter: Specific Questions

Once you've broken ground with your general questions, it's time to bring the negotiations down to earth. For this purpose, you'll want to start asking specific questions.

Unlike general questions, *specific questions* call for fairly confined, detailed answers. You can use specific questions at any point during a negotiation, but they're best asked in the later stages, when you're more apt to know exactly what you're after when asking.

Watch how you phrase your specific questions. The more precise your question, the better the chance you'll get a precise answer—without exposing your bargaining strategy or opening yourself up to other questions.

For example, let's say you're in the market to buy property and build a restaurant. If you're concerned about zoning, you should ask, "Is the property fully zoned for use as a restaurant?" Don't ask, "What's the property's zoning?" The first question is more likely to get you the information you want.

Negotiable Terms

A **leading question** is one that, by its very wording, makes it difficult for your opponent to give any answer other than the one you want.

Taking the Lead

General and specific questions are asked to convey your interest in the subject at hand and, more importantly, to increase your store of information in hopes of bettering your bargaining position. *Leading questions*, on the other hand, are designed to influence your opponent's receptivity to your position. Questions of this type are simply statements turned into questions.

Leading questions always call for "yes" answers. When you ask a leading question, you already know what response you expect to get from your opponent. Leading questions help you maintain control of the bargaining and may push your negotiating momentum further along. They also put your opponent in a receptive, "yes" mood.

You Can Lead a Horse to Water . . .

You form leading questions by making a statement of fact that you already know (or that you want your opponent to agree to) and twisting it around to make a question out of it. Take a look at the following examples:

> *Leading question:* "It's a very profitable company, isn't it?"
>
> *What you want your opponent to admit:* "It's a very profitable company."
>
> *Leading question:* "The property across the street leased for only $15 per square foot, didn't it?"

What you want your opponent to admit: "The property leased for $15 per square foot."

Leading question: "I've done an excellent job and really earned a raise, haven't I?"

What you want your opponent to admit: "You've earned a raise."

Leading questions calling for a "yes" response from your opponent are powerful, not only because they call forth the answer you want to hear, but also because they put your opponent in a "yes" mood—exactly the mood you want your opponent to be in.

Take the question, "I've earned a raise, haven't I?" Once you've gotten your boss to answer "Yes," then it's going to be more difficult for your boss to weasel her way out of giving you a raise, unless there are major company problems that prevent *anyone* from getting a raise.

. . . But You Can't Make It Drink

You've probably seen more than one courtroom drama where the star witness shocks the court with an answer that no one—not even the lawyers—saw coming. That's the risk of asking a leading question: You'll bomb big-time if you're not sure what the answer will be. Never ask your opponent a leading question to which you don't already know the answer. If you do and your opponent's answer surprises you, you'll automatically go on the defensive; you'll find yourself scrambling to regain some control, and you'll lower your chances of winning the negotiation.

The Art of the Deal

Just picture how quickly your campaign for a raise will come crashing down if you say, "I've earned a raise, haven't I?" and your boss says, "Frankly, Snively, you haven't," and then launches into a list of reasons why. Even a master negotiator would be hard-pressed to recover from a blow like that.

This is another reason why it's important to do some solid research before you open your negotiation. From your research, you can identify information that might be particularly useful in forming leading questions—questions that will powerfully move the negotiation in the direction you want it to go.

Planting Suggestive Seeds

Sometimes you can use questions to achieve the same effect as extrapolation (discussed in Chapter 5): to get your opponent to arrive on his own at a decision or conclusion that's favorable to you. You do this by asking *suggestive questions*. As the name implies, embedded in suggestive questions is a specific course of action or a suggestion. Examples of suggestive questions would include these:

➤ "Don't you think it's better to sign the contract now?"

➤ "Wouldn't it be best to give me my money back now?"

➤ "Isn't it a good time to give me a raise?"

In all these suggestive questions, your opponent must either commit himself to the course of action suggested in your question or explain why not. If he agrees with your suggestion, congratulations! You've won. If he tries to explain away your suggestion, he must go on the defensive. Any way you cut it, suggestive questions are excellent bargaining tools. Use them often.

Although suggestive questions seem to be similar in form and style to leading questions, they are really quite different. Just think of all the times you've shopped for a suit or dress, only to have the salesperson say, "How about this shirt (or blouse) to go with it?" The salesperson is using a suggestive question because it's well-known that once a customer has committed to one purchase, he or she is more likely to be open to the suggestion of buying another related item.

Talking Points

"The man who is afraid of asking is afraid of learning."

—Danish proverb

The salesperson might have asked a leading question instead. In that case, he would say, "You can use this new shirt to go with it, can't you?" But more than likely, that approach wouldn't work. A leading question feels more aggressive and more like bullying than a suggestive question, so it's likely to put the customer off.

Setting Up Some "Yesses"

Obvious questions—questions that call for particular, obvious answers—are a negotiator's tactical delight. As with suggestive questions, these appear similar to leading questions, but they work directly on your opponent's ego: Obvious questions are designed to get a favorable response because your opponent doesn't want to look stupid even though he may not know the correct answer.

By definition, obvious questions relate to matters of common knowledge. If you're negotiating a raise, you might cry, "Doesn't everyone know that the cost of living has gone up?" If you're trying to buy a home, you might say, "Don't we all know it's a buyer's market?" Even if your opponent doesn't know a buyer's market from a super-market, he will probably still answer "yes"—just so he doesn't look stupid.

Skillfully used, obvious questions accomplish a couple of goals at the same time. For one thing, they help to condition your opponent into a general "yes" mode. For another, they can subtly nudge your opponent toward your own bargaining position, often without him even realizing that this is happening.

Giving the Illusion of Choices

No one wants to feel bullied or pressured—especially in the middle of a bargaining situation. But if you're trying to win a negotiation, you are *trying* to make your opponent leave his or her position and come over to your own. One great technique for this is to use *choice questions*—questions that present your opponent with at least the appearance of several alternative responses.

Dealmaker

Use questions that call for obvious answers liberally when you bargain. Not only do they put your opponent in an agreeable mood, but they also provide you with good negotiating momentum.

The trick is to make certain that the alternatives you present when asking these *choice questions* are all favorable to you. Let's say you've got your eye on some new furniture for your home. You've identified your price range and a couple of sets that would suit your needs nicely, so you ask: "Would you give me that sofa and chair combination for $700, or the other living room set for $600?"

If you're negotiating for a bonus, you might take a different tack. You've decided how much you want, but you don't really care whether it's paid annually or quarterly. In this case, you'd ask: "Would you rather give me my bonus in one lump sum at the end of the year or in quarterly payments?"

Or, say you're trying to get your teenager to buckle down on her schoolwork. You'd ask: "Would you prefer to do your homework before dinner or after?"

Notice how the choices in all the three questions are favorable to you. You'll take either living room set, as long as your price is met. You're after a bonus, but the payment schedule doesn't really matter to you. And you don't care when your child does her homework—as long as it gets done.

Dealbreaker

Badly worded choice questions can backfire. If you allow an undesirable alternative to slip into the choice, you'll have to live with the high likelihood that that's precisely the option that your opponent will select.

If the salesperson tries to sell you the $1,000 imitation-leather sofa, or if your boss attempts to switch the subject back to the Smithers account, or if your child still evades the homework subject, your choice questions will pin them down.

A-One, A-Two, and A-Three . . . Successive Questions

Momentum is very important in negotiating. You want to do whatever you can to get the process moving in such a way that your negotiation begins to roll on its own toward the outcome you desire, like a snowball increasing in size and speed as it rolls down a steep hill. *Successive questions* are an excellent way to maintain control of your negotiation and to develop positive bargaining momentum.

Say the lease on your apartment is about to run out. You want to renew, but at a lower rent. Here's how you use successive questions to help get what you want:

"Why shouldn't I get a rent reduction? Haven't I been a good tenant? Haven't I kept the place in perfect shape? Haven't I cooperated with you every time you needed to get into the apartment? Shouldn't all of that be worth something? Don't you think it's fair and reasonable to give me a 10 percent rent reduction?"

Notice how your questions build up to your final question, the grand finale, the pièce de résistance, your ultimate objective: a lower rent. You can add as many questions as you like—building successive questions is like piling layers on lasagna. (Just make sure you don't run out of breath before you get through your questions.)

Your purpose when using successive questions is not to bully, annoy, or intimidate. It's to make your case without being interrupted, so the total sum of your questions has a much greater impact.

Dealmaker

Throughout your negotiation, it's important to appear cooperative and positive. When faced with potentially damaging questions from your opponent, do your best to couch your refusal to answer in friendly, reasonable terms.

When the Questions Are Aimed at You

Of course, you're not the only one who's likely to be asking questions during a negotiation. How you handle your opponent's questions can have a powerful impact—good or bad—on your bargaining position. If your opponent asks you a question that you feel is appropriate, don't hesitate to answer. If you refuse, your opponent may become suspicious of your motives. She may also begin to resent you for appearing uncooperative.

But you'll sometimes encounter questions that you shouldn't answer. Here are some tactful approaches you can use to dodge a question without turning off your opponent:

➤ *Plead irrelevance.* Say something like, "I'm not sure how that question fits in here," or "I don't see where you're coming from." Your response is mild and won't turn your opponent off, but it may get your opponent to drop the question.

➤ *Plead ignorance.* Simply say that you don't know the answer. Realize, though, that with this approach you risk looking uninformed or unprepared.

➤ *Take the fifth.* Tactfully suggest that the question calls for information you'd rather not disclose—at least not at this point in the bargaining process.

➤ *Answer that it's too personal.* If the question calls for personal information you'd rather not disclose, say so. Your opponent should respect your right to privacy.

➤ *Answer with your own question.* Answering your opponent's question with a question of your own is an excellent way to avoid the question and regain control of the bargaining momentum.

At all times, keep your responses friendly and tactful. Don't respond with anger—it will make further negotiation difficult. In addition, if you let emotions run away with you, you're more likely to blurt out information that will give the bargaining edge to your opponent.

The Least You Need to Know

➤ Questions are excellent probing tools that help you to get information to which you might not otherwise have access.

➤ General questions are best at the beginning of the bargaining; specific questions call for more confined answers and are useful at any stage of the bargaining.

➤ Leading questions seek a "yes" answer and put your opponent in a "yes" mood; never ask them unless you are certain that your opponent's answer will be "yes."

➤ Use suggestive questions and questions that require a choice to get a commitment from your opponent.

➤ Questions that call for obvious answers put your opponent in an agreeable mood and give you good bargaining momentum. Use them liberally.

➤ Successive questions help you control the bargaining. Ask them without pausing because you don't want your opponent to reply until you finish.

Chapter 9

The Paper Chase

> **In This Chapter**
>
> ➤ Incoming: The importance of paperwork
>
> ➤ Gathering your data
>
> ➤ The keys to organization
>
> ➤ Outgoing: Preparing professional correspondence
>
> ➤ To whom does it concern?

Negotiation isn't entirely done face-to-face across a desk or a bargaining table. You already know from Chapter 2, "Bargaining Essentials," and Chapter 3, "Scoping Out the Other Side," that there's a pre-negotiation phase of research you need to do, for example. But there's also a lot of negotiating that can—and sometimes *must*—get done on paper. You'll often want to document your position, clarify a tricky point, and protect your legal rights.

All this involves paperwork—often the most neglected aspect of negotiation. In this chapter, you'll learn about the documentary side of bargaining, from amassing and managing information to communicating effectively through position papers, letters, and other documents.

Doing Your Homework

Back in Chapter 2, you learned to identify your primary base and secondary bases. Now it's time to harness all the arguments that support your position. The more hard facts, statistics, and documentation you have, the more difficult it will be for your opponent to turn you down.

Of special importance is any information you can come up with from your opponent. I don't mean her correspondence or materials produced specifically for the negotiating session. I mean product brochures, warranties, tags, user's manuals, and so on. Even furniture usually comes with tags that brag about its quality and durability. Save these items long enough to be sure that the product is performing up to expectations.

Dealmaker

When preparing your case, look for claims you can use to your advantage. If the manual that comes with your computer frequently praises its dependability, underline the word "dependable" every time it appears. Then when you negotiate, emphasize how "dependable" your computer was supposed to be, and how *un*dependable it actually is.

Singling Out the Problem

In simple negotiations, a quick mental rehearsal of your arguments may be all you need. If you're returning your computer, for example, you should simply gather all the reasons why you think you got a piece of bum equipment. The more specific you can be, the better. ("The mouse freezes up every five minutes, the hard drive spits out my disks, and it deleted the file that contained my great American novel.") The only documentation you'll probably need in this case will be your receipt, the owner's manual, and a copy of the warranty. (You did keep them, didn't you?)

Carefully think out what kind of information you need to buttress your case, and then do a thorough search—through your records, in the library, or over the Internet—to locate documentation that you can use. After that, it's a good idea to plan how you're going to use the written material during the actual negotiation and when you'll introduce it.

More complex negotiations (such as bidding for a company, or buying or selling a home) will require more elaborate files and documentation. You don't want to rely on memory alone during the heat of the discussion, when you may be under a lot of pressure. Having all the information you need on paper will also free up your attention to focus on what the other person or people are saying—which is where your concentration *should* be.

Let's say you are about to ask for a raise. You should prepare a file that documents all the backbreaking work you've done. Your file might include the following:

➤ A list of the successful projects you've spearheaded, the new products rolled out under your supervision, and the employees you supervise.

➤ Any favorable financial reports, such as those that show increased sales or profitability for which you can claim credit.

➤ Any letters of praise or recommendation from coworkers or clients.

➤ Comparable salary surveys, if they show that the average salary for your position is substantially higher than what your company is paying you. (One source of this information is the U.S. Department of Labor's Bureau of Labor Statistics.)

Doing It the Write Way

As you can see, virtually anything that's relevant to your bargaining and that is in writing can be used to add authority to your negotiating position: invoices, receipts, brochures, letters, and memos— even your kid's report card if the issue involves his or her grades (or the lack of them). That's why you should be on the lookout for useful written information. This can be very helpful and frequently means the difference between success and failure, as you'll see later in the chapter when we take up the issue of correspondence during negotiation.

Dealbreaker

Don't go into negotiation thinking you can turn up necessary backup documents as you go along. Have everything prepared beforehand, or you'll find yourself frantic when you can't find that darned (but crucial) receipt at the last minute.

Writing That Works

You've heard the expression "A picture is worth a thousand words." Written information can have the same impact. Those D's on your kid's report card make your point ("You've got to buckle down on your homework, son!") better than any lecture you might give. Similarly, that computer brochure advising you that you've bought "the best there is" comes in handy when you call the company to report that it has turned out to be a lemon. And that canceled check proves beyond a doubt that you've paid up and will get that pesky bill collector off your back.

Not yet convinced about the power of written information? Here are just a few of the benefits of using it when you negotiate:

➤ You have a written record to rely on and to work from during the negotiating process.

➤ Anything in writing carries extra authority; it has more credibility than the same information if you were to just speak it.

➤ This provides an excellent way to refresh your memory—and your opponent's memory as well. This is particularly important if you're negotiating something that happened a long time ago.

➤ This provides a way to impeach your opponent's bargaining position, when necessary.

➤ This gives your opponent something "to hang his hat on," as lawyerly slang puts it. (Skilled lawyers know that they must provide the judge with a sound basis for his or her ruling in their favor—they call it "something the court can hang its hat on.") In negotiation, anything in writing that you can produce to support your position gives your opponent a legitimate reason to go along with you.

When Writing Works Against You

Written information that's relevant to your position dramatically increases the odds that you'll get what you want. But keep in mind that if there's any documentation that hurts your bargaining position, your opponent is likely to use it against you. Be prepared to come up with a strategy of dealing with it before you begin bargaining. That will help to neutralize its impact on your position.

Your opponent is only human—and it's human nature to try to deny or downplay anything that's contrary to our interests. When confronted with an incriminating piece of written information, some opponents will put on an acting job that even the pros can't equal. Be prepared for such a denial—here are some tips on how to do it:

➤ *Defusing a denial:* Hand your opponent a copy of the item in question, and review it in detail as he or she reads along. This not only defuses your opponent's denial, but it also allows you to underscore your own position through repetition.

➤ *Derailing an attempt to downplay:* Explain in detail why the documentation is both relevant and beneficial to your position. Don't assume that your opponent fully appreciates how important the document is. (And, once again, you get a chance to employ repetition to further advance your position.)

Remember what you've learned about body language in Chapter 6, "Getting Physical." When your opponent attempts to deny or downplay your documents—and while you're countering that denial—watch your opponent carefully. If he looks away or blinks excessively, he's faking. The same is true if he turns his body away from you or folds his arms tightly across his chest: Both are signs that he doesn't really believe the position he's taking.

Making an Impact

Because of the power of written information, I rarely negotiate any important matter without thoroughly investigating to see if any written information relevant to my bargaining position exists. Then I strategically use it during the negotiation.

But keep in mind that once you use written information, the genie is out of the bottle—you have to live with its impact, for good and for ill. So you must think through every interpretation of your written information before you use it.

I learned this the hard way early in my negotiating career. I used written information that I thought was beneficial to my cause, only to later learn that it could be used *against* my interests. If it turns out that the written information you used isn't really supportive or, worse yet, that it actually bolsters your opponent's position, you've got basically two choices:

1. Deny or play down the written information. This is usually a mistake. It calls your credibility and integrity into question, which will seriously reduce your chances of getting your opponent to give you what you want.

2. Admit it. When you do, you've substantially increased your credibility and integrity in your opponent's eyes. Your opponent will perceive you as someone who can be trusted and will be favorably motivated to strike a reasonable deal.

Get Organized

All the research and information in the world won't help you if they're spilling out of your briefcase onto the floor. You don't want to break a deep discussion while you fumble for a document or search for an important piece of information. If you aren't organized, you will appear less effective and less competent, and you could lose your negotiating momentum.

The Art of the Deal

When I walk up to a negotiating table, I like to have the documents related to each major subject under negotiation separated into individual folders. I label each folder with a large, boldly written title that's easy to read. I sometimes use different-colored inks to help me instantly locate specific paragraphs or ideas in a file. It helps me make a smooth, knowledgeable presentation that always impresses my opponents.

Find an organizational system that works for you—one that is clear, well-marked, and easily understood. Here's one that you might use when you're negotiating to buy your dream home:

➤ *A Financial file:* This file contains information on all matters financial, including the offering price, real-estate taxes, and sewer, water, or street levies. It should also include any add-ons that may raise the price of the home, such as appliances.

➤ *A Comparable Sales file:* This file contains sales data on similar homes, especially those in the immediate area of the home you want to buy. During the negotiation, you'll want to call special attention to comparable homes whose sales prices are lower than your seller's offering price.

➤ *A Correspondence file:* This file contains any and all written offers or counteroffers made by you or the seller. It should also include all correspondence relevant to the transaction, placed in chronological order.

➤ *A Title file:* This file contains all matters relevant to title, including title insurance and any title defects (such as a neighbor's tree that encroaches on the property) that must be cleared by the seller before a title can pass to you if you purchase the property.

➤ *A Contingencies file:* This file contains information on all the conditions that must be met before the deal can be finalized: financing, house inspection, property surveying, and so on.

If you decide to bring pictures or other graphic data, keep them in a separate file. Do the same with physical exhibits such as posters. You don't want them to detract from your presentation until you are actually ready to use them. (In Chapter 6, you learned all about using props in negotiation.)

Dealbreaker

Once negotiations have begun, never leave your files unattended. They'll be too vulnerable to prying eyes. Always take them with you, even during short breaks in the bargaining process.

Putting It in Writing

A client of mine once negotiated a large and intricate deal with a group of business people anxious to seal an agreement. At the eleventh hour, however, he reviewed the terms and decided that he just couldn't go through with the arrangement. He asked me if I could untangle the situation.

As I reviewed his case, I realized that if my client didn't make his wishes clear, he could easily get slapped with a number of lawsuits.

I drafted a letter on his behalf and, over a period of three days (this was a *big* deal), pruned and fine-tuned it. I tried to imagine how my opponents would feel and what they would likely do when they received it.

When I was finally convinced that I had the letter right, I sent it out. Then I waited and waited—and waited some more. Finally, I received a response: They were not going to pursue the deal or prosecute my client.

As you can see from this example, correspondence can play a powerful role in the bargaining process. It allows you to clarify your position, and it provides a clear paper trail in case you need to protect yourself if negotiations turn sour. The key is to learn to prepare your correspondence professionally. Never just dash something off without fully thinking about the impact it will have on your overall negotiation.

The Uses of Correspondence

Correspondence and any other type of paperwork serve many purposes throughout the negotiation process, from the opening bargaining through the offer and counteroffer stages, and on to closing.

Opening the Negotiation

Many negotiations, particularly business negotiations, begin with a written offer or other bargaining "position paper." This document sets forth the issues you want to negotiate and clarifies your hopes for the negotiation process.

If you must prepare a position paper, craft it carefully because it will set the tone and direction for the upcoming negotiation. Also, if any expectations or promises are set forth in the opening paper (for example, stipulations as to fees or legal rights), you'll be held to them, and it will be very difficult to back out once you've committed yourself in writing.

Dealmaker

Think of your correspondence as an important part of your bargaining image. If it looks professional, you look professional; if it looks sloppy, so do you.

Here are some pointers on how to prepare effective written offers or other opening position papers:

➤ Keep them brief. The less you write, the less you are committed to.

➤ Be concise.

➤ If you're in doubt about a particular term or proposal, leave it out! You can always raise the issue later.

➤ Arrange your ideas and positions so that each point flows logically from the previous one. This avoids confusion about what you've written.

➤ Put yourself in your opponent's shoes and read your letter. How does it sound? Does it make sense? This will help clarify your writing.

Clearing the Air

I'm sure you've heard the saying, "Don't make a mountain out of a molehill." That often happens when you're bargaining; simple issues sometimes snowball into complicated ones.

Correspondence can be the perfect vehicle to get back to basics. By outlining and organizing the issue on paper, you can separate the crucial issues from the negligible ones.

The Art of the Deal

I once had a client who wanted to rezone his property. What began as a simple request turned into a bureaucratic nightmare as numerous government agencies, planning commissions, and local community boards all got involved and expressed competing viewpoints, interests, and requirements. I had to craft a simple letter that clearly stated the current status of the request to bring everyone involved in the negotiation back on track.

By reporting on the issues that are important to you first, you also can control the direction of the negotiation. You can de-emphasize issues that are not important to you by placing them in parentheses or by mentioning them in a brief postscript.

You can also de-emphasize any matters you feel are unimportant by using language such as, "I place little emphasis on. . ." or "I see little merit in. . . ." Then you can go on to explain why you feel that way.

Getting It in Writing

As you can see, putting your own position down on paper serves several important purposes. Equally important is getting your opponent's promises on paper once you've achieved agreement on some or all of your negotiation. Details can be interpreted differently, or perhaps even forgotten. Your understanding of the agreements reached can be different than your opponent's understanding of them. Restating your interpretation can head off serious problems down the road when you're anxious to close the negotiation.

Following up your discussions with a letter detailing the issues resolved is an excellent way to avoid any such misunderstanding. The printed or written word lends credibility. People are much more likely to believe what they see and read than what they hear. This approach is especially useful when the negotiation is complicated or drawn out over more than one bargaining session.

Blazing the Paper Trail

Not only do follow-up letters clarify issues, but they also serve as official proof of promises made, terms agreed on, and actions taken. Sign and date all your correspondence, and keep a file of every letter you send out and receive. You never know when you'll need it.

Regular mail, Federal Express, UPS, faxes, and electronic mail (e-mail) are fine for sending standard documents and letters. If you are sending particularly sensitive or crucial documents, the U.S. Postal Service offers several options that guarantee your letters will get where they are going:

➤ *Certified mail* provides you with a mailing receipt, and a record of delivery is kept at the recipient's post office.

➤ *Registered mail* is regarded by the postal service as its most secure mailing option. Once again, you get a receipt, but both your post office and the post office on the receiving end are able to track delivery.

➤ *Restricted delivery* means that delivery is made only to the addressee or to someone who has written authorization to receive mail for the addressee.

Professionalizing Your Paperwork

How you present yourself in writing is as important as how you present yourself in person. I'm amazed at how many people still submit handwritten letters or badly smudged Xeroxed copies. If you want to be taken seriously on paper, you should follow a few basic rules:

➤ *Be accurate.* Proofread everything you send to your opponent—twice. In negotiation, even one little word can make a substantial difference. If you want to inform your opponent that her offer is not acceptable but then you leave out the word *not*, you've got a lot of explaining to do.

Dealmaker

In many negotiations, proof that you've filed a required document—and proof of *when* it was filed—can be very important. For those situations, sending it certified and registered mail are useful options to consider.

➤ *Be neat.* Type your letter to your opponent. If you want to add a personal touch, write a handwritten note on the page (but be sure your handwriting is clear).

➤ *Use a conservative design, with a classic typeface and generous margins.* This isn't the time to display your hip sensibilities or funky design style.

➤ *Use highlighting elements such as bold, underline, or exclamation points sparingly.* If you emphasize too many points in your letter, you will appear obnoxious, strident, or too opinionated.

➤ *Avoid jokes, sarcasm, or irony in your letter unless you're certain the recipient will understand and appreciate your humor.* Your letter won't be able to communicate the subtle voice intonations and gestures to signify that you're just kidding.

➤ *Be prompt.* By delaying correspondence, you will appear unprofessional, disorganized, or not confident in your negotiating position.

Using Forms

A number of matters you negotiate will involve printed or standard documents such as apartment leases, car leases, service contracts, repair contracts, or employment contracts. The use of forms in particular negotiations is covered in more detail in Part 7, "Real-Time, Real-World Negotiating." For now, these are some general rules you should follow when you are confronted with a printed or standard document:

➤ Never sign a document on the spot. If possible, get a copy early in the bargaining process so that you (or someone you trust) can review the document in detail. (Be sure to read the fine print.) If you are apartment hunting, for example, you might want to pick up a standard lease in a stationery store. Then when you are presented with a lease to sign, you will have a rough idea what will be in it.

➤ As you negotiate, make notes directly on the document so that you have a quick and accurate reference to work from. If you aren't comfortable marking up the original, make a copy and use that.

➤ Printed documents are often worded in dense legalese. Don't let that intimidate you! Seek an explanation of any language you're unsure about.

➤ Pay attention to any pre-existing conditions that may affect the terms of the document. For example, if an apartment lease states that you are financially responsible for any damages you cause, you should check the apartment before you move in and document any damages (holes, stains, faulty heating or plumbing, and so on) that are already there. Otherwise, under the terms of the lease, you could be held responsible for damages you didn't even cause.

➤ Realize that no document is official until all concerned parties have signed it. Oftentimes, any changes, additions, or deletions marked on a document also have to be initialed by all parties before they are official. Everyone involved in the negotiation should have an identical copy of the form.

➤ All parties should keep a signed copy of the document for their records.

Who Should Receive Your Correspondence?

If you bargain with more than one opponent, send the original to the "yes" person and send copies to everyone else involved in the negotiation.

If you are not bargaining directly with the "yes" person, send the original to the person you are bargaining with and a copy to the "yes" person.

If your negotiation is controversial and you're not sure how it will turn out, your written correspondence should contain a reference that you have sent a copy to your lawyer (if you are using one). This lets your opponent know that you're serious and that the negotiation is being monitored by a professional.

Dealmaker

It's only polite to make certain that all parties concerned with your negotiation are copied on all your paperwork. And it's more than a courtesy—if everyone is working with the same information, you're much more likely to avoid misunderstandings further down the line.

The Least You Need to Know

➤ Correspondence helps you control the bargaining process.

➤ Use correspondence to clarify your position and create a paper trail of promises and accountability.

➤ Your correspondence should be neat, error-free, and timely.

➤ Send the original correspondence to the person you are bargaining with directly. Send copies to anyone else involved in the negotiation.

➤ Send a copy of your correspondence to your lawyer when you feel you need additional bargaining leverage.

Chapter 10

Top Negotiating Techniques

In This Chapter

➤ Techniques from the pros

➤ Different strokes for different negotiating folks

➤ What to do, when to do it

➤ Pitfalls to avoid

No two negotiations are the same, even if they're about the same types of issues. That's because every negotiation involves different personalities. Even if you're negotiating with someone you've dealt with before, your opponent may be in a different mood or may be working with a new set of constraints on his or her actions. That's why it's useful to have a variety of negotiating techniques in your bargaining arsenal—you want to be able to tailor your negotiation to the needs of the moment.

In this chapter, I'll pull back the curtain on some of my favorite negotiating techniques, tricks of the trade that can significantly boost your negotiating prowess. Here you'll learn a variety of approaches to getting what you want, and you'll learn how each one of these approaches works. When you prepare to bargain, it's up to you to decide which of these techniques will work the best to persuade your opponent. Use as many of them as often as you feel is necessary—and at every window of opportunity, no matter how small.

The Professional Negotiator's Arsenal

In previous chapters, I've shown you how to develop a number of skills you'll need in negotiating. These range from communication skills (both verbal and nonverbal) to questions, from correspondence to timing and information gathering. But skills are one thing—technique is another.

This is not to say that you should approach negotiating like a programmed robot—you should always be prepared to respond flexibly to situations as they arise during the bargaining process. But when it comes to trying for a particular reaction from your opponent, there are several sure-fire, tried-and-true techniques you can use, including these:

➤ The "Building Block" technique

➤ The "Vinegar and Honey" technique

➤ The "Exhausting" technique

➤ The "Gear-Shifting" technique

➤ The "Conduit" technique

➤ The "Talk-Show Host" technique

➤ The "Self-Deprecating" technique

➤ The "It's-A-Shame" technique

Negotiable Terms

A **technique** is a constellation of specific skills used in a particular way to attain your negotiating purpose.

Each of these negotiating techniques is designed to handle a particular type of problem or issue. Read on to see how they work.

Doling Out the Info: Building Your Case

The "Building Block" technique is specially designed to impress your opponent with your preparation and your knowledge of the negotiating situation. With this technique, you carefully build your case with facts and figures, thus bolstering your position (and your image) in your opponent's eyes.

Taking Your Time

If the bargaining lasts for only one meeting (as many will), your goal is to parcel out your facts throughout the entire meeting rather than all at once. This "rationing" of information makes it appear as if you have much more supportive data available to you than is actually the case. The cumulative effect leaves your opponent with the impression that your bargaining position is stronger than it really is.

For longer negotiations, the same principle holds, only this time you'll be trying to parcel out your facts over several bargaining sessions.

Leading with Your Strength

Whether you're parceling out your facts over one bargaining session or over the course of several sessions, always lead off with your strongest facts, but keep a few in reserve. Communicate your weaker facts during the middle part of your negotiation, but always finish up with a few new pieces of strong supportive data. The effect you're going for is something like a roller coaster ride.

Dealmaker

Practice using the various negotiating techniques before you sit down at the bargaining table. If you can use them easily and naturally, they'll have a much greater impact.

This building block approach leaves a strong impact because we tend to retain the first and last pieces of information the longest; everything in between is largely forgotten. This also gives the impression of inevitability: As you build your position, point by point, with supportive facts offered every step of the way, your opponent has less chance to avoid reaching the conclusion that you're trying to get him or her to reach.

To use this technique most effectively, you must cultivate patience (see Chapter 7, "Timing Is Everything"). Don't be too anxious to reveal your supporting facts too quickly: Dribble them out like drops from a leaky faucet.

Catching Negotiating Flies with Vinegar and Honey

The "Vinegar and Honey" technique relies on skillfully manipulating your opponents' expectations so that they are more receptive to your proposed deal than they otherwise would be. Here's how it works: You structure your argument so that you present your opponent with what he might consider to be bad news (the vinegar), and then you follow up with good news (the honey). This makes the good news seem even sweeter, even if it isn't as good as your opponent might have expected.

A Taste of Vinegar and Honey

Say you're a boss and a valued employee asks for a 10 percent raise. While 10 percent is too high, you're secretly willing and able to give him 5 percent because you want to keep him on your team. So you don't reject the 10 percent outright. You say, "Oh, I really don't know . . . . There's a wage freeze on the entire company, and as much as I'd like to give you a raise, I just don't know what I'll be able to do. But let me see what I can do."

The Art of the Deal

"Vinegar and honey" situations occur every day. Recently, I was on a flight that was about to land when the pilot announced that there would be an hour's delay because of heavy traffic at the airport. All the passengers grumbled and settled in for a long, boring wait. A few minutes later, the pilot announced that the delay had been cut to a half-hour. Five minutes later, the pilot gave us the good news that we had been cleared for immediate landing. We were thrilled with the news—even though we were already late.

Your employee is obviously going to be disappointed because you haven't agreed to the raise on the spot. But you haven't closed the door entirely. You reschedule a later meeting.

At the next meeting, you begin with the bad news. You say, "Well, I really tried, but I just couldn't get that 10 percent raise for you. There was just no way." At this point, your employee may be worried that absolutely *no* raise is forthcoming. Then comes the honey: "But I did manage to get 5 percent for you." Your employee will be elated, even though he didn't get the entire raise he was asking for.

If you're the one asking for the raise, you reverse the process. If your goal is a 10 percent raise, you ask for 20 percent and then, when your boss gives you a sob story about why 20 percent is too high, you *gradually scale back* until you're at your final 10 percent target.

Avoid Large Concessions

The "Vinegar and Honey" technique works best when you make concessions in small increments. If you make a large concession all at once ("What's that, Mr. Smith? No 20 percent raise? Well, in that case, 10 percent is fine!") you can devastate your entire case (more on this in Chapter 19, "Offers and Counteroffers"). Smaller concessions are more convincing and leave you more room to negotiate. And be careful: This technique requires that you are skilled at keeping a poker face (See Chapter 6, "Getting Physical," for more details on how body language can give you away during negotiations.)

The "Exhausting" Technique

When you're working on a complex negotiation, sometimes it's best to make time your ally: You're essentially trying to wear your opponent down, subtly and smoothly. I call this approach the "Exhausting" technique. It calls for you to map out a long-term, strategic type of negotiating rather than a more cut-and-dried style.

Wear 'em Down, Wear 'em Out

I once handled a negotiation in which my opponent was after more than $13 million. I knew I faced a difficult battle—it usually is, when there's that much money involved. For this reason, I decided that the "Exhausting" technique was called for.

I arranged to conduct the bargaining over a number of smaller sessions rather than one or two drawn-out meetings. My game plan was to get one concession at every meeting. We had six meetings, and I did get a concession at each one. Finally, the $13 million was reduced to less than $1 million.

Dealbreaker

You can carry the "Exhausting" technique too far, until you've strained your opponent's patience to the breaking point and he walks out on the deal. Stay alert to warning signs that this might happen, and be prepared to shift techniques if necessary.

Watch Your Opponent's Limits (and Your Own)

When you use the "Exhausting" technique, there's always the risk that your opponent will threaten to break off the bargaining out of sheer frustration—not exactly the outcome you were hoping for. For that reason, you need to keep a careful eye on how your opponent is holding up—you've got to be prepared to give him or her some sense that progress is being made every once in awhile, just to keep the negotiation open. Obviously, this technique works best when you're bargaining about something that your opponent can't afford to walk away from, such as selling a home or settling a customer dispute.

An additional potential problem is that you may find that the drawn-out nature of this bargaining technique is difficult to maintain on *your* side of the table—your confidence or concentration may begin to waver. If that happens, take a break; use strategically timed recesses to keep yourself sharp and at your negotiating best.

Making Like Mario Andretti: Shifting Gears

Not every negotiation is straightforwardly about a single goal—in fact, most major negotiations have several issues that need to be resolved at the same time. These situations are tailor-made for what I like to call the "Gear-Shifting" technique.

Keeping 'em Guessing

Gear shifting means changing from one issue to another, the way a racing car driver shifts gears during a long race. When you use this technique, your opponent can never quite figure out when you are about to shift to other issues. This keeps your opponent off balance and swings the advantage to you.

Taking Gear-Shifting on the Road

Let's say you're negotiating to buy widgets for your company. The representative from Wonder Widgets promises you a discount if you buy a 1,000-lot case, but that's more widgets than you could ever possibly need. He can also guarantee delivery by October 1, but you want your widgets at least a month sooner. Finally, he wants the bill settled with 15-day net terms. Your company's accounting department doesn't usually operate that way.

Dealmaker

Done well, gear shifting can leave your opponent *so* off balance that you can positively resolve all your issues, when other techniques might require you to concede one to get the rest.

You have three items on your negotiating agenda, which make this a classic case where you can successfully use the "Gear-Shifting" technique to your advantage. Here's how you would use it in this situation:

Start by negotiating about the amount of widgets you need, but don't agree to a final amount—not just yet. Instead, shift to the delivery-date issue. You consult your calendar and start tossing out possible dates by which you need the widgets. Once again, you leave that issue before it's resolved. At this point, you take on the problem of payment terms. Here, again, you confuse the issue without settling anything.

You might go through this routine a second or even third time—each time taking up one of your negotiating issues and then dropping it before it's fully resolved. Soon, your opponent will be disoriented and receptive to any reasonable offer. You are then able to tailor your proposals on each issue to what you want.

Negotiable Terms

A **conduit** is any means by which something is conveyed from one point to another. When you're negotiating, what you're conveying is information—and you want to channel it to your opposing side's "yes" person as effectively and completely as possible.

The "Conduit" Technique

A conduit is a channel for conveying something. When you're negotiating, you are, in effect, conveying information—in the terms and with the interpretation that is most beneficial to your bargaining position. Your goal is to make certain that you are conveying that information to the right person—the "yes" person.

Making Allies

In Chapter 3, "Scoping Out the Other Side," I told you how to prepare for a negotiation in which you would be facing several opponents, including the "yes" person. This is precisely the type of situation in which you might want to pull the "Conduit" technique out of your negotiating arsenal.

When you're forced to deal with your "yes" person's associates, or when you simply can't persuade the "yes" person, you're best advised to focus your efforts on his colleagues. Your goal is to persuade them to see the issues under negotiation from your point of view, and to use them to help you persuade the "yes" person. In effect, your goal is to make them conduits, which thus makes them your bargaining allies.

Channeling Your Way to Success

One reason the "Conduit" technique is so effective is that it takes advantage of a powerful bargaining weapon: repetition. When you face the "yes" person's colleagues, you repeat the arguments you may already have made to the "yes" person, but you're careful not to repeat them word for word. You take a fresh approach—preferably a fresh approach for each one of the "yes" person's colleagues, pointing out other benefits and possibilities of your proposal. This makes it likely that these colleagues will each carry an independent message to the "yes" person that is supportive of your position.

Another reason the "Conduit" technique is so powerful is that it allows you the advantage of indirection: The "yes" person isn't influenced directly by you. Instead, she is influenced by her trusted colleagues and coworkers, who have bought into your proposals. Because these are her trusted coworkers, she is more likely to listen to them than she would have been to you.

The Art of the Deal

I once negotiated with five opponents. I wasn't getting through to the "yes" person, so I focused on convincing the other four. As I kept speaking, I noticed one opponent begin nodding her approval. That improved my odds from 5 against 1 to 4 against 2. I kept on talking, and eventually three of the four were on my side. And with their support for my position, the "yes" person was convinced as well.

The "Talk-Show Host" Technique

I'm sure you've seen those daytime talk shows (even the nighttime ones do it, too): Oprah or Dave or Jay has a guest on, and they're trying to get him to give some scandalous personal information. They'll say to a guest: "I don't want to get too personal, but . . ." or "I don't mean to pry, but . . . ."

The "Talk-Show Host" technique hinges on the use of four key words: *but, however, nevertheless,* and *except.* When a question is phrased using one or more of those words, it's nearly impossible to turn down. The next thing you know, the guest is admitting that he truly *is* the son of three-headed aliens with serious personality disorders.

"I'm on Your Side, but Do It My Way"

The subtlety of this technique is why it's one of my favorites—you can get water from a rock using it. This technique gives you a way to approach delicate or touchy matters without offending your opponent. That's also why this technique is very useful when you negotiate with family or friends.

Hosting at Home

Say your son is asking for the car again, but he hasn't done his homework. That's against house rules, so you have to turn him down. You can just say "no," but that's a sure way to send him stomping off to his room to sulk behind a closed door. Better to approach it like this: "I know how much you want to go out tonight. You know I always let you have the car after you've finished your homework, but . . . ." This is a much sweeter pill for your son to swallow than a direct refusal would be, because you're acknowledging that a.) the car means a lot to your son, and b.) you'd let him have the car, if only he would keep his end of the bargain. Deep down, your son will know you're right (even though he won't admit it).

Negotiable Terms

Self-deprecation is making a statement or statements that contain an admission of a failing or a shortcoming.

The "Self-Deprecating" Technique

When you present a proposal to your opponent and think you might meet with some resistance, try a little self-deprecation. You'll be amazed at how much it helps.

Self-deprecating statements break down barriers between you and your opponent. They make your opponent "like" you. They persuade your opponent without your opponent even knowing it.

Bonding Through Strategic Confession

With self-deprecation, you are giving your opponent something about yourself that he or she can identify with—something that makes you appear more accessible and makes your opponent more comfortable when dealing with you. All of us are at least a little bit insecure, so the kind of bond that this technique helps you forge is very powerful— it can make an ally out of a potential adversary.

The trick is to make sure that you chose your "confession" carefully—you want to choose something that achieves the effect of self-deprecation without destroying your credibility. Sometimes it's easy to spot the kind of topic that will lend itself to a constructive self-deprecating remark. Other times, you'll need to know something about your opponent before you select your remarks.

Bringing It Out to the Real World

So, how does self-deprecation play out in a real-world situation? Suppose your child is having problems at school and you are asked to speak with the principal. As you check out the pictures in the principal's office, you discover that she is a parent, too. So you open the discussion by admitting how difficult parenting is. The principal will immediately relate to what you said. She will also be more sympathetic toward you, your problem, and any solutions you can suggest.

The "It's a Shame" Technique

When you're negotiating more than one issue and a few issues have already been settled, you may find that you can get the rest of the problems solved by using easy language that's hard to disagree with and that nudges your opponent into being more receptive. "It's a Shame" is merely the name I've given to the technique that accomplishes this goal.

With "It's a Shame," you can use a variety of phrases, such as "It's too bad that . . ." or "It's unfortunate that . . ." or "We've come this far, let's try to . . . ." The point is, by using a key phrase, you use the issues already agreed upon as a basis for motivating your opponent to continue bargaining on the unresolved issues.

It's simple to employ this technique. Let's say that you've hit a stalemate on a few sticking points in your negotiation after having reached agreement on four important issues. You break the impasse by saying, "Look, we've taken care of so much. *It's a shame* to make that much progress without settling the remaining two issues. Let's give it a shot." Most of the time your opponent will go along with you. If you reach an agreement on the fifth issue and your opponent again resists about the last one, just repeat the "It's a Shame" technique.

Dealmaker

Avoid language that paints you into a corner, such as "I won't" and "I can't" when using the "It's a Shame" technique. If you have to reverse yourself later, you'll lose credibility and will look weak in the eyes of your opponent.

The Least You Need to Know

➤ As you prepare to negotiate, you should consider which negotiating techniques will work in your negotiation.

➤ Use the "Building Block" technique to impress your opponent with the strength of your case by parceling out facts favorable to your position.

➤ The "Vinegar and Honey" technique works by making a bad negotiating situation or concession seem better than it really is.

➤ The "Exhausting" and "Gear-Shifting" techniques work best on large, complex negotiations.

➤ Use the "Conduit" technique when you are facing more than one opponent and can't convince the "yes" person directly.

➤ The "Talk-Show Host" and "Self-Deprecating" techniques work to form a bond with your opponent.

➤ The "It's a Shame" technique works when a negotiation is nearly settled and only a few points remain to be resolved.

Part 3
Making Minds Meet

In the final analysis, successful negotiation means influencing your opponent's mind—his way of thinking—to get him to agree to your bargaining positions. So, the more you know about how the mind works—and specifically about how a negotiator's mind works—the more effective a negotiator you'll be.

As you gain bargaining experience, you'll begin to see how easy it is to read your opponent's mind, as long as you pay attention to the meaning behind his actions and words. In this part, I'll clue you in on that meaning and show you how to use that knowledge to bargain successfully.

Chapter 11

Identifying Your Opponent

In This Chapter

➤ Just who *is* your opponent?

➤ Identifying decision-making types

➤ Spotting the weak spots

➤ Tailoring your negotiation to suit your opponent

In negotiation, as in life, you will face all kinds of people—people whose skills and talents lie in very different directions. Some can patiently plod through lists of figures, integrating complex statistics into one convincing analysis; others have a distinctively visual flair: a keen eye for color, shape, and design. Still others are keen judges of character, capable of "reading" the new people they meet rapidly and with surprising accuracy.

If you can figure out which skills and preferences your opponent brings to the negotiating table, you can form a strategy that's best suited to persuading your opponent to give you what you want. In this chapter, you learn about the different types of negotiating opponents and how to best influence each one.

It's All a Question of (Negotiating) Style

While it's impossible to pigeonhole all people into neat categories, you can get a fairly good idea of what type of information your opponent values most highly. There are three broad types of negotiators, defined according to the kind of information that will have the strongest influence on their decision making:

➤ Analytical

➤ Aesthetic

➤ Intuitive

Think of these categories as a psychological shorthand that you can use to size up your opponent. While most of us employ a combination of these types, we usually find one of the three more dominant or more readily understandable, and we are therefore more likely to be influenced more strongly when offered information of that type. By identifying the one most favored by your opponent, you'll be better able to determine an effective negotiating strategy.

Dealmaker

Practice distinguishing among "types" with all the people that you meet. When you're bargaining, this insight will come in handy and make it easier for you to figure out the type of opponent you're up against.

Back in Chapter 3, "Scoping Out the Other Side," you already learned about the importance of researching your opponent. You'll now want to review that research to see if any of the information you've dug up clues you in to which type of opponent you face.

Calling Mr. Spock

The analytical opponent is most profoundly influenced by all things financial, statistical, and factual. Balance sheets, cost-benefit analyses, time and motion studies—they're all grist for her decision-making mill. She likes to be fully prepared before she enters into any discussion or negotiation; she wants "all the facts" before she makes a decision.

An analytical type is capable of making decisions that run counter to her personal preferences, if the numbers bear it out. For example, she might buy a house she isn't crazy about if it promises a good investment opportunity. On the job, she might roll out a new product that she wouldn't buy personally if the marketing research suggests that it will be an instant best-seller.

Not surprisingly, analytical types can be found in occupations that require a head for figures: accountants, financial analysts, business managers, chief financial officers, and tax consultants. Frequently, corporate presidents and business owners also have an analytical side because they are constantly asked to analyze profit and loss statements, expenses, budgets, and so on.

How can you tell if you're bargaining with an analytical type? Here are some telltale signs to consider:

➤ They immediately ask for hard facts, such as sales figures, price, profit potential, financing options, or fees.

➤ They are interested in the financial history of the product or service you are negotiating for. How well did the widgets sell in the past? How much of a return did you make on the investment property? How much of a raise did you receive last year? These figures will give them a sense of the future potential of the deal.

➤ They ask to see documentation (sales figures, reports, receipts) of your assertions.

If your opponent is an analytical type at heart, here are some hints to help you influence the course of your negotiation:

➤ Be fully primed and prepared with any information related to the financial or factual side of the deal. For example, if you're bargaining to sell your home, have figures on the cost, the price you paid for the house, the cost of the repair work you've done, the taxes you pay, and so on.

Dealbreaker

Beware of making assumptions about negotiating types based on occupation alone—not all accountants are analytical by nature, nor are all artistic types necessarily influenced by aesthetic considerations. Take all relevant factors into account before deciding on your opponent's likely type.

➤ Downplay aesthetic or intuitive arguments, such as how nice your house looks or what a good neighborhood it's in. The analytical opponent wants the hard facts first.

➤ The more you can document on paper—sales graphs, receipts, or cost estimates—the more you will influence the analytical type (see Chapter 9, "The Paper Chase," for information on organizing your documentation).

Everything's Beautiful, in Its Own Way . . .

The aesthetic opponent focuses on how things look and feel, and on the visceral impact that they have. He may be openly dismissive or even scornful of facts and figures in favor of more artistic considerations. In terms of selling your home, for example, an aesthetic type might actually be willing to pay more for your house (if he really likes the way it looks) than an analytical type would.

Artists, writers, actors, designers, and other people who work in creative occupations tend to be aesthetic types.

Here are some signs that you're bargaining with an aesthetic type:

➤ They place great importance on the way things look. For example, if you're showing your home, they may become wide-eyed at the sight of your beautifully landscaped lawn. On the other hand, nothing turns them off so quickly as an unkempt or dirty room or yard.

The Art of The Deal

Real-estate agents recommend a useful aesthetic trick to anyone who wants to encourage a prospective home buyer to write out that check. They suggest that, just before the prospect comes over to view the house, the homeowner pop a sheet of chocolate chip cookies into the oven. The aroma of baking cookies provides a strong but subtle message to the buyer: "This is a happy home."

➤ They are quick to point out sights (and even smells and sounds) that they like or dislike.

➤ Aesthetic types may also be more tactile than other types: They often like to touch objects (run a hand over a countertop, feel a piece of drapery or fabric, and so on).

Here are some hints to help you influence an aesthetic type:

➤ Emphasize the appearance, condition, and quality of the product or service you are negotiating for. Make sure the product or service has spectacular "eye appeal."

➤ Beyond the obvious appearance of whatever you are negotiating for, emphasize subtle but important aesthetic concerns. For example, if you are showing your house, point out the flow of the floor design or the play of light and shade from the windows.

"I Can Feel It In My Gut . . ."

The intuitive type is influenced by one major consideration: how he "feels" about what you're bargaining about. If his gut feeling about you or the negotiation is good, he'll be happy to work with you. If he doesn't have a good feeling, on the other hand, you'll have to work extra hard to overcome his bad impression and seal the deal.

Intuitive types tend to make decisions very quickly. If pressed for an explanation, they often can't even verbalize why they make the decisions they do. That's because they operate primarily on instinct.

People who work in jobs that require rapid analysis, diagnosis, and action (such as doctors, lawyers, and salespeople) are often the intuitive type. Lawyers, for example, often spend a lot of time analyzing a client's problems and then must make on-the-spot decisions when they try the case in front of a jury.

Here are some signs that you are bargaining with an intuitive type:

➤ They give you plenty of verbal and physical feedback to show what they think of your proposal. If they like what they're seeing and hearing, they may nod frequently and say "Uh-huh" or "I see." If they don't like what you're saying, they may frown, shake their heads, or express their displeasure in some other way.

➤ They may make quick, generalized snap judgments: "I don't like it. It doesn't feel right." Or: "I have a good feeling about this. I think it's going to work out."

Intuitive types can be tricky to negotiate with because if they simply don't like you, you will be hard-pressed to win them over. But here are some hints to help you influence an intuitive type:

➤ Be especially careful to cultivate a bond with this type. (See Chapter 13, "Goodwill Hunting," for more detailed advice on this topic.) While you should do this with all negotiating opponents, intuitive types place especially strong emphasis on trusting and liking the people they negotiate with.

➤ Emphasize how well the deal will suit both of you. Intuitive types are keen to act on negotiations that feel right and that are fair to everyone involved in them.

A Word of Caution About Types

It's impossible to boil down a person of myriad experiences, emotions, and preferences into a single type, even though one type may be dominant. For one thing, many people may straddle one or more types. A marketing manager, for example, may be equally concerned with the aesthetics of a product design and the financial analysis of how well the product will sell. A salesperson, on the other hand, may operate on both intuitive and analytical levels as she tries to clinch a sale.

Dealmaker

Intuitive types pride themselves on their ability to get an instinctive "feel" for the appropriate decision. If you're getting a sense that your opponent doesn't "feel" right about your position, probe gently for the source of that feeling, and address your efforts to overcoming it.

Accordingly, as you prepare for a negotiation, you should be well-versed in arguments that will convince all three types. Don't assume, for example, that because you are negotiating with an aesthetic type, you can completely ignore or fudge the financial aspect of your negotiation. That's unrealistic and insulting to your opponent.

Your goal is to be prepared for all contingencies, so prepare thoroughly before you begin negotiating, and use these "types" only as a general guideline, not as the final word on your opponent's psyche.

From Weakness, or From Strength?

There's another refinement you can use as you try to size up your opponent. In addition to discovering the way your opponent is most strongly influenced, you can quickly determine *how* she makes decisions.

Whether your opponent is primarily analytical, aesthetic, or intuitive, she also operates on a continuum of decision-making, from strong (quick, assertive) to weak (hesitant, doubtful). An aesthetic type who is a strong decision-maker, for example, probably has highly developed views on what looks good and what does not; she has a strong design sense. An aesthetic type who is a weak decision-maker, on the other hand, may have less firmly set views.

Just as the analytical-aesthetic-intuitive labels are guidelines, not final judgments, so is the strong-weak continuum. Most negotiators will fall somewhere in the middle. Use this as a general guideline to determine how best to negotiate with your opponent.

Dealmaker

Once you've figured out the type of opponent you're negotiating with, don't let on that you've got him or her pegged. Continue on as you've always done, but inwardly you should be developing your strategies to fit your opponent's particular type.

Strong, but Not-So-Silent

Whether they operate primarily on analytical, aesthetic, or intuitive levels, strong types make decisions quickly and confidently. They analyze complicated information rapidly—but sometimes, when they pass judgment too quickly, their hasty decisions turn out to be wrong.

Identifying the Strong Decision-Maker

If you're trying to sell your home to a strong type, for example, she will go after your property aggressively if she really loves it. She may want to rush the deal through without bargaining—even if it means that she has to pay a higher price for your place.

Most strong types display some or all of the following traits:

➤ They interrupt frequently and often answer your questions before you've finished asking them.

➤ They use "I" a lot because they have a strong desire for recognition.

➤ They speak in a firm, unhesitant tone of voice. They always talk and act like they know what they're doing—even if they secretly have doubts.

➤ They get angry quickly and take a long time to calm down.

Negotiating with a Strong Type

While strong types seem commanding and authoritative, they're easy to deal with if you use the following strategies:

➤ Strong types respond best to clear, logical positions that leave no unanswered questions or areas open to interpretation. So if you're negotiating with a strong type, present your proposals clearly and back them up with as much documentation as you can.

Take that house you're selling as an example. The strong type is likely to give you the price you're asking for without question if you've got a written appraisal that proves the house is worth it.

➤ Strong types tend to stick to their views or judgments, even after they've been proven wrong (which, incidentally, doesn't happen often). That's because it's excruciatingly difficult for these types to admit that they've made a mistake.

➤ Strong types get angry quickly, and they stay angry. Don't do or say anything that will set them off.

One of the easiest ways to make strong types angry is by not taking them seriously. If you have to reject a strong type's offer, you should explain in detail why you're turning him down. And never laugh at or belittle a proposal made by a strong type, no matter how off-the-wall it seems.

Dealbreaker

If you catch a strong type making a mistake, be tactful—don't gloat when you point out the error. Most strong types have a definite sense of right and wrong, so if you catch an error and point it out diplomatically, they'll usually make concessions—sometimes large ones—to "put things right."

Foiling the Fence-Straddler

Unlike the strong type, who will have immediate and decisive views on any issue or negotiation, the fence-straddling type needs more time and likes to reach a consensus before taking any action.

Spotting the Fence-Straddler

Fence-straddlers can be frustrating to work with unless you've got a good plan in place, so it's helpful to know if this is the type of decision-maker you're dealing with early on. Here are some clues to help you spot this type:

➤ Fence-straddlers like to feel that they've examined all possible approaches before they make a final decision. They hoard all paperwork related to the issue, and they tend to consult with others (colleagues, family, friends, experts) to get a wide variety of opinions.

113

➤ They will usually ask for time to consult with others before they make a final decision on any major proposals, but they are quick to concede minor points.

Negotiating with a Fence-Straddling Type

Here's how you can break through the fence-straddler's indecision:

➤ When a fence-straddler leaves a negotiation to consult with others, he often comes back to the bargaining table with all kinds of changes and variations. Don't let him get away with this! Explain your proposals to him in great detail, and try to force him to make a decision on the spot.

➤ If other people whose opinions are important to your opponent agree with your negotiating position, you should mention this to the fence-straddling type, who likes to reach consensus. For example, you might say, "I've heard that your business manager thinks that 50 cents a widget will work with your budget."

Talking Points

"Indecision is debilitating; it feeds upon itself; it is, one might almost say, habit forming . . . often greater risk is involved in postponement than in making the wrong decision."
—H. A. Hopt

The 98-Pound Weakling

Weak decision-makers, whether analytical, aesthetic, or intuitive, make for unfortunate negotiators. They just don't want to commit to anything that could turn out wrong.

Indications of Indecisiveness

Weak decision-makers are reluctant to make any decisions—they would much rather pass the responsibility on to family members, business associates, or friends. They stall, they stammer, they beg for more information and more time. They try to postpone any decision until it's forced upon them. Here are some other clues to help you spot weak types:

➤ They tend to be timid and speak quietly. They let you do all the talking and only occasionally offer a nod or an "Uh-huh." They almost never interrupt.

➤ Because decision-making is nerve-wracking for them, they are prone to bad habits such as nail-biting and squinting.

Avoiding the Hesitation Shuffle

If you apply too much pressure on weak types, they will simply abdicate and turn the decision over to someone else. But there are things you can do to overcome the weak decision-maker's fear of commitment. Here are a few:

➤ Be very patient.

➤ Explain every major proposal you make in detail.

➤ Encourage them to ask questions so they can participate in the bargaining process.

By going through the negotiation process step by step, you can reduce your opponent's resistance. Keep in mind that the weak type of negotiator needs a great deal of reassurance, so you'll probably be well advised to concentrate on building a bond of trust with him or her as early in the negotiation process as possible (see Chapter 13 " for more on building a bond with your opponent).

The Least You Need to Know

➤ Analytical types are most influenced by figures, statistics, and hard data.

➤ Aesthetic types are most influenced by things that look, feel, taste, smell, and sound good to them. Cultivate a lot of "eye appeal" when you negotiate with these types.

➤ Intuitive types often operate on gut feeling and instinct. Concentrate on developing a bond with them before you negotiate.

➤ If you are negotiating with a strong type, take every proposal seriously, and provide a lot of documentation for your proposals.

➤ If you are negotiating with a fence-straddling type, press for a decision without giving your opponent a chance to consult with others.

➤ If you are negotiating with a weak type, be patient and explain every detail of your proposal.

Reaching Out to the Other Side

None of us are immune to appeals to our self-perception or our emotions—even if we aren't 100 percent consciously aware of what those perceptions and emotions might be. That's why the psychological aspect of developing your negotiating strategy can be so important: It's how you enlist your opponent's own personal and emotional responses to your cause.

In this chapter, you'll learn about two very important elements that have a strong but usually unrecognized influence over your opponent's decision-making process: his sense of "self" and the emotions that color every decision that he makes. Once you understand how these influence decision making, you'll be better able to use them to further your own cause and to reduce your own vulnerability to an opponent who tries to use them against *you!*

An Appeal to Image

Shortly after she moved to a new neighborhood, Sally visited the local diner for breakfast. She wasn't crazy about the food and thought the service was poor. The next day, she mentioned how bad the place was to her neighbor.

A few weeks later, Sally revisited the diner. This time, the owner came out to greet her personally. He served her himself and made sure everything was perfect. Sally reported the welcome change to her neighbor. "I wonder what happened? Did you tell the owner about my complaints?" she asked.

"Actually," her neighbor said, "I told him you were very impressed with his service and said that was how he must have built up such a good business."

The lesson here? You will always get more out of people if you compliment rather than criticize them. We negotiators call this appealing to your opponent's *self*. In this chapter, you learn how to recognize—and appeal to—the essential parts of your opponent's self.

Talking Points

"The first care of diplomatists and monarchs and all who wish to rule or influence is . . . to find out their victim's strongest principle of self-regard, so as to make that the fulcrum of all appeals."

—William James

Who *Are* You?

Quick—describe yourself, in 10 words or less.

Difficult, isn't it? That's because there are so many different elements that contribute to the person you call your "self." Here's just a partial list of the kinds of elements that contribute to your image of your self:

➤ The people you associate with—family and friends

➤ Your pets

➤ Your job, employer, and coworkers, or your business

➤ The things you own: your clothes, house, money, and car

➤ Intangibles, including your reputation and values

Literally everything you are connected to is part of your identity. You are emotionally attached to all of them, but not with the same intensity. You're more strongly attached to your family, for example, than to your neighbor or your car (I hope!). Your degree of attachment depends on how closely you consider anything to be part of your self.

If you have children, think about how fiercely protective you are of them. When anyone criticizes them, you immediately rise to defend them—not just because of the criticism, but because, in your mind, when someone attacks your children, it feels like that person is attacking you. Likewise, when your kids do well, you glow with pride—not just for them, but for yourself. Your kids are that much a part of you. Whatever happens to them touches your self.

If you can discover what is an important part of your opponent's self, you can establish a bond with, and thus motivate, your opponent—and this will make negotiating easier, more fruitful, and more enjoyable for both of you.

Discovering What Turns Your Opponent On

Back in Chapter 3, "Scoping Out the Other Side," I talked about how important it is to research your opponent before you begin negotiating. During your research, try to discover some of your opponent's interests and values. Better still, look for those interests and values that you and your opponent have in common.

See if you can find any mention of the following facets to your opponent:

➤ Professional achievements

➤ Family life

➤ Artistic pursuits

➤ Athletic ability

➤ Intellectual accomplishments

➤ Volunteer work

➤ Hobbies

If you can't discover anything beforehand, you'll have only a few minutes before negotiating begins to look for tip-offs to your opponent's personality. Look around his office, if that's where you are. (Of course, you'll try *not* to be there, because that's his home field—see Chapter 4, "On Your Mark . . ., Get Set. . ., Negotiate!" for a discussion of picking the place for your negotiation.) Study any plaques on the wall, books on the shelf, or pictures or knick-knacks on the desk. If your opponent has come to you, make a quick study of his physical appearance for clues (but don't stare).

Dealmaker

It's best to introduce references to shared personal interests right from the start of a negotiation. It helps you form an instant bond that will make the rest of the session run more smoothly.

The initial conversation you make with your opponent before negotiation begins can also offer you a wealth of chances to learn more about her. Ask questions about her business, her schooling, or even her hobbies if you feel it's appropriate.

Do this tactfully and sincerely, however. You don't want your opponent to think that you're snooping into areas that are none of your business. But most people like to talk about themselves and will tell you a lot without hesitation.

The sooner and the more you can learn, the better. You want as much time as possible to use what you've learned during the bargaining.

Working the Self-Image Angle

You have three objectives when you appeal to your opponent's self:

➤ You want to create a more compatible relationship with your opponent as a person.

➤ You want to form a bond between the two of you.

➤ You want to know the best way to influence and persuade your opponent.

Difficult though it may be, you have to separate the *issue* that you are negotiating from the *person* you are negotiating with. Even if the negotiation is controversial and the discussions become intense, you still have to treat your opponent as a person.

You can be a tough-as-nails negotiator but a respectful, courteous, and patient person. That's the only way you'll ever reach your opponent's self. Once that cardinal rule is forgotten and negotiating breaks down, cases end up in court, unions go on strike, and friends become enemies.

Negotiating is much easier once you and your opponent have a bond, such as belonging to the same organization. Having a bond makes you a part of your opponent's self.

The Art of the Deal

When I'm negotiating with a lawyer, I always check his background to see if we have anything in common (such as belonging to the same legal fraternity). If I find something, I mention it as early in the bargaining as possible. That makes me a part of my opponent's self and he a part of my self.

Building Bridges

Say your daughter is having a problem with one of her teachers at school, and you have to talk to the principal about it. You've read in the last PTA bulletin that the principal recently received an award for outstanding school administrator. You can assume that the principal is very proud of that award. It represents her accomplishments and all she has worked so hard for so many difficult years. It's a part of her self.

When you sit down to speak with the principal, you open with a compliment: "You know, I'm so happy that Margie is enrolled in this school. The classes and activities are great. And congratulations on winning the Outstanding School Administrator award! You must be really proud." That does the trick. You've touched your opponent's self.

Now you're both relaxed and can move into your discussion in an atmosphere of mutual cooperation and agreement.

Or, say your opponent mentions that she belongs to the same charitable group as you—you both volunteer for the Salvation Army during the holidays. Talking about your mutual interest will appeal to your opponent's self and will form a bond between you that will make your negotiation proceed more smoothly.

A lot of times your opponent may be fishing—even hoping—for a compliment. Stay alert, and you'll be able to pick up the clues. If your opponent is vain about his appearance, for example, he may make unconscious gestures such as smoothing down his tie or brushing imaginary lint off his suit. If you sense that a compliment is in order, go for it. Tell your opponent what a great suit he has on. You'll see an immediate reaction. Your opponent will warm up to you. You've hit him where he's most responsive: his self.

Open Mouth, Insert Foot

You're flustered. You're late to meet with your opponent because your plane was delayed. You show up at his office and say, "Sorry, but the terminal was a zoo. None of the attendants knew what was going on, and I ended up sitting on an unmoving plane for over an hour before we got cleared for takeoff. You know how those damned airlines are."

Your opponent frowns and says, "Yes, actually I do. My father, brother, and sister are commercial pilots."

Dealbreaker

Always make your compliments sincere. Your opponent will be insulted if he detects or even suspects that you're faking it.

Oops! Anything can happen once you make the mistake of offending your opponent's self. Your opponent may seethe quietly or even tell you off. Whatever the reaction, one thing is certain: Negotiating with this person won't be easy.

Say your opponent casually tells you that she and her family just returned from a fabulous two-week camping trip. (Yes, the love of camping may be a part of your opponent's self.) If you hate the outdoors and just the thought of camping makes you itchy, keep it to yourself. Say something neutral like, "That's great. Sounds like a lot of fun." You've kept your comments positive and, more importantly, you didn't injure your opponent's self.

Avoid these subjects so that you don't attack your opponent's self:

➤ Negative opinions or gossip about your opponent's company, product, or colleagues

➤ Negative opinions on hobbies, movies, books, or interests—unless you know for sure that your opponent agrees

➤ Jokes (unless you know your opponent's sense of humor well)

➤ Anything to do with religion or politics

Of course, you're only human and there will be times when you unintentionally offend your opponent. What do you do if that happens? Simple: Apologize! Right there, on the spot. If you wait too long to apologize, your opponent may think you're insincere—and then you're a goner.

Feelings, Nothing More than Feelings

Every one of us is a bundle of emotions. Fear, anger, grief, joy, rage, and shame, to name only a few, lay quietly within us, waiting for the right stimulant to wake up. And playing on emotions is an age-old practice—a trade that politicians, playwrights, and poets, among others, have been plying for centuries. Negotiators do, too.

Playing the Emotional Angle?

When you're emotionally involved in something, you don't look at it objectively and impartially. You substitute your emotional judgment for a judgment based on the merits of a position. Appealing to your opponent's emotions is thus a separate form of persuasion from trying to persuade your opponent on the merits of your bargaining position.

Therein lies its real worth: If your bargaining position is weak on merit, you can appeal to your opponent's emotions. You want to get your opponent to forget about your weak negotiating position and be emotionally motivated to give you what you want.

An Emotional Triad

There are many ways to influence your opponent's emotions. In negotiation, the three most direct routes to emotional influence are by making appeals to your opponent's needs or desires:

➤ Desire for wealth

➤ Thirst for recognition

➤ Need for self-preservation

Each of these emotional appeals can have a powerful effect on the success of your negotiation—and one of the three is usually dominant. Your goal is to discover which is dominant in your opponent and to focus your attention on that one. This will help to emotionally influence your opponent to give you what you want in return.

Give Me Money (That's What I Want)

For many of us, a part of the great American dream is to get rich. We all have a strong desire for wealth, which includes money, property, valuables, or anything else to which we attach value. Wealth gives us power, freedom, and security (not to mention the ability to take off for Bora Bora whenever we feel like it). Most of us have a strong desire to accumulate more wealth and protect what we have.

Many of your opponents will have a strong desire for wealth. If your bargaining strategy is to cut a deal that will either increase their wealth or help them preserve their existing wealth, you'll strike their emotional nerve.

Dealmaker

Once you learn which emotion is your opponent's strongest motivator, you can develop a strategy that appeals to it, especially if the merits of your bargaining position are weak.

Here's how to recognize opponents with a strong craving for wealth:

➤ They like to talk about and show off their possessions: expensive car, house, clothes, and so on.

➤ They often like to talk about anything that relates to money, such as the killing they made in the stock market or their company profits.

➤ Expressions dealing with money—"bucks," "big ones," "moola," "greenbacks," and the like—often pop up in their conversation.

➤ They frequently talk about other people's money with a hint of envy.

➤ They tend to have a negative, almost condescending attitude toward people who don't have a lot of money.

I Love the Spotlight—Recognition

Legendary actress Kate Hepburn perhaps characterized this desire best when she said: "When I started out, I didn't have any desire to be an actress or to learn how to act. I just wanted to be famous." Now *that's* a classic case of a strong desire for recognition.

People have a strong desire to be recognized and acknowledged for their achievements. A skillful actress wants her fans and colleagues to notice and admire her technique. A high-powered businessman wants others to pay tribute to his flamboyant wheeling and dealing. An all-star athlete wants to win medals for her athletic prowess.

Here's how to recognize opponents with a strong craving for recognition:

➤ They're often driven to get themselves and their accomplishments splashed across any media that will have them, whether it's a local newspaper, magazine, television, or even word of mouth.

➤ They are usually well-groomed and may wear flashy clothes.

➤ Their material goods are usually impeccable—they have well-tended homes and cars (often with custom license plates).

➤ They may refer to themselves frequently in conversation; their favorite words are "I" or "me."

➤ They often work in the public eye (actors, politicians, athletes, executives, celebrities).

➤ They often work in uniform (military officers, airline pilots, police).

Gimme Shelter: Self-Preservation

Talking Points

"When dealing with people, remember you are not dealing with creatures of logic, but with creatures of emotion."

—Dale Carnegie

Self-preservation is the desire to be physically and financially safe and secure. Anything that ensures or threatens that security will get an emotional response. If someone sticks a gun in your face and tells you to do something, you'll do it because you value your life. If someone threatens your job, you'd have the same self-preservation reaction, but to a less extreme degree.

Self-preservation will be the strongest desire of many of your opponents. We all want to be safe and secure, but some people take that desire to extremes. They squirrel away every dime, even though they have enough money to last a lifetime. They obey the speed limit, cross only at the intersection, and observe every rule and regulation because it gives them a feeling of safety.

Here's how to recognize opponents with a strong craving for self-preservation:

➤ Generally, they are not aggressive.

➤ They are good listeners who will let you talk because they feel more secure when they know what's on your mind.

➤ They are usually low-key. They don't get excited or angry easily.

➤ They dress plainly because they don't crave recognition.

Making Your Appeals

Once you know which emotional appeal is strongest for your opponent—wealth, recognition, or self-preservation—you have an additional weapon in your negotiating arsenal. This gives you more bargaining flexibility.

Money Makes the World Go 'Round

Any of your bargaining positions that increase or preserve your opponent's wealth will prompt an emotional response. The more your opponent wants wealth, the quicker and stronger your opponent's emotional response will be.

The Art of the Deal

I once had a job collecting debts for a luxury car dealership. Because the cars were expensive and prestigious, I figured wealth was the strongest emotional approach. I sent a simple letter to the debtors, promising that if they didn't pay, the dealership would take "appropriate action" that would cause them "additional expenses." Aside from using fear as a motivator, I was really advising them that they could preserve their wealth if they promptly paid off their debt. I was appealing to their desire for wealth.

If you're negotiating to collect payment on an overdue bill, for example, you might offer your customer a 10 percent discount for paying promptly. That would be a direct appeal to preserving their wealth. It would be the same if you offered a $100 gift certificate as an incentive because the customer would then be $100 richer.

To give another example, say you're selling your home, which has an additional acre attached that's worth $10,000. You've just about persuaded the buyer to pay full price for your house, but he hasn't signed on the dotted line. So you throw in a sweetener—the right to buy the attached lot for $8,000 any time within three years from the date you sell your home. If your opponent's strong desire is wealth, he will emotionally respond to the opportunity to get a good deal on the attached property.

Offering Your Opponent Recognition

If your opponent craves recognition, he will be receptive to any deal that will increase his visibility. And if his desire for recognition is strong enough, the money part of the deal becomes secondary. Anything you do that appeals to his desire for recognition will emotionally motivate him.

Dealmaker

When you're appealing to your opponent's emotions, give in on minor concessions. You don't want to get bogged down in petty disputes and run the risk of angering your opponent. If you do, your opponent will not respond to your emotional appeals.

For example, during one negotiation I suggested to my opponent that if we reached an agreement, we should hold a press conference to announce it. I knew his strongest emotional desire was clearly for recognition that he would welcome with open arms the opportunity to shine in front of the camera. Slipping the press conference suggestion into the negotiation emotionally stimulated my opponent to reach an agreement.

Or, say you're bargaining with a landscaper to redo the design of the shrubbery and flowers around your front lawn. You promise the landscaper that you will leave her sign on your property for 30 days after the job is completed so that everyone who passes by your house will know that Smith Landscaping did the job. Not only does this promise good business for Smith, but it also directly appeals to her desire for recognition for a landscaping job well done.

Offering Your Opponent Security

Anything you say or do that preserves and ensures your opponent's self-preservation will cause him to emotionally respond.

For example, say you own a beautiful and intricate grandfather clock, passed down from your grandparents to your parents and now to you. You intend to pass the clock on to your own children someday. But time has taken its toll, and the delicate clock mechanism needs repairs. A specialist examines the clock and estimates that a full repair will cost nearly $1,000.

You don't really have that kind of money, but you do have a strong desire for self-preservation. The repair person senses this and clinches it by suggesting that the clock mechanism will completely break if you don't take action soon.

Your urge to preserve the clock will be very strong because it's a part of your family and a part of your self. You'll probably fork up the money because you want to preserve the things that are closest and dearest to you. By preserving those things, you're preserving a part of your self.

Staying Above the Fray

I once negotiated with an opponent who opened the discussions by accusing me of insulting his intelligence. I was negotiating to buy his property—a golf course he had helped to design—and I mentioned that my client needed to make changes on the property. I was trying to get the purchase price lowered to cover the cost of the changes.

My opponent was so personally attached to the course and his design that he attacked me for suggesting that anything should be done to change it. I stayed cool, smiled, and then carefully explained that nothing personal was intended by the suggested changes. The issue was return on our investment, and the changes were proposed solely for economic reasons—not to personally offend him. That did the trick. He calmed down and we resumed bargaining.

Keeping Cucumber Cool

Your goal is to be thick-skinned when you negotiate. (I know, I know, it's a lot easier said than done.) You'll bargain with a lot of opponents who may offend you, either because they lack experience or because they are just mean-spirited. Don't let that get to you. Keep your eye on the issues, not the people involved. (See Part 5, "Problem Solving" for advice on this and other related issues.)

Talking Points

"Emotions come wholly from within, and have only the strength we allow them . . . . But we must control those emotions, or they will control us."

—John M. Wilson

Staying Alert to Opponent's Appeals

While you are saying nice things about your opponent's professional expertise, beautiful family, or well-tended widget collection, your opponent will be equally quick to stroke you about your accomplishments, your family, and your interests. You know she's trying to appeal to your self or to your emotions. What do you do?

Be gracious. Thank your opponent. Then move on with the discussion as quickly as possible. Don't dwell on your opponent's remarks—you're increasing the chances that they will influence you to make concessions.

We all like people who stroke us and build up our ego. But don't let a little flattery persuade you to make concessions that work against your interests. That's a high price to pay for a little buttering up.

The Least You Need to Know

➤ Appealing to your opponent's self creates a closer relationship, which makes your opponent more likely to give you what you want.

➤ Sincere compliments will appeal to your opponent's self. So will finding that you share something in common, such as belonging to the same club or working for the same charity.

➤ When your negotiating position is weak on its merits, you should consider appealing to your opponent's emotions to get what you want.

➤ All people have a desire for wealth, recognition, and self-preservation; determine which most strongly motivates your opponent and appeal to it during negotiations.

➤ Don't make any concessions because your opponent has appealed to your self; keep your focus on getting what you want.

Goodwill Hunting

Earlier in my career, when I worked with the Treasury Department in Chicago, I was constantly called upon to negotiate with high-powered lawyers who represented the estates of wealthy decedents. In one case, a lawyer didn't want to include a particular asset in his late client's estate because that would raise the estate taxes. But I knew of a tax loophole that would offset the added tax, and I told him about it. We concluded our business successfully and cordially. He later called me to thank me again for letting him in on that inside information.

By doing my opponent that small but significant favor, I built up goodwill with him—goodwill that was ultimately helpful to me. In this chapter, you learn what goodwill is and how you can harness its powers in your negotiations.

Compatibility Counts!

Goodwill simply means establishing a relationship with your opponent that will make her more likely to deal favorably with you. That sometimes means doing your opponent a favor, just as I did when I pointed out that tax reduction to the estate lawyer. When you build goodwill with your opponent, what you're really doing is developing a relationship of mutual trust and compatibility.

Negotiable Terms

Goodwill is defined as benevolence and willingness—a relationship built on trust and compatibility. When a business is sold, goodwill is so important that it is treated as an intangible asset, and figured into the selling price, along with the physical assets.

A goodwill-based bargaining environment, with mutual trust and compatibility, is one in which both you and your opponent are most likely to seal a successful deal. Your opponent will concede points and issues he normally wouldn't dream of giving in on, solely because he has a favorable perception of you.

The Benefits of Benevolence

There are innumerable political, social, and psychological benefits of doing good things for others. In strictly negotiating terms, however, there are four specific reasons why you should build goodwill:

➤ It serves as a bridge of trust between you and your opponent. Once your opponent trusts you, it will be easier to persuade her. She will accept your words, assertions, and any written material you offer. Then you are practicing the art of persuasion at its finest: You're reaching and influencing your opponent.

➤ Goodwill ensures that your opponent will like you. I admit, likability doesn't sound like a quality tough negotiators should boast about, but it is. If your opponent likes you, he'll be more likely to give you what you want.

➤ If you build goodwill with your opponent the first time the two of you negotiate, you'll have an easier time whenever you negotiate again.

➤ Once you build goodwill with an opponent, he will tell others how pleasant it was to work with you. It's basic human nature to talk about people we like—and dislike.

Dealmaker

People who like each other tend to reach agreements fast. People who don't, won't.

This last point is very important. If you can make your opponent into a goodwill ambassador for you, it sets up a ripple-like effect. Sooner or later the benefits will surface—sometimes in surprising contexts. I frequently negotiate with new opponents who tell me they feel comfortable with me solely because of what they've heard about me from my previous opponents. That's in spite of the fact that I have a reputation as a tough, tenacious negotiator.

Building the Goodwill Bridge

There are many ways you can build a bridge of goodwill to your opponent. Here are just a few:

➤ *Tip off your client to any hidden benefits in your proposal.* That's what I did when I informed that estate lawyer about the tax benefits he wasn't aware of. That's one of the best ways to get your opponent in the right frame of mind. Each favor you do for your opponent builds a plank in the bridge of trust—even if you're hard-hitting at the bargaining table.

➤ *Cultivate a personal touch.* This is where the research you've done on your opponent comes into play (see Chapter 3, "Scoping Out the Other Side"). Ask about your opponent's family, career, hobbies—whatever you can think of. Just make sure you're sincere. If you genuinely don't care or can't stand your opponent, don't try to "make nice."

➤ *Express your appreciation.* Anything you think will go over well with your opponent is something to do. Think of all the generous, dramatic gestures that companies make to woo important clients: tickets to sports and theater events, holiday gift baskets, celebratory bottles of champagne on completion of a project. You don't have to send your opponent to a sporting match or a Broadway show to earn goodwill, but a nice card acknowledging that you enjoyed meeting and working with your opponent wouldn't be a bad idea.

➤ Point out any errors your opponent makes, as early in the negotiations as possible and as tactfully as possible. Your opponent will owe you a big favor when you help save his face in a negotiation.

But be careful—pointing out your opponent's errors requires a diplomatic touch. Still, it's well worth your while to learn how to do this skillfully. I once negotiated with an opponent who mistook an asset valued at $750,000 for only $75,000. I quickly corrected him before he completely embarrassed himself and botched the deal. From that point on he trusted me and was very receptive to my proposals.

Realize here that I'm referring to obvious errors that have an important impact on the negotiation. You don't have to monitor your opponent's entire case, but obvious errors will come to light sooner or later. You can both head off problems and build up goodwill by pointing them out sooner.

A final thought: Make suggestions that help your opponent once the bargaining is successfully concluded. When you negotiate a deal to buy something—clothes, a car, a new house—you can always promise good word-of-mouth to your opponent if you're happy with your purchase. That will make your opponent feel good about the deal and about you. (See Chapter 12, "Reaching Out to the Other Side," for some more ideas about how to do this.)

Dealbreaker

Always point out obvious errors immediately. If you wait too long, your opponent will suspect that you were trying to think of a way to benefit from the error. This will make your opponent suspicious of you, and a suspicious opponent is not one very likely to agree with your bargaining position.

Getting to Goodwill

There's more than one way to establish goodwill with a bargaining opponent. So far, you've learned several: building an emotional bond through appealing to his sense of self, playing to your opponent's emotional response, and even doing favors. But that's just the beginning. You can also build goodwill by the very image you present as you negotiate.

If you're like many people, you may think that a tough, tenacious negotiator means someone who is unfair or unfriendly or someone who spends the entire negotiation with a scowl permanently fixed on her face, angrily barking out demands like a junkyard dog. That's just not true: Any negotiator who behaved like that would consistently fail.

The only real way to get anybody to do anything is to make them want to do it. And if you spend your negotiation in anger, or come on too strong, you're following a formula for failure.

Instead, you should try to cultivate what I consider to be the three key personal attributes of a successful negotiator:

➤ Fairness

➤ Sincerity

➤ Friendliness

Climbing the Fair-Way to Negotiating Heaven

Fairness always attracts a positive response—people tend to like people who are fair, even if they disagree with them. For example, let's say that your neighbor's dog likes to dig up your manicured lawn. You're fully aware that your neighbor loves his big old mutt, so you know you've got a sensitive, touchy problem to negotiate. What to do?

Talking Points

"The ability . . . to make people believe in you and trust you is one of the few absolutely fundamental qualities of success."

—John J. McGuirk

Of course, you can give your neighbor an ultimatum: "Keep your dog off my lawn, or else!" But that will only infuriate your neighbor and make him dig in his heels—by attacking his beloved pet, you are in effect attacking *him*. Alternatively, you can put up a fence. But that's a drastic solution that penalizes you more than anyone else—you'll have to dig into your pocket to pay for it, and it'll probably hurt the value of your property (there are very few attractive fences).

Here's where your sense of fairness can quickly pay off. You can open your negotiation with your neighbor by first mentioning what a nice dog he has and how you, too, are an animal lover (assuming, of course, that you are one). Than you can calmly and carefully explain the problem and come straight out with your dilemma about how to solve it. Notice, here, that you haven't proposed a solution—you know that the only true one would be to keep the dog off your property.

By soliciting your neighbor's idea for a solution, you're sending an extra message—one that has to do with your fairness. What you're really saying to your neighbor is something like this: "Look, your dog is ruining *my* lawn. I could get tough and take steps to keep your dog out, but you're my neighbor and I want to be fair to both you and your dog."

Following this strategy permits you to create a negotiating climate that allows you to both resolve your problem and keep your friendship with your neighbor. That last is no small benefit: Good neighbors frequently have a falling out over relatively trivial matters when a little bargaining skill can quickly and favorably settle the matter.

Sincerely Yours

Lack of sincerity is a major cause of negotiating failure. If, in the above example, your neighbor detects any hint of insincerity on your part, you run the risk of turning him off not only to your dog problem but to all your future encounters with him as well.

No Phonies, Please

If you want a quick and easy gauge of the positive impact that sincerity has on a party to a negotiation, just review your own experience. The next time you meet a new person—if she's sincere, you'll instantly feel as though you like her; if she asks a favor you'll almost immediately agree based on the strength of your positive feelings. You'll find yourself bending over backward to agree to nearly any reasonable request, whether she wants to borrow a couple of eggs or asks you to watch her place while she's off for a few days' vacation in Vegas. You'll find that you simply *want* to help.

If that new person is insincere, though, you'll respond quite differently. You'll do just about anything you can to get out of doing the favor. You simply don't want to get involved with someone you feel lacks sincerity—life's just too short to spend it dealing with someone you feel is a phony.

Dealbreaker

Nervousness and defensiveness on your part can easily come across as insincerity—you're more likely to have trouble looking into your opponent's eyes, and you're likely to be fidgety. The best way to overcome this problem is to go into negotiations fully prepared. That will give you confidence in your position, which will translate into personal confidence.

The Impact of Sincerity

When you're negotiating, your opponent is much more apt to go along with your bargaining position if he feels that you're being sincere. If he feels that you're being open and honest with him, he is unlikely to raise unnecessary roadblocks to reaching an agreement. This frees you to focus on your bargaining strategy without constantly having to put out brushfires caused by personality problems.

Your New Best Friend

I guarantee you that *everybody* wants to be appreciated—even your opponent when negotiating. Your bargaining goal is simple: You want to favorably influence your opponent toward your negotiating goal. If you want a raise, you want your boss to want to *give* you that raise. If you're after the lowest price possible for that new home, you want to influence the seller (and broker) so that they *want* to give you your price.

Building Bonds

One powerful way to motivate your negotiation opponent to feel this way is through establishing a bond of friendship. But being friendly means more than slapping a smile on your face. It means being courteous even in bargaining situations that may become heated or emotional (see Chapter 16, "Don't Get Your Dander Up," for more on coping with anger when negotiating).

Dealmaker

No one likes to be turned down on a deal or a request, but you can make your opponent feel better about such an event if you take the time to acknowledge his feelings. A sincere "I'm sorry, but I can't do that for you right now" takes some of the sting out of rejection.

Courtesy is an expression of friendliness, and it helps keep you from creating unnecessary bargaining problems. If, for example, you first approach that dog-owning neighbor of yours angrily, don't be surprised if he reacts to you by slamming the door in your face. On the other hand, if you approach him courteously, making friendly small-talk about his favorite pet (as suggested earlier), you're far more likely to get him into a receptive mood for solving your problem.

And that's the point: When planning negotiation, your goal is to resolve—or minimize—any problems that might get in the way of getting what you want.

Friendly, but Firm

The fact that you are being friendly doesn't mean that you can't be firm in advocating your position. For example, you can maintain courtesy with your neighbor while still holding your ground about keeping your lawn from getting dug up. In fact, your friendliness will give your firmness even greater impact—your neighbor will be hard-pressed to refuse to recognize your claims if you present them in a pleasant, courteous manner.

Here's how it might play out in real life. Let's say you're the manager of a department, and one of your most valued employees has come to you asking for a raise. Your budget just won't cover such an increase, at least not now. You need to hold your bargaining position, but you don't want to antagonize this employee. What do you do? You might say something like this:

> *You*: "Well, Smithers, you know I consider the work you did on the XYZ account to be instrumental in improving our sales figures. And there's no doubt about it—you are certainly due for an increase. If there were any funds in the budget for raises, you'd be the first person I'd think of. But, right now, there's just no funds. I'll gladly take your request to the people over in accounting and see if there's anything that can be done, but it's likely to take some time. You're a highly valued member of this department, so I hope you'll bear with us during this temporary payroll freeze."

Such a statement expresses all the important elements of goodwill building. You've been fair in giving credit where credit's due by acknowledging Smithers' contributions to the department. You've shown yourself to be a good friend by expressing a willingness to at least make an effort to look into the possibility of a raise. And you've expressed a sincere appreciation of the fact that Smithers deserves a raise. But you've nonetheless held firm in your position: There are no raises to be given out at present.

By handling the matter with fairness, friendliness, and sincerity, you've made it likely that Smithers will be willing to accept your decision—after all, while the pay raise is no doubt important, appreciation and recognition also count heavily toward keeping an employee on the job.

When Not to Give Goodwill: A Cautionary Note

As you can see, in almost every instance, goodwill—established through fairness, sincerity, and friendliness—is an important asset in your negotiation. But there's one important exception: when your attempts at goodwill harm your bargaining position. This should never be permitted to happen. Establishing goodwill does *not* mean that you have to reveal your negotiating strategy, point out any flaws in your own argument, relinquish your terms, or compromise your own position. Remember, it's not your job to help win your opponent's case.

The Least You Need to Know

➤ Always try to build goodwill with your opponent. Goodwill builds trust, makes negotiation easier, and will build your reputation as a good negotiator.

➤ You can build goodwill by doing your opponent a favor, pointing out errors your opponent has made, agreeing to help promote your opponent's interests, showing concern for your opponent, or doing anything else that benefits your opponent.

➤ Three important elements to creating goodwill are fairness, friendliness, and sincerity.

➤ Anything you do to build up goodwill with your opponent should not harm your bargaining position.

Part 4
Increasing Your Negotiating Power

The word "power" is defined as "the ability to accomplish objectives." When you bargain, you have a primary base, your objective: It may be to get back money, to buy something you want at a fair price, or to gain some peace of mind.

That's where power comes in. If you have negotiating power, your task of accomplishing your negotiating objectives will be much easier. In this part, I show you how to increase your negotiating power by honing the skills you've developed up to now. You'll soon see how this increased power helps you get any of the things you decide to negotiate for.

Chapter 14

Power, Unleashed

In This Chapter

➤ Your power sources

➤ Letting loose: tapping your negotiating power

➤ Speaking powerfully

➤ The power of the mind

The word "power" usually calls to mind physical strength or far-reaching financial or political influence. When you think of powerful people, you might picture Michael Jordan, billionaire Bill Gates, or the President of the United States.

Fortunately, negotiating power doesn't rely on a commanding presence or influential job (although both *can* be part of it). That's because when you bargain, you pit your mind against your opponent's mind. The resources you bring to your negotiating power palette include all your preparation for the negotiation, your knowledge of the subject matter and your opponent, and how you play your bargaining hand.

The trick is to discover what power you already have and then learn how and when to use it. After you read this chapter, you'll know all about power and how to use it when you bargain.

What's Your Power Source?

Negotiating power is anything you can use to motivate your opponent to give you what you want. This broad definition includes these aspects:

Dealmaker

Power is meaningless unless you learn to use it effectively. Develop your power sources carefully, and know them well. They'll boost your rate of negotiating success into the stratosphere.

➤ Your knowledge of the negotiating situation

➤ Your knowledge of what motivates your opponent

➤ The negotiating options open to you and to your opponent—and how you play them out during the bargaining

➤ Your negotiating experience and how you use it

➤ Your reputation or your company's reputation

➤ All the bargaining techniques you have at your disposal (see Part 2, "Bargaining Table Techniques")

It helps to have a clear idea of the sources of your power—and that's easiest done by making a list. Use the "Sources of Negotiating Power" worksheet that follows—once you've filled it in, you will be better able to pinpoint the exact sources of your negotiating power.

Sources of Negotiating Power

1. What am I willing to offer my opponent to meet my goals?

   Money: _____

   Payment schedule: _____

   Time: _____

   Service: _____

   Improvements: _____

   Returns: _____

   Future business: _____

   Volume deals: _____

   Other: _____

2. How badly does my opponent need what I am willing to offer?

   Money: _____

   Payment schedule: _____

   Time: _____

   Service: _____

   Improvements: _____

   Returns: _____

   Future business: _____

Volume deals:_____

Other:_____

3. How can I appeal to my opponent's self as I negotiate?

   _____

4. How can I appeal to my opponent's emotions as I negotiate?

   _____

5. What is my negotiating reputation or the reputation of those associated with me? (broker, company, and so on)

   _____

6. How can I build up goodwill with my opponent?

   _____

7. What else do I have or can I do to motivate my opponent?

   _____

When you skillfully use your negotiating power, your opponent *will* be favorably motivated to reach an agreement. That's a certainty.

The Rules of the Game

A few basic rules exist when it comes to making your opponent aware of—and, if necessary, using—your negotiating power. A truly skilled negotiator understands these rules and appreciates how to employ them to his or her best advantage. Read on to learn the different types of negotiating power and their most effective uses.

Knowledge Is Power

As you bargain, remind yourself of the negotiating power you have so that if you have an opportunity to use it, you can.

But first, it's important to distinguish between *knowledge* of power and the actual *use* of that power. Making your opponent aware of your power is different from—and sometimes just as powerful as—actually using it.

Remember the Woody Allen movie *Take the Money and Run*? Woody's hapless character tries to rob a bank but gets nowhere because the teller misreads his note: "I have a gub." A small phalanx of bank representatives crowd around the teller, and

Dealbreaker

Never hold back knowledge of the full extent of your bargaining power. Tactfully let your opponent know what power you have, or you'll lose the advantage that your power could provide.

Woody—the would-be robber armed with a deadly weapon—watches helplessly as they all try to decipher his note. Needless to say (as usual in his movies), Woody doesn't get very far.

In negotiating terms, Woody's effort failed because his opponents didn't recognize the source of his power—his gun. I'm not advocating that you bring a gun along to your next negotiating session, but you, too, must always make your opponent aware of your bargaining power.

Don't Hold Back!

Many negotiators think they should hold knowledge of their power in reserve in case it's needed later. Their negotiations usually fail as a result. I recommend never with-holding any information that constitute your negotiating power.

As a matter of strategy, you may withhold *use* of your power. But even if you do that, you must be absolutely sure your opponent is aware of the full extent of your power.

Keep in mind, however, that you should always use tact when alerting your opponent to your bargaining power. If you hit your opponent over the head with a demonstration of your power, he may resent it—and that could backfire on you.

The Art of the Deal

If you're interested in buying a house and you know the seller is having a tough time finding a buyer, you might say, "You can't sell the place, can you?" But with that approach, the seller may be so angry that he refuses to sell the house to you. Instead, you might engage in a general, low-key discussion about how many houses there are on the market and how so many sellers are finding it tough to make a sale. The seller will get your subtle message: He'll have to give you a bargain to make you sign on the dotted line.

How does that work? A seller's difficulty in finding a buyer for his house translates into bargaining power for you. But if you respond to that difficulty by gloating or making light of his difficulties, you're likely to irritate him. If he's angry with you, your bargaining power diminishes. You can still use the seller's difficulty to your advantage, however—all it takes is tact.

How's Your Timing?

In any negotiation, the key question to ask yourself is: When will revealing or using my power have the greatest impact and the greatest influence on motivating my opponent to make a deal? In Woody's bank robbery, the key was to present the gun before demanding the money. He missed his moment, so he flubbed the deal.

In some negotiations, however, you may not want to reveal or use your power—your connections or your inside knowledge of the situation—until *after* you've built up an understanding with your opponent. As you prepare to bargain and determine the source of your negotiating power, you should also be thinking about the best time to use it.

That's why it's wise to develop a game plan during your preparation and to decide how and when you'd like to disclose your negotiating power. But keep your plan flexible. Don't lock yourself in.

When the bargaining begins, stay alert to see if your game plan is still the best approach. If it's not, don't hesitate to change directions and reveal or use your power sooner or later. Trust your instincts to decide when the time is ripe. The more experience you gain, the more your instincts will be right.

Keep Recharging Your Negotiating Power

Once you've determined and revealed your negotiating power, you must make sure your opponent is continually aware of it. If your negotiation is high-pressure, protracted, or involves a large exchange of information, your opponent can easily forget about your power. If that happens, your power is useless.

Say you want to hire a contractor to remodel your kitchen—he's going to install space-age appliances, skylights, new cabinets, the works. It's a tremendous job, and you know you'll have to haggle over the price. As you prepare to negotiate, you realize that you've got several sources of negotiating power:

Dealbreaker

If your opponent underestimates your bargaining power, immediately correct her. If you don't, you'll lose your power and weaken your own bargaining position.

> ➤ You've waited until the winter because contractors will be looking for inside work at that time of year.
>
> ➤ Your neighbors, the Joneses, are also thinking about remodeling. They've said that they would consider hiring your contractor, if he does a good job on your kitchen.

➤ You're willing to pay 25 percent of the total cost before any work begins, as an added incentive to get a good price.

At your first meeting with the contractor, Rick Wrecker, you reveal your three sources of power. Still, Rick comes back with a price that's too high. You speak with other contractors and get a few more estimates. Some of those estimates are lower than Rick's, so you decide to see Rick again—those lower estimates are now an additional source of bargaining power for you. How do you remind Rick of your negotiating edge? There are two good ways to keep your power fresh in your opponent's memory.

Repeat Yourself . . . Repeat Yourself . . . Repeat Yourself . . .

Repetition is the best way to remind your opponent of your negotiating power and magnify its impact. As with most negotiating skills, this technique involves a little diplomacy—and a lot of good timing. You want to remind your opponent of your power, not beat him over the head with it.

At your second meeting with Rick, for example, you should tactfully repeat your three elements of power to refresh his memory. You could then say something like, "I've spoken with quite a few other reputable contractors whose prices are lower than yours, and they seem eager for this job. Between my kitchen and the Joneses', they'll have work lined up for the entire winter." Now you've really set the stage to get the price that you want.

Dealmaker

Forgetful opponents are common, especially if your opponent is a busy person juggling a lot of balls. Never hesitate to repeat yourself when you bargain. Remind your opponent of your bargaining power—tactfully— every chance you get.

Questioning Your Power

Another way to keep your bargaining power fresh in your opponent's mind is to ask questions about it. (Chapter 8, "Questions, Questions, and More Questions," provides you with very useful information on the creative use of questions during negotiation.) You might ask Rick: "It'll be nice to work inside when the snow is piling up, won't it?" He'll be forced to answer yes, and you will have made your point.

Make sure your questions aren't too obvious—they'll have greater impact and your opponent won't resent you for asking them.

Mental Practice: The Way to Boost Your Negotiating Power

Many performing artists and athletes have long known the power of visualizing their performances. You can harness that power to boost your negotiating power as well.

When you think of "practice," you probably envision physically performing a certain act. When you drive golf balls at a driving range, you're physically practicing your golf game. But mental practice can also improve your performance.

That's important when it comes to negotiation because you're not going to have an opportunity for a real dress rehearsal before you start bargaining. Still, mental practice can serve the same purpose.

What Mental Practice Really Means

When you mentally practice, envision yourself at the bargaining table. Think about everything you intend to say and do. Imagine how your opponent might respond. Be specific in your imagined details of the scene—include everything you can. Your mental rehearsal should include not only your presentation, but also your best estimation of your opponent's responses.

When you get into the actual bargaining, you'll often find that the negotiation will unfold closely to how you've envisioned it. That gives you an edge. In a sense, you've "been there before." With mental rehearsal, the actual negotiation will be easier on your system (you won't be as nervous or stressed out) and you'll enjoy the bargaining process a lot more. Moreover, you'll quickly discover that your success ratio will increase dramatically.

Picture This: A Sample Mental Rehearsal

Say you've decided to go after that long overdue raise. Get comfortable and visualize every detail of the entire bargaining process. Picture yourself walking into the office and making some small talk. Watch yourself confidently launching into your request. (Imagine at least two, preferably three, approaches you'll take. That gives you the flexibility to choose the best approach when you're actually negotiating.) Visualize yourself making good eye contact and sitting up straight, like your mother always told you to.

Be realistic, even in your imagination. (It's not likely that your boss will say, "A 15 percent raise? Why not make it 50!") Visualize every possible excuse your boss might use to turn you down ("We're under a wage freeze right now," "There's no money for raises—it was a bad year for widgets") and mentally come up with an answer. This when, when you're actually sitting in front of your boss, you'll be able to respond easily and calmly, because you've already anticipated his or her objections and practiced answering them.

Be graphic. Picture your boss's face and her physical reaction when you pop the question. Visualize the whole event, from start to finish, in great detail.

Dealmaker

Remember that when you negotiate, you're pitting your mind against your opponent's. The more you prepare in your mind, the greater negotiating power you'll have.

Finally, imagine your boss saying yes.

Rehearse a half-dozen times, or even more until you've got the entire process down cold. When you finally do get to negotiate, you'll be more comfortable, more confident, more powerful, and more likely to get what you want.

The Least You Need to Know

➤ Determine your negotiating power as you prepare to negotiate.

➤ Always make your opponent fully aware of the true extent of your bargaining power, even if you don't have to use it.

➤ Reveal or use your power when your instincts tell you the time is ripe.

➤ Repetition and questions are good ways to keep the true extent of your bargaining power fresh in your opponent's mind.

➤ Before you negotiate, mentally rehearse the entire negotiation to increase your negotiating power.

Chapter 15

Taking Control

> **In This Chapter**
>
> ➤ Developing good negotiating habits
>
> ➤ Succeeding through strategy
>
> ➤ The power of unpredictability
>
> ➤ Controlling factors: taking charge of your negotiations

Now that you've learned the basic techniques and skills of successful negotiating, it's time to pull them all together into a single, effective package. That means making these new skills a natural part of your day-to-day life—ways of behaving that you do without even having to think about them. And it means understanding the role of strategy—of building those skills and techniques into a plan of action tailor-made to achieve your particular negotiating goal.

In this chapter you'll learn how to do all this. You'll learn the value of habituating yourself into your new negotiating skills and incorporating them into a strategic package. And in so doing, you'll learn to take charge of your negotiations, boosting your effectiveness in any bargaining situation.

It's Habit Forming!

Think about the way that many of the things you do are governed by habit. Brushing your teeth, combing your hair, driving to work or school—your brain is on "cruise control" through most or all of these activities. That's because they have become habits.

Habits, as William James points out in his book *The Principles of Psychology*, are nothing less than pathways through your brain. The more you repeat an activity, the deeper the pathway gets. By developing habits, your mind is free to focus on other subjects. But as any of us who have tried to lose weight or stop smoking know, the deeper the pathway, the harder it is to change. To enhance your bargaining power, you need to learn how to make the most of your good negotiating habits—and minimize or eliminate your bad ones.

Habit and Negotiation

Because anything can (and often does) happen in a negotiation, good negotiating habits that will put you in a better position to deal with the unexpected. They will allow you to focus on the changing situation without any distractions, because you can respond to changes effortlessly.

On the other hand, bad negotiating habits will hurt your bargaining position, because they'll hinder your performance. For example, if you frequently interrupt when someone else is talking, you'll interrupt during negotiation, too—even though it will work against you. That may cause you to miss important information, and will certainly annoy your opponent. Similarly, if you constantly fidget, you'll distract your opponent when you don't want to. That, too, can work to your disadvantage.

Good Negotiating Habits

There are a number of qualities every good negotiator should have. Practice the following good habits every day and they'll spill over into your negotiating:

➤ Make good eye contact with everyone you meet. Looking away from people suggests that you lack confidence—and that's not the impression you want to make when you negotiate!

➤ Dress neatly and professionally.

➤ Speak clearly.

➤ Eliminate fillers ("you knows" and "ums") from your conversation.

➤ Listen carefully (no interrupting!) and ask pertinent questions.

➤ Sit with good posture.

➤ Stand and walk with your head up, shoulders back, and body straight.

➤ Develop a standard method of preparation for every meeting and negotiation. (See Chapter 2, "Bargaining Essentials," and Chapter 3, "Scoping Out the Other Side.")

➤ If you're chronically late, try to arrive early at all of your appointments. Set your clocks ahead a few minutes (or more!) if you must.

These habits have two immediate benefits. They help you become a good conversationalist, capable of listening carefully, asking pointed questions, and thinking well on your feet. They also help you convey an air of confidence that bolsters your negotiating position. Your confidence makes you seem more believable and your opponent will therefore be more likely to respect and be influenced by your bargaining position.

Hard Habits to Break

Were you ever shocked by the sound of your own voice on someone's answering machine? Have you ever been surprised to catch sight of yourself in a store window? Most of us don't realize the way we appear to others. Many of our bad habits—speaking rapid-fire or in a slow drawl, slouching or hunching over, avoiding eye contact—go unnoticed, unless someone tips us off. And who's willing to do that?

Unconscious mannerisms can be deadly to effective negotiating. They can make you appear uncomfortable or, even worse, incompetent.

The best way to get rid of your bad habits is quickly and decisively. William James put it this way: "in the acquisition of a new habit, or the leaving off of an old one, we must . . . launch ourselves with as strong and decided an initiative as possible . . . . Never suffer an exception to occur till the new habit is securely rooted in your life."

Dealbreaker

You can't carry bad habits around wherever you go and expect them to suddenly disappear when it's time to negotiate.

A few nasty habits you should immediately eliminate before you begin any negotiation:

➤ *Fidgeting with pencils, eyeglasses, cups, or anything that distracts your opponent.* I once negotiated with an opponent who beat a pencil on the table like a drummer in a rock band. Your opponent won't concentrate on what you're saying if you're fidgeting while you're talking. (Don't confuse bad habits that disturb your opponent with situations in which you want to effectively break your opponent's concentration. In the latter case, you are taking a deliberate action to achieve a specific result as part of your bargaining strategy. In the former, you are repeating an unconscious gesture that may jeopardize your bargaining position.)

➤ *Interrupting your opponent.* Have you ever talked to someone who constantly interrupts? It's annoying. You don't want to frustrate your opponent and perhaps make him angry.

➤ *Using fillers.* I'm sure you know people whose conversation is perpetually sprinkled with "you know" or "ummmmmm." They don't sound particularly articulate or intelligent, do they? Make some tape recordings of yourself running through your arguments. Play them back and listen carefully. What unnecessary fillers do you rely on? Concentrate on eliminating them from your everyday speech.

➤ *Taking extensive notes.* This isn't a good bargaining practice because it diverts your attention from your opponent. For example, if your opponent makes an offer and then looks away, that's a clue that she lacks confidence in her offer. If you're busy taking notes and miss that small but crucial clue, you might think that your opponent is making a good offer when, in fact, she isn't.

I limit my note-taking to writing down key matters (such as the terms of agreements reached), or to recording facts or documents that I've promised to provide to my opponent. Other than that, my pen stays in my pocket.

➤ *Jotting down or reading from notes that your opponent can't see.* Your opponent will get suspicious—even if you're just doodling or writing a grocery list. It's the appearance of surreptitiousness that can cause problems. If you must rely on notes, hold them so your opponent can see what you're doing. But while you should let your opponent see that your *using* notes, you should hold them far enough away so that he or she can't read what you're writing or reading.

Dealmaker

When you're negotiating, notice any bad habits your opponent has, such as avoiding eye contact. After you've finished negotiating, think about whether you have the same behaviors. That's an excellent way to spot your own bad habits.

Dealing with Your Opponent's Bad Habits

Your opponent's bad habits make him less effective, but they also prevent you from concentrating on what your opponent is saying. For example, I once had an opponent who liked to click his briefcase latch open and shut. That sound was as inescapable as the ticking of a large clock when you're trying to drop off to sleep.

How do you deal with an opponent who has a distracting bad habit? You can either grin and bear it, or tactfully get your opponent to stop it until the bargaining is over. In the briefcase example, for instance, I said something like, "That briefcase must be in your way. Would you like me to put it with your coat so you have more room?" If you can break your opponent's bad habit, you strengthen your own concentration and throw your opponent slightly off-balance. This swings the bargaining edge in your favor.

150

Controlling Concepts

Having developed good negotiating habits, you're now ready to move on to pulling your newly developed negotiating skills into an effective package that allows you to take control. Control over any negotiation falls to whoever is best prepared to cope with any and all contingencies that might arise. That means being able to handle the unexpected—and even to *introduce* the unexpected to throw your opponent off balance. Both of these skills require strategic planning. In fact, strategy—and the judicious introduction of unpredictability into the negotiation—can be the ultimate key to your negotiating success.

Strategizing for Success

You bought a computer and the day after the warranty runs out it goes haywire. You've been a long-time customer of the store that sold you the machine. How do you get the computer fixed or replaced? What's your strategy? Or, you just had a $500 repair job done on your car, but a week later it conks out on you with the same problem it had before. You already paid the bill, so you can't withhold payment until the garage does its job. What's your strategy?

"What's my strategy?" has to be the first question you ask yourself before you approach every negotiation. "What's the best way I can effectively communicate my bargaining position in order to persuade my opponent to give me what I want?" When you ask these questions, you're thinking strategy.

Negotiable Terms

Strategy, is the science of planning, directing, or maneuvering yourself into the most advantageous position for achieving your goal.

In the case of your computer troubles, you know that when you go back to the store to make your pitch for repairs or replacement you'll be fighting an uphill battle. But not an impossible one. The same applies to getting your mechanic to make good on your car repairs, without another dime coming out of your pocket. In either case, the strategy you devise and use will make the difference between success and failure. In other words, it's not the cards you hold that makes the difference, it's the skill with which you play them.

Thinking Strategically

Your first, and perhaps your most important step, is to make strategic thinking a habitual process (we discussed the importance of habits earlier in this chapter). Once you've grown accustomed to strategic thinking, you'll do it automatically—before *and* during every negotiation.

So how, exactly, do you think strategically? You run through a careful assessment of your goals, your knowledge of your opponent, and your alternatives, and then you methodically build a step-by-step game plan. Most winning sports teams—no matter what the particular sport—develop a game plan prior to the contest. They even diagram that strategy on blackboards so they fully understand what it is and how to execute it. That's a very good process to adopt for negotiating, as well.

Let's take the two examples that began this section and see how they might be subject to strategizing:

Problem	Strategic Advantages to Your Position
Computer dies after warranty expires	You're a regular customer of the computer store
	You have a long-standing relationship of goodwill with the customer service representative there
	You've researched the problem and you know it's not due to normal wear and tear (or your own error)
Car breaks down again after repairs were done	You've got the work receipt detailing the problem that should have been fixed
	You've identified the cause of the current breakdown—it's the same problem, all over again
	You're a first-time customer at the repair shop—so the garage owner wants your repeat business.
	The garage owner wants to preserve his business's reputation for good service.

As you can see, in each case you've got several possible "cards" you can play when you go in to negotiate. Once you've identified them, you can start to figure out the best way to incorporate them into your overall negotiating game plan.

When I handle complicated negotiations, I make it a standard practice to come up with alternative approaches to achieving my goal, and jot down the pros and cons of each one. This way, I can develop a strategy that answers the cons and emphasizes the pros. It works for me, and I think it will for you, too.

Talking Points

"You've got to know when to hold 'em, and know when to fold 'em."

—Kenny Rogers hit, "The Gambler"

Knocking 'em off balance

A sound strategy makes it easier for you to stay tightly focused on your primary bases. But if your opponent knows what your bargaining strategy is going to be, you're in a very vulnerable position, no matter how good that strategy is. After all, he'll be able to anticipate everything you're going to say and do, and then equalize it. That leaves you out on a limb waiting for your opponent to saw off the branch, sending you plummeting down to a losing situation.

But if your opponent has no idea what your strategy is likely to be, his or her uncertainty will work to your advantage. Your opponent be less able to counter your arguments, and he or she is likely to be thrown off balance. In any case, he or she will be interested in learning what you're up to, and therefore much more receptive to your bargaining position.

Let's go back to that problem with your $500 car repair that didn't work. If you stride into the repair shop angrily and blast the owner, demanding that the job be done right, you are behaving predictably—the garage owner has probably frequently had to face that strategy and won't be particularly moved to remedy the situation. In fact, he probably has developed a set strategy of his own to handle such confrontations.

If, on the other hand, you approach the garage owner reasonably, you're likely to catch him off-guard, and you'll be more likely to win the negotiation.

Putting Unpredictability into Practice

Now, let's go back to the computer that worked fine until your warranty ran out. You've done business with the store before—even bought several large items, including a CD player, TV set, and a washer and dryer. You've saved the receipts in every case.

First, you want to make certain that you're dealing with the "yes" person—the one who can grant you the relief you're seeking (repair or replacement of your computer, at no cost). You sit down with the manager (if it's a large chain) or the owner (if it's a smaller store) and, after a pleasant greeting, begin your negotiation:

Your Comments/Actions	Their Strategic Meaning
"I've got a little problem and I'm hoping you can help me with it?	You're not demanding action; instead, you're raising the issue and tactfully getting your opponent into a cooperative frame of mind. You're building up goodwill by indicating your belief in the owner's fairness and showing him that you're a reasonable person.

continues

153

continued

Your Comments/Actions	Their Strategic Meaning
You bring out receipts of your prior purchases, describing each and handing them, one by one, to the owner	You're displaying that you're a very good customer, and implying that you might take your business elsewhere. At the same time, you're showing him that losing your patronage means a substantial loss of business for him.
"I bought this computer for $2,000, and it worked great until the week after the warranty expired. Can you help me out?	By bringing the warranty problem right up front you're watering down the impact of that issue, making it difficult for the owner to brush you off. This is an unpredictable move—the owner won't be expecting it, so he'll be less prepared to deny your request.

You might take a very different tack in dealing with the car repair problem. You already know that by bursting into the shop owner's office you'd be doing the predictable thing. What might be a more unpredictable (and potentially more successful) strategy?

Your Comments/Actions	Their Strategic Meaning
You open with a cordial greeting	Right away, you're behaving unpredictably—the owner or manager is probably expecting you to rant and rave.
You initiate a brief conversation about how complicated today's computer-reliant cars are to repair	You're building goodwill and laying a foundation for the owner to justify errors in the original repairs.
You request the repairs be done again, still speaking reasonably and calmly.	You're appealing to his sense of self as a fair and reasonable businessman, and you're placing the blame for the faulty repairs on the complicated cars, not on his (or his mechanic's) competency.

In each of these examples, keep in mind that you have to pull off these strategies with complete sincerity. Any sarcasm, any hint that you're insincere, will make your opponent dig in his heels and send you packing.

Taking Charge

Strategy, as you can see, is the way that you can take control of negotiating situations, even when your bargaining position is weak. By strategic use of the material discussed throughout the first part of this book, you're able to set and control the pace, and thus improve the odds of guaranteeing your desired results. Here's a breakdown of the stages of any negotiation, and a summary of bargaining strategies that are the most effectively employed at each stage in the process.

Before the Negotiation Begins

You can begin to assert yourself even before you sit down at the bargaining table by controlling the negotiation setting:

➤ Bargain on your home field (see Chapter 4, "On Your Mark. . ., Get Set. . ., Negotiate!").

➤ Set the negotiation for the time when you are mentally at your sharpest (again, see Chapter 4).

➤ Mentally rehearse the negotiation (see Chapter 14, "Power, Unleashed").

Gaining Control When Negotiation Is Underway

Once you're actually facing your opponent, you can continue to control the bargaining process with a few more well-planned actions:

➤ *Ask questions.* Questions place your opponent on the defensive. When your opponent is answering your questions, she can't ask you questions or focus on her negotiating strategy. (Good use of questions is discussed in Chapter 8, "Questions, Questions, and More Questions.")

➤ *Focus on your primary base (your objective) until it is settled—even if your opponent is trying to skip to another issue.* Salespeople do this all the time. Say you're interested in buying a plush new couch for your living room. The salesman starts hawking a set of matching chairs, a coffee table, and a lamp. He says he'll sell it to you for a special price as part of a package. You say you don't want to spend that much money. The salesman describes the store's special financing options—instant credit for all you can buy, and you don't have to pay until the year 2001!

Suddenly, instead of focusing on pricing the couch, you're hip-deep in discussing an entire room renovation. A lot of people would get sucked into buying these new items. Don't let it happen to you. Keep your eyes on the prize and say firmly, "No thanks. All the room needs right now is a couch. How much is it?" And start pulling out your wallet. That will keep both of you focused on your primary negotiating base—namely, buying just the couch—(primary bases are discussed in Chapter 2, "Bargaining Essentials") and it will also help you maintain control of the negotiation.

Dealbreaker

The more complicated the bargaining issues are, the greater the danger you'll lose sight of your primary base. That's why you should firmly tattoo your base in your mind, especially when you prepare.

Negotiable Terms

Funneling means setting aside points once they are resolved. They may be returned to later for review or summation, but *not* for renegotiation.

➤ *Don't raise new issues once the bargaining begins.* This needlessly broadens the discussion and creates an air of uncertainty that will harm your bargaining position.

➤ *Don't introduce any new parties or new elements once the bargaining begins.* If you do, it gives your opponent a perfect opportunity to raise new ideas of his or her own, or even to have second thoughts on issues already agreed upon.

➤ *Close off settled issues from further discussion once they've been resolved.* This technique, called funneling adds to your negotiating control because it prevents your opponent from reopening or rehashing issues that have already been settled.

The more negotiating experience you gain, the better you'll become at funneling. When your opponent tries to reopen a closed issue (they often do), tactfully remind him that the point has been settled. If he still insists on discussing the issue, quickly explain what the agreement on the issue was. Then move on to something else. Don't allow yourself or your opponent to begin discussing and renegotiating closed issues.

Regaining Control Once You've Lost It

Have you ever lost an argument with your kids, your spouse, or your boss? Then you know the sinking feeling that accompanies a loss of control. You're on the defensive, struggling to explain yourself, stammering for answers. You may find yourself sidetracked onto an issue that has nothing to do with the one you want to discuss. Everything you say is misinterpreted. You can't win.

When you lose negotiating control, you're most vulnerable to making concessions. Before that happens, you must regain control—and the quicker the better.

Once you've lost control of the bargaining, there are ways to regain it:

➤ Immediately ask for a recess or time-out. Then reassess the bargaining and think about what went wrong and how you can remedy it.

➤ Look for ways to take the offense.

➤ Immediately after the recess, start by summarizing what's happened in the bargaining process to date. That will help give you control. Once you've finished with your summary, begin to launch your own bargaining position(s). You're now back in control of the negotiation.

Dealmaker

It's almost always better to act than to react. When you act, you're on the offense. When you react, you're on the defense—and that's not where you want to be when you bargain.

The Least You Need to Know

➤ The best way to develop good negotiating habits—such as making good eye contact, standing up straight, and arriving on time—is to practice these good habits even when you're not negotiating.

➤ If you must ask your opponent to stop a bad habit (such as fiddling with something or smoking), do it tactfully.

➤ Strategic planning, and the judicious use of unpredictable tactics, can swing the negotiating momentum in your favor.

➤ Prior to the negotiation, you can gain control by choosing the place and time for negotiation and mentally rehearsing the negotiation.

➤ During negotiation, you can gain and maintain control by asking questions, avoiding new elements, and funneling the discussion.

➤ When you sense you've lost control, ask for a recess. Use your recess time to figure out what went wrong and why.

Part 5
Problem Solving

You're going to encounter problems when you bargain—there's no way to avoid them. Negotiating difficulties are kind of like mosquitoes on a hot, muggy day—the more you swat, the more you are attacked. Or so it seems.

But you don't have to let those pesky problems slow you down. Not if you've discovered the many tools you can use to help overcome some common negotiating problems. In this part you'll learn those tools. You'll learn how to ease through the bargaining process with fewer headaches—and maybe even start to have fun!

Hmmm...

Chapter 16

Don't Get Your Dander Up!

In This Chapter

➤ Anger's destructive effects

➤ Using anger to your advantage

➤ Coping with an angry opponent

➤ Cooling down an overheated encounter

I once represented a client who was involved in a three-car accident but wasn't at fault. Another driver—let's call him Crash Carson—was the true instigator of the accident.

My opponent, who represented Crash's insurance company, refused to admit that my client was not in the wrong. He insisted that I cut the amount of settlement money I was asking for.

I held my ground, tactfully insisting that the amount was reasonable because his client was at fault. I could see his anger and frustration building as he realized I was not going to give way. Finally, he erupted, pounding his fist on my desk and yelling, "Okay! My driver caused the $#@!$# wreck. So what?! I'm still not paying what you want!" Then he threw his papers in his briefcase and stomped out.

It's rare to get an opponent to admit liability, and it would never have happened if my opponent hadn't gotten so angry. His temper was my ally. Within a week I received a check for the full amount for my client.

There's a saying that the person who angers you also conquers you. That's what happened to my opponent. In this chapter, you learn what to do if anger—yours or your opponent's—disrupts the negotiation.

Anger's Disruptive Potential

Anger has many physiological effects on your body. When you get angry, your blood pressure rises and your heart rate increases.

The behavioral consequences of anger aren't pretty, either. You can't think or act logically when you are angry, and usually nothing you do when you're angry is particularly constructive. In negotiating, anger has two downsides, which are described in the following sections.

Talking Points

"Heads are wisest when they are cool."

—Ralph Bunche

Vengeance Is Mine!

Usually, anger is supplanted by a desire for revenge. (Think of scorned girlfriend Glenn Close killing the rabbit in *Fatal Attraction*.)

Once you're set on revenge, chances are good that you'll say or do something that will jeopardize your bargaining position. It happens all the time, as my previous story shows. Just think of some of the things you've blurted out in anger in personal relationships, and you'll know what I mean.

Dealbreaker

The person who gets angry during negotiation usually loses—either because a favorable agreement is not reached, because the negotiation is terminated entirely, or because he or she makes a damaging admission while angry.

My Way or the Highway

Anger may also make you obstinate. Once you're angry, you may become stubbornly insistent on all your negotiating positions, allowing no room for concession or bargaining. You may become unwilling to countenance any changes, even reasonable ones. You can see how this makes you difficult to negotiate with.

The general rule is this: Never become angry when you're bargaining. Stay cool even if your opponent says or does something designed to provoke your anger. Here are a few ways to stay cool in the midst of a hot situation:

➤ Take a deep breath and count to ten.

➤ Suggest a five-minute break. Take a walk, drink some cold water, give yourself a chance to calm down.

➤ If your opponent gets personal, say that you are negotiating issues and that personal remarks are not appropriate. (See Chapter 20, "Closing with Class," for more on personality and principle conflicts and how to handle them.)

The Constructive Use of Anger

Based on the previous paragraphs, you might think that there is never a place for anger in negotiation. But there is one very potent exception. You can use anger in a negotiating technique I call controlled anger.

If your opponent says or does something that fully justifies your anger, keep your cool—but fake anger. Speak and act like you're angry—frown, speak in a tight, stern voice, and use commanding gestures (discussed in Chapter 6, "Getting Physical").

Use the controlled-anger technique when you don't want to be taken for a pushover. This allows you to display your displeasure over your opponent's tactics without letting you fall victim to the drawbacks of real anger.

I once assisted in a negotiation that had drawn out over a long period of time with no progress. I was asked to assist a man who was selling a company.

Many corporate buyouts are subject to delays because the buyers aren't really that serious about buying and actually have other motives in mind, such as learning as much as possible about the other company. (That's called "going to school.") Usually, the more drawn out the bargaining, the more the buyers can learn. Once the pseudo-buyers have discovered all they need to know, they either drop the talks or make such far-out proposals that the other side walks away.

I suspected that my opponent was deliberately stalling because he was not responding to my client's proposals or making any proposals of his own. The discussions were going nowhere. That gave me a good reason to get angry, and my opponent knew it.

Talking Points

"Anger is momentary madness, so control your passion or it will control you."

—Horace, *Epistles*

So I did get angry—but with controlled anger. I kept my emotions under complete control. Only my voice, gestures, and facial expressions revealed my displeasure. I advised my opponent that my client intended to walk away from the bargaining unless meaningful proposals were laid down on the table. That did it. The bargaining got down to serious business.

You should realize that controlled anger has its limits. I had to limit my controlled anger to my opponent's delaying tactics. If I had gone too far, my opponent would have had full justification to get angry at me, and that would have jeopardized my client's interests. By controlling my anger, I turned my opponent's delaying tactic into a bargaining advantage for my client.

Controlled anger can be risky, so use it judiciously. Be certain that your anger is justified, and limit your controlled anger only to the issues that justify it.

If Your Opponent Gets Angry

If you're stuck in a negotiation that has reached a standstill and you have no other way of breaking the log jam, your opponent's anger might be just the dynamite to do it. Angry people frequently say and do things that they shouldn't—that's why you may want to get your opponent angry. But be careful. If you decide to provoke your opponent's anger, you don't want to get that person so worked up that the negotiation is terminated.

Usually, when discussions are at a standstill, both you and your opponent are prone to getting angry because you'll each blame the other for blocking progress. This is where you have to keep your cool.

Probing Your Opponent's Reactions

In some situations, you can tactfully state that your opponent's unreasonableness is what is blocking the agreement. Notice how mild and tame the word "unreasonableness" is—it's not provocative enough to infuriate your opponent, but it may be severe enough to get him to break the stalemate.

Or, you might suggest that your opponent never really intended to reach a fair and reasonable agreement. What you're really saying is that your opponent is not a fair and reasonable person. Most people consider themselves to be fair and reasonable, so this approach will usually cause your opponent to launch into a lengthy explanation of why she *is* being fair—and she may even suggest a fine deal to prove it.

You also might want to get your opponent angry when he is holding a far stronger bargaining position—most, if not all, of the aces—and you're searching for a way to weaken your opponent's hand and strengthen yours.

Dealbreaker

Once you've lit your opponent's fuse, be a good listener! If you interrupt at this stage, you risk provoking your opponent to uncontrollable anger—and that's not what you want to deal with.

I once represented a client who was an investor in a real estate development. He wasn't happy with the way the development was progressing and wanted out of the deal, but he had no legal means of getting out.

Even though my client had a legally weak position, I kept pushing the developer to cut my client loose, on my terms. The developer became angry at my sheer persistence and finally gave in to the deal I was proposing.

Here again, frame your remarks mildly. Your goal is to make your opponent mildly angry, not uncontrollably enraged.

A Sure-Fire Fuse Igniter

Whenever you deliberately make your opponent angry, you take a risk. Everybody's fuse ignites differently—some opponents will fly into a tantrum at the slightest provocation, while others will take a lot more before they lose their temper. So try to gauge your opponent's boiling point before you attempt to provoke him.

As you learned in Chapter 12, "Reaching Out to the Other Side," one potent way to provoke your opponent is to make a personal slight that attacks his self. The closer anything you say touches upon your opponent's self, the more likely your opponent will become genuinely, irrevocably angry.

For example, if your opponent is a real estate agent, any snide comments you make about the real estate market in general may be enough to provoke him to mild anger. Take a crack at the real estate agency he works for, and you come one step closer to touching his self. Disparage his abilities to do his job, and you've made direct contact with his self. Now you're risking genuine anger that will only make negotiation more difficult (if not impossible). You don't want to go this far.

Dealmaker

Confine your remarks to the subject matter of the negotiation. If you broaden them and get into areas beyond what you're negotiating, you run the risk of inadvertently setting off your opponent's fuse.

When you decide to deliberately provoke your opponent's anger, always consider how close to his self your actions or remarks will get. Personal attacks have no place in successful negotiation.

Pouring Oil on Troubled Waters

If your opponent gets uncontrollably angry with you, there are five approaches you can take to calm the situation.

➤ Anger is a temporary emotion, and it is usually entirely curable by a good dose of time. If your opponent is mildly upset, a short break will be fine. If you think a little more time is necessary, let your opponent cool off over lunch or overnight. If your opponent is truly angry, you should allow a few days or a week to pass. Eventually your opponent may even feel foolish about becoming angry.

➤ Show that there's no reason for your opponent's anger (if this is indeed the case). Explain that no insult was intended by your actions or remarks.

➤ Remedy the situation. If you've somehow personally slighted your opponent, a simple, sincere apology will do. Don't be reluctant to apologize, and don't let pride or stubbornness stand in your way. Admitting fault is not a

Talking Points

"If anger proceeds from a great cause, it turns to fury; if from a small cause, it is peevishness; and so it is always either terrible or ridiculous."

—Jeremy Taylor

165

sign of weakness—it's good negotiating. You're there to successfully negotiate something important to you. Stay focused on that objective.

➤ If your opponent is furious over something you've said or done, you may have to make a concession or two to regain his goodwill and get the negotiating back on course. This is risky because your opponent may construe your concessions as a sign of weakness and may demand even more from you. Use this approach only when you've exhausted all your other options.

➤ Send someone to bargain in your place. However, this is risky because it can be interpreted as an admission that you were in the wrong. If your opponent has any kind of bargaining skills, she'll start asking for large concessions.

A Calming Scenario

Say your car is five days out of the shop and already is making that strange pinging noise again. Disgustedly, you take your car back to Rocky's Repairs, where Rocky tells you it's a new, more intricate and costly problem than the one he's fixed before. You've already paid for the first set of repairs and don't want to pay anything more. Rocky says, "Too bad." In a surge of anger, you accuse Rocky of running an incompetent shop. Rocky's shop is part of Rocky's self, so now you've accused Rocky himself of being incompetent—and he doesn't take that lightly.

That's enough to bring the negotiating process to a grinding halt (no pun intended). You still have the pinging car, and Rocky still has your money. The stalemate will continue until you can calm him down.

Dealbreaker

Effective negotiation is knowing how to make your point without making the opponent your enemy. A twice-angered opponent will be your enemy.

Time-Out for a Cool-Down

The passage of time will help. Ask Rocky if you can come back in two or three days. If he refuses, apologize for losing your cool. Then point out that it's really in both of your best interests to reach a friendly solution: You'll have a well-running car, and Rocky will have a satisfied customer.

Once you've rescheduled, do nothing. Let time be your ally. It'll eliminate a lot of Rocky's anger.

Picking Up Where You Left Off— Only Better

When you next show up at Rocky's Repairs, immediately offer an apology. If you think it's necessary, go further and throw in an explanation for your bad behavior. Perhaps you were having a bad day, or that your car is vital to your life and you were frustrated by its problems. Any legitimate, genuine explanation will help get rid of Rocky's anger. Then explain again why you're there: to either get your car back in working order or to get your money back.

Once Rocky is calm, be extra careful not to get him angry again. It's difficult enough to assuage an opponent once—it's nearly impossible to do it twice.

The Least You Need to Know

➤ Except for very special situations, anger should be avoided because it disrupts negotiation by making both you and your opponent obstinate and vengeful.

➤ If your opponent gives you cause, use the controlled anger technique to express your displeasure, and thus gain the bargaining edge.

➤ If the negotiation has reached a stalemate, you might try mildly provoking your opponent to break the impasse.

➤ Avoid making personal attacks on your opponent—they may irreparably damage the negotiation.

➤ If your opponent becomes genuinely angry, take a break, apologize, or show that your opponent's anger is unjustified. As a last resort, you may have to make small concessions to assuage your opponent.

Chapter 17

Fear and Trembling

In This Chapter

➤ The effects of fear

➤ The three most common negotiating fears

➤ Introducing uncertainty in your negotiations

➤ Using your opponent's fears in negotiations

➤ Overcoming personal fears

Every week, a kindergarten teacher I know visits the local library to check out a load of books for all her students. At one point, the librarian complained about all the books she was checking out. My friend offered a solution: How about if she brought all 20 of her kindergartners in to scramble around and look for their own books? The librarian never complained again.

That's a sweet, simple lesson on the power of fear and how strongly it motivates our thinking and decisions. What could be more frightening to a librarian than the thought of so many 5-year-olds zooming through her library? Not much. In this chapter, you learn how fear and uncertainty affect negotiation.

The Effects of Fear

You learned about the powerful effects of fear at an early age. Think about how you feared your first day of school, the first time you drove a car, the night of your first big date. Fear still accompanies you on many occasions such as job interviews, opening-night performances, and wedding days, to name only a few.

When we fear something, we imagine the worst. That's a powerful motivator to act. Think about your first date. You were afraid you'd sprout a noxious rash before the big night, so you took extra-careful care of your skin. You didn't want your date to think you looked like a geek, so you chose your clothes with extra care.

Fear also almost always shows up when you negotiate. And the more important the negotiation, the greater your fear will be.

Fear and Negotiation

I had my first brush with fear when I was fresh out of law school. My job was to collect debts for a large company, but many of the debtors weren't paying up. I wanted to motivate them to pay without getting involved in a lot of messy, time-consuming lawsuits.

I managed to motivate most of them to pay out of fear. I constructed a simple letter that consisted of only two sentences. The first acknowledged the amount of the debt. The second read as follows:

> "If payment is not received within two weeks, appropriate action will be taken, which will result in additional expenses to you, the debtor."

What was "appropriate action"? What were the "additional expenses"? I deliberately left those phrases vague because I wanted the debtor's imagination to run wild over the possibilities. My strategy worked. Within a few days, the checks started arriving in the mail.

The Top Three Negotiating Fears

The fears you'll face in negotiation usually center on three subjects:

➤ Fear of loss

➤ Fear of the unknown

➤ Fear of failure

Two of those fears motivated the debtors to pay up. They feared both the "additional expenses" (fear of loss of money) and what the "appropriate action" would be (fear of the unknown). Let's take a closer look at each.

Fear of Loss

Many negotiations hinge on the fear of losing something of value—money, a dream house, a raise, or even a good deal.

Crafty people know how to harp on our fears of missing out on a good thing. Stockbrokers call with promises of investments that will double your money—but only if you buy now, before the price of the stock climbs too high. Landlords tell you that several other people want the apartment, so you'd better sign the lease fast. Store advertisements trumpet "unbeatable, one-day-only" sale prices.

The Art of the Deal

The fear of loss is really two fears in one: a fear of missing out on something special, and a fear of losing something of (usually monetary) value. When you can harness both those fears into a single negotiating tactic, you've got something powerful indeed. That's why successful negotiators often combine a presentation that suggests their offering is of great value with a tight deadline for accepting their offer.

Every negotiation that involves something of value will make both you and your opponent highly prone to fear of loss. For example, you finally find your dream home. The broker tells you several other buyers are ready to make offers on the house.

That revelation is a deliberate ploy to make you fear losing the home and thus motivating you to make an immediate offer—maybe one that's higher than the seller's asking price. (Chapter 21, "Real Estate Negotiations," covers how you can protect yourself from experiencing fear of loss from such tactics when buying a home.)

Here are some tips that will help you when you fear losing a deal you very much want:

➤ Never give your opponent any hint that you have a great desire to make the deal (buy the house, take the job, sell your car for the opponent's price).

➤ Be mentally prepared to walk away from the deal if it's not on the terms and conditions that you want.

➤ Find an alternate solution before you bargain (a comparable house, another prospective job, another potential car buyer). That helps prevent you from experiencing fear of loss—you'll know that if this particular deal doesn't go your way, there will be others.

Fear of the Unknown: The Uncertainty Factor

When you fear the unknown, you imagine the worst. (If you're like me, you probably experience this every time you visit your doctor or dentist.) As far as negotiation is concerned, fear of the unknown is a great motivator. What if the home sellers laugh at your offer? What if your negotiating opponent turns you down flat?

Here are some tips on how you can conquer your fear of the unknown:

➤ Prepare thoroughly. It'll give you confidence, and fear can't survive in the face of confidence.

➤ Remind yourself that most, if not all, of the horrible outcomes you are imagining will never happen. Sweep away those fears by concentrating on your preparation and strategies.

➤ Again, find an alternate solution before you bargain.

➤ And again, be prepared to walk away from the deal.

Fear of Failure

All negotiators, even the most experienced and most prepared, have a slight panic attack before stepping in to a new negotiation. That's natural. Negotiating is a performance, like acting or speaking in public, and a little performance anxiety is understandable.

You can deal with this fear in several ways:

➤ Acknowledge your fear instead of repressing it—but don't get obsessive.

➤ Prepare thoroughly and examine the negotiation from as many angles as possible. The more you know, the less you will fear being caught off-guard during the negotiation (see Chapter 2, "Bargaining Essentials," and Chapter 3, "Scoping Out the Other Side," for more on preparation).

➤ Mentally rehearse your negotiation before you go in (as explained in Chapter 15, "Taking Control").

➤ Dress for the negotiation in clothes that make you feel good about yourself.

➤ Make sure your notes or files (if you have them) are in order before you begin.

➤ Act confident. Your opponent won't detect your fear unless you show it. Take deep breaths so that your voice is controlled and firm, not shaky. Stand up straight. Make good eye contact.

Using the Fear Factor on Your Opponent

Closely linked to the fear of the unknown is the fear of uncertainty. Uncertainty is one of our greatest natural enemies. We worry and stew more about what we think *might* happen than we do about what actually *does* happen. Once an anticipated event occurs—even if it's unpleasant or downright bad—we actually feel relief. Now we have a known quantity that we can deal with.

Lets say you receive a telephone call from a close friend who says, "There's been a disaster at your house," and then hangs up. You can imagine what would be going through your mind—the worst possible situation. You're going to think that maybe the house burned down, or somebody was deathly ill—maybe even a robbery! You'll drop everything and try to contact your house to find out what's happened—you need to relieve the pain of your uncertainty.

That same process occurs when there is uncertainty in a negotiation. If one party to the bargaining process is in a state of uncertainty, he or she will be motivated to do everything that can be done just to get rid of the feeling.

The techniques in this book are your own personal insurance policy against negotiating from a position of uncertainty. But now it's time to look at how you can harness fear's motivational power to get your opponent to give you what you want.

Talking Points

"To know the worst is peace—it is uncertainty that kills."

—Elbert Hubbard

Introducing Doubt

Let's say you're in the market for a new home. You find the ideal house, but you don't tip off the seller or the broker that you love the place. On the contrary—you're smart and shrewd, so you maintain a poker face as you tour the property, and you keep that poker face during all your contacts with the seller and broker. You've begun to create some uncertainty in them because you're going to make an offer that is a lot lower than the asking price. You can do this in two ways:

1. You give the seller or broker only 24 hours to accept your offer.

2. You inform the seller or broker that you have two other houses in mind and will be making offers on them, too, in the event you can't make a fair and reasonable deal.

Each strategy is designed to generate uncertainty as to whether or not you'll withdraw your offer—unless, of course, your offer is so ridiculously low that no one takes it seriously. The seller wants to sell the house—that's why it's on the market. And the broker wants to make his or her commission. So, to relieve their uncertainty about making this sale, they're likely to come up with a counteroffer (see Chapter 19, "Offers and Counteroffers").

Dealbreaker

Arbitrary or "lowball" offers (or counteroffers) will not create uncertainty in a seller—and may very well offend him. Keep your initial offers low, but still within the reasonable range. Otherwise you run the risk of ruining your own deal.

Constructive Uncertainty

Let's say that you're happy with your current job, but not with your paycheck. You know you've been doing a good job and that your boss wants to keep you, but when it comes down to getting a raise, you keep hearing excuses about the company's tight budget and so forth. Creating a little uncertainty may be just the ticket to push your negotiations for a raise over the top. Carefully let word leak out that you need more money and are thinking about contacting a competitor about coming on board. Once the news filters back to your boss, you'll have created a sense of uncertainty on his part—he's not sure he'll have your services for much longer.

Losing a good employee is always a negative for the boss and the company (good employees are hard to find and expensive to train), so your boss is likely to want to relieve his uncertainty about your future with the company. That means your odds in favor of getting a raise have just increased substantially.

Uncertainty as Strategy

In almost any negotiation, certain facts and circumstances can provide you with the opportunity to create uncertainty. Early in your planning, you should ask yourself:

Dealmaker

Be subtle in your efforts at creating uncertainty—if your opponent discovers what you're doing, your chances of making this strategy work are slim to none.

"What can I do to create a constructive state of uncertainty in my opponent that will motivate him to act in my favor?" Once you've spotted a likely avenue for this sort of tactic, go for it!

But keep in mind that timing is critical in this, as in any other element of your negotiating strategy. In the previous example about getting a raise, the appropriate timing for creating uncertainty might come just after you've done something very beneficial for the company, such as successfully completing an important project or scoring a major sales coup—these are times when your boss is likely to be especially unwilling to lose you as an employee.

Taking the Fear Tactic Further

We all know how to use fear to get what we want. Parents warn their children, "No fighting . . . or else!" Police officers threaten to revoke licenses. Lawyers threaten to sue. And skilled negotiators may (tactfully) paint a picture that creates fear and

174

motivates you to agree to their positions. Unskilled negotiators may be more blunt and say, "Take it or leave it!" because they know that you want the deal.

A photographer I know was desperate to collect overdue bills. He hit upon a fear-inducing solution. He leafed through his files and found the most unflattering picture he had for every deadbeat customer. He attached each picture to each bill—along with a note suggesting that if he received permission to display the terrible picture in his window, he'd consider the bill paid in full. Fearful of having every wrinkle and double chin prominently displayed in the store window, the customers paid up quickly after that.

Stay alert during the bargaining to pick up clues as to how badly your opponent wants to close the deal. If your opponent is afraid of losing the deal, you can add more demands without worrying about the deal falling through.

Here are some tips on how you can spot your opponent's strong desire to clinch the deal:

➤ Your opponent was the one who initiated the bargaining (for example, he approached you about buying your home or car).

➤ Your opponent makes an offer or counteroffer that's especially generous—more than you expected.

➤ Your opponent quickly responds to any suggestion you make that indicates you're not certain about completing the deal (for example, if you say, "I'm not so sure I want to sell" or "I'm not in a hurry to buy right now.").

➤ Your opponent doesn't strongly protest when you make a proposal very favorable to you.

Dealmaker

A skillful opponent will frequently probe during bargaining to see how badly you want to close the deal so that he can take advantage of your fear of loss. Stay alert and don't tip your hand.

The "Greater Fear" Technique

This technique will work in any negotiation in which your opponent is likely to play on your fears.

Let's use buying a car as an example (now there's a scary experience). At the dealership, you see a car that you like, but you want to shop around before you make a decision. The salesperson tells you that the special sale on the model you want ends tomorrow, so if you don't sign now you could lose out on a great deal. That's a subtle way of saying, "You'd better buy the car today, or else . . .," and it's designed to cause you fear of loss.

Many people might take the bait. But you're prepared: You realize that this is the perfect time to use the "greater fear" technique. You know the salesperson works on a commission and is anxious to make the sale. So you tell the salesperson that you're sure other dealers will meet—and even beat—his price. Now the salesperson is afraid of losing the sale, and you're in a position to get an even greater discount than advertised.

Let's take another example. You decide to stop payment on the out-of-control computer you bought at Erratic Electronics. The store owner threatens to turn the matter over to a collection agency if you don't pay up. He mentions how a nonpayment notice will badly damage your credit rating.

You advise the store owner that if he jeopardizes your credit rating, you'll report the bad workmanship and unhelpful service to the Better Business Bureau. If absolutely necessary, you'll take legal action for damaging your credit rating without cause. You're now in a good position to get a new computer.

Fear and Time

Fear diminishes with time. If your opponent is afraid of losing the deal, take every opportunity to tactfully remind him that the deal may not go through. The longer the negotiation takes, the more times you should remind your opponent of his fears.

Talking Points

"The proper course with every kind of fear is to think about it rationally and calmly, and with great concentration, until it has become entirely familiar. In the end, familiarity will blunt its terrors."

—Bertrand Russell

Never Let Them See You Sweat

Never, never, never let your opponent know that you want to seal a deal, no matter how desperate you may be. Let's return to the home-buying example. The real estate agent takes you through the house. Your spouse praises the backyard. You ooh and ahh over the working fireplace. You both mention how anxious you are to move.

You've both just tipped off the salesperson that you're strongly attached to the house and that you fear losing it. The salesperson takes advantage of your fear by telling you that the house will be shown to several other couples that very day. Faced with the possibility of losing that home, the chances are good that you will be motivated to buy the house for more than what you wanted to pay.

The best way to protect yourself from this kind of manipulation is to never disclose, by either your words or your acts, that you're strongly attached to whatever you're bargaining for. Don't praise any aspects of the deal in front of your opponent; don't express delight. Keep as bland a poker face as you can. This will prevent your opponent from cashing in on your fears.

The Least You Need to Know

➤ Fear motivates us to act.

➤ The three most common fears you'll encounter when you negotiate are the fear of loss, the fear of the unknown, and the fear of failure.

➤ Recognizing your opponent's fears will increase your chances of negotiating successfully.

➤ Use the "greater fear" technique when an opponent tries to manipulate you through fear.

➤ Avoid displaying your fears during negotiation. Keep a poker face, and carefully monitor what you say about the deal.

Chapter 18

When Principles or Personalities Collide

In This Chapter

➤ When your opponent gets personal

➤ When negotiations founder on matters of principle

➤ Respecting your opponent's principles

I once negotiated to buy a business. The seller wasn't happy with the way the deal was progressing, and he began to make snide comments about lawyers—knowing full well that I was one.

I remained calm, smiled slightly, and made the mild observation that most lawyers are good, hard-working people trying their best to represent their clients; but, like any other profession, there probably were a few rotten apples in the bunch.

That took the wind out of my opponent's sails and got our discussions back on track. In this chapter, I show you how to handle negotiations that get too personal.

The Risks of Getting Personal

No matter how tempted you are (and how much justification you may have), never make a personal attack on your opponent. If you do, it will threaten all the goodwill, respect, and diplomacy you've brought to the negotiation thus far, and it may prevent your opponent from wanting to work with you.

Negotiable Terms

Personality is used here in its broadest sense, defined by *Webster's New World Dictionary* as "the distinctive individual qualities of a person, considered collectively."

Keeping your emotions to yourself is easier said than done. You may be deeply offended if your boss turns you down for a raise, if a client laughs at your proposal, or if the driver who smashed your fender claims that your driving is at fault.

It can be especially tempting to get personal if you're bargaining with someone close to you, such as a family member or friend (rather than a business associate). It's easier to get personal when the restraints of polite office behavior are removed.

If you feel you're about to lose control, take a break, take a deep breath, or get a drink of water. Do something—anything—that calms you down and prevents you from personally attacking your opponent. You've got to resist the temptation, no matter how difficult it is and even if your opponent gives you full justification—as my opponent did with his unpleasant lawyer-bashing.

Take the high road and follow the Negotiator's Golden Rule: "Treat your opponent the way you want your opponent to treat you." It's not a sign of weakness; it's a sign of inner strength and great negotiating skill.

If you can overcome your temptation to attack your opponent personally, you'll be in total command of both yourself and the negotiation. The bargaining momentum will be all yours.

Five Things You Should Never Mention When You Negotiate

Dealbreaker

No matter how you personally feel about your opponent, never express disdain or contempt by word *or* deed. You'll never recover from the ill will that such behavior generates.

Never let the negotiation disintegrate into an insult contest. Avoid any mention of personal characteristics of your opponent, from sly insinuations to outright barbs. Those characteristics include any reference to these aspects:

➤ Appearance, personal hygiene, or clothing

➤ Race, gender, ethnic background, or religion

➤ Profession, company, or business

➤ Competence or experience

➤ Age

Five Things You Should Never Do When You Negotiate

As you learned in Chapter 6, "Getting Physical," body language can communicate just as clearly as words. Avoid all physical gestures that translate into, "Your proposals are a joke, you stupid idiot." Aside from the time-honored upraised middle finger, you should avoid these actions:

➤ Exasperated eye-rolling

➤ Disdainful sneering

➤ Finger-pointing or fist-shaking

➤ Book, paper, or furniture throwing

➤ Any gesture your opponent can construe as physically threatening

If you do attack your opponent personally, you'd better be prepared for a searing counterattack. Don't escalate the verbal war! Stop it right there. Offer an apology—say something like, "Look, I was out of line. We're here to work out a deal, not insult each other. Why don't we take a break and try to talk this over again." Usually that'll do the trick, especially if you combine a gracious apology with a little self-deprecating humor.

Managing an Opponent Who's Become Personal

I've had more than one opponent call me names my publisher won't allow me to print here. I practiced what I'm now preaching—I stayed cool, gently smiled, and said, "I'm sorry you feel that way. I hope we can put this behind us and arrive at a fair resolution." In most cases, we did.

So what can you do when faced with an opponent who calls you a jerk or—worse?

➤ Don't join in, no matter how witty your comeback. Remember, your goal is to get what you want, not conduct a verbal war.

➤ Think about the consequences if the negotiation breaks down—you won't get to buy the house, you'll lose the client, your boss will fire you. That alone should be enough to convince you to rescue the situation.

The Art of the Deal

Count to 10, then count to 10 again—that's the ticket for keeping your cool when a hot-headed opponent tries to lure you into a personal fight. If counting doesn't work for you, try taking deep breaths or politely excusing yourself on some pretext so you can leave the room and recover your equilibrium. Do whatever it takes to keep yourself above the fray.

➤ If you can't figure out why your opponent is getting personal, ask. Say something like, "I thought we were discussing a deal here. Why are you getting so offensive?" Maybe something you've said or done has touched a nerve in your opponent. Get the cause out on the table.

➤ If an apology is in order, make it.

➤ If there's a misunderstanding, discuss it and clear it up.

Remember, if your opponent deliberately provokes you, nothing will be more difficult or disconcerting for him than your cool, fair, and impartial reaction. Your control will disarm him. It will make him feel foolish and, in most cases, will bring him back to his senses.

Neutralizing Personality Conflicts

On occasion, you'll bargain with an opponent whose personality clashes with yours. That can make it difficult for the two of you to even sit in the same room together, let alone try to work out a deal. Here are some tips on how to handle a personality conflict:

➤ *Stay low-key.* Moderate your tone of voice and your attitude. That will make you less threatening to your opponent and will help minimize the personality differences between the two of you.

➤ *Be frank.* Tell your opponent that although neither of you seems to have much in common, that's no reason why you can't reach a satisfactory agreement.

➤ *Use the magic words "fair and reasonable."* Tell your opponent that, whatever your personal differences, you know your opponent is "fair and reasonable"—and so are you.

A Matter of Principle

I once negotiated with an opponent who made it clear that he never discussed business after 6 p.m. For him, closing business at that hour was a matter of principle. Maybe he felt that way because of family commitments, or religious beliefs, or some other reason.

I didn't ask him to explain himself—I didn't have to. I knew from experience that when he uttered the words "a matter of principle," he meant it. If I insisted on bargaining beyond 6 p.m. he would be in no mood to gratify my request. So whenever I negotiated with him, I made sure that when the clock neared 6 p.m., we quit for the day and planned to resume some other time—even if we weren't finished negotiating.

When you negotiate, you may not always agree with your opponent's principles, but that's not important. What is important is to understand that your chances of changing your opponent's principles are slim to none. So don't try.

Never—I repeat, never—attack your opponent's principles, even if you think your opponent is naive or deluded. If you attack your opponent's principles, you're attacking the inner core of your opponent's self, and you can kiss any bargaining progress good-bye. (See Chapter 12, "Reaching Out to the Other Side," for a detailed discussion of the concept of "self" in negotiations.)

Talking Points

"If principle is good for anything, it's worth living up to."

—Benjamin Franklin

How to Overcome Matters of Principle

If your opponent is insistent on a trivial point, claiming that "it's the principle of the thing," concede the point. Don't jeopardize the entire negotiation by trying to force your opponent to surrender a principle for a point that's not important. I routinely concede unimportant matters almost every time I negotiate. It's a great strategy. It promotes progress and makes my opponent feel good, and it paves the way for further negotiating progress on the bigger issues.

If your opponent is immovable on a major bargaining point because of her principles, however, you have three options:

➤ Concede the point (the most dissatisfying option).

➤ Prove that the point doesn't apply to your opponent's principle.

➤ Find a way around your opponent's principle.

Notice that *none* of these options involves trying to make your opponent abandon his or her principle. That's never a good idea.

I once negotiated the sale of an interest in a residential development. One issue was the payment of $50,000 for improvements made to the development. My opponent stubbornly refused to pay any part of the $50,000 and said that, for him, not paying was "a matter of principle." He had never done it before, and he wasn't about to now. As he spoke, his jaw clenched and his face turned red. He was drawing a line in the sand and wanted me to know it.

At that point, bargaining came to a halt. I couldn't attack his principle. That would have made him even more furious. I didn't want to concede the point, either ($50,000 is a lot of money!). But I still had those two other options to try.

Dealmaker

Whether you share your opponent's principles or not, it's important that you recognize their importance to your opponent—and that you respect his or her desire to live in accord with those principles. By showing such respect, you greatly enhance your chances for bargaining success.

183

First, I tried to show him that his principle didn't apply. I pointed out that the improvements I wanted him to pay for would also benefit the neighboring property—which he also owned. By paying $50,000 now, he could actually save some money down the road. That didn't move him. He repeated he'd never paid for these kind of improvements before and he wouldn't start now.

That left me with the second option: to find a way around our disagreement that satisfied both of us. I proposed that he not pay the $50,000, but that we receive a $50,000 increase in the purchase price of the development. This solution allowed him to keep his principle intact. He agreed, my persistence paid off, and the stalemate was broken.

When All Else Fails

What if you simply cannot overcome the conflicts that you face with your opponent? If you've tried every suggestion recommended in this chapter and you still can't reach an agreement, there are professionals who can help you finalize the negotiation:

➤ A *mediator* is a neutral third party who is trained in conflict resolution and who makes suggestions and proposals to help you reach an agreement with your opponent. Mediators are commonly used to help negotiate divorce settlements.

➤ An *arbitrator* is another neutral third party who can resolve disputes. When a case is brought before an arbitrator, both parties agree in advance to be bound by the arbitrator's decision. Arbitration is commonly used to settle labor agreements and construction contracts.

Mediators and arbitrators are especially useful when negotiations become emotional, or when the two sides to a dispute find it impossible to work together directly. A neutral third party helps to keep the discussion calm and businesslike, thus reducing the likelihood of a stalemate when one side or another refuses to listen to reason. For more information about mediators and arbitrators, call or write the following organizations:

➤ American Arbitration Association
140 West 51st Street, New York, NY 10020
212-484-4041

➤ National Academy of Arbitrators
Office of the Secretary, 20 Thornwood Drive, Suite 107, Ithaca NY 14850
607-257-9925

➤ Academy of Family Mediators
1500 South Highway 100, Suite 355, Golden Valley, MN 55416
612-525-8760

The Least You Need to Know

➤ Never attack your opponent personally, even when you have just cause. Avoid insults or threatening gestures.

➤ If your opponent gets personal, don't retaliate. Stay cool, resolve the misunderstanding, or apologize, if necessary.

➤ Neutralize personality conflicts by staying low-key, concentrating on the business at hand, and reminding your opponent that you both are "fair and reasonable" people.

➤ If your opponent is insistent on a trivial point as a matter of principle, concede the point.

➤ If your opponent insists on a major point as a matter of principle, never attack the principle. Try to show why the principle doesn't apply, or find a way around it.

Part 6
Sealing the Deal

Two key elements of any negotiation are the offer/counteroffer process and the closer. Offers and counteroffers are sort of like marriage proposals. First, it takes a little courting (bargaining). Then, you have to say the right words at the right time if you want a "yes" to your proposal.

As in a marriage proposal, the offer and counteroffer stage is a critical part of the bargaining process. One wrong move or badly timed gesture, and the whole negotiation is off—and all your bargaining has gone down the drain.

Closing, too, is a crucial stage in the bargaining process. If you can't close, you're just talking, not negotiating. In this part, I explain how to make offers and counteroffers and then seal the deal.

Offers and Counteroffers

When you make an offer or counteroffer, you put your beliefs on the line. You say, in essence, "This is my proposal and what I *believe* is a fair bargain." You commit yourself to a course of action. If your opponent accepts, the deal is done.

Obviously, then, you'll need to be firmly convinced that your offer—or your counteroffer—is something you can comfortably live with. As with all other aspects of negotiation, there is skill involved in developing and presenting appropriate offers and counteroffers. In this chapter, I'll show you the strategies and techniques you'll need so that you can sail through the offer and counteroffer stage with confidence.

The Negotiation Rumba

The offer and counteroffer stage resembles a rumba—there's plenty of apparent motion, but only a limited number of steps you can take. After the first offer has been laid on the table, you and your opponent can choose one of three alternative maneuvers:

➤ Reject the offer on the table.

➤ Accept the offer on the table and seal the deal.

➤ Propose a counteroffer.

Dealmaker

When you receive an offer or counteroffer that you can't accept, your first thought should be: "What can I suggest in a counteroffer?"

Later in this chapter, you'll see why the last option is almost always the one to go with. But before you can even begin to formulate a counteroffer, you need to have an offer on the table.

Let Your Opponent Make the First Move

There's no rule that says which side has to make the first offer, but in nearly every negotiation situation, you'll benefit if you let your opponent lead off. Here's why:

➤ When your opponent makes the first offer, she sets the upper or lower limit. Say you want to sell your used car for $6,000. You find an interested buyer and name your price. Now you've set the upper limit. What if the buyer had been willing to pay $6,500? You'd never get it. And if the buyer has any sense at all, she'll already be trying to negotiate down from $6,000.

Likewise, if you're the buyer and you offer $6,000, that's the lowest you can expect to pay. The seller is going to bargain to work up from that figure.

➤ When your opponent leads with the first offer, you immediately have the three options mentioned earlier. You're always in a good bargaining position when you have plenty of options.

It's like the old story about the medieval serf who was sentenced to death by the king. The serf promised to teach the king's horse how to fly if the king let him live for another year. The king agreed. The serf's friends said he was crazy because horses can't fly. The serf pointed out to his friend that in a year the king might die, the horse might die, or, hey!—maybe he'd even figure out how to make the horse fly.

Three Opening Move Strategies: The Good, The Bad, and The Ugly

When you're approaching the offer stage of a negotiation, things begin to get very delicate. Say you've found someone who wants to buy your house. If you want to get the top price, it's important that you begin the bargaining with the right approach. There are three ways you can proceed, but only one of them is best. Read on to learn about these options and to discover the best one to take.

The Ugly Opening Move

Let's take the worst opening scenario first. It would go something like this:

> Buyer: "How much do you want for the property?"
>
> You: "$150,000."

What's wrong with this picture? Simple: With one utterance, you've committed yourself to the maximum price you can get, which any smart buyer will begin to chip away. No one in his right mind will ever offer even one penny more than the $150,000 you've just quoted, so you've put yourself in a defensive bargaining position. That's not where you want to be.

Dealbreaker

People often try to back out on deals for all sorts of reasons. Avoid getting stuck this way! Keep a paper trail going from the moment the first offer hits the table—that way you'll have proof of your opponent's commitment to you.

The Merely Bad Opening Move

There's a slightly better way to go:

> Buyer: "How much do you want for the property?"
>
> You: "I haven't made up my mind. How much are you willing to pay?"

This at least has the advantage of not committing you to a price right off the bat. Instead, you've put the burden on the buyer, which is good because she may come in with a higher price than you intended. But your reply is too general, and it's unlikely that she will take the bait and open up with a dollar figure right away. She will probably fish around for details, then ask you again to name your figure. In effect, you've moved no closer to closing the deal.

The Good Opening Move

What the merely bad opening move had working against it was that it made you look pretty clueless. What it had going for it (so that it wasn't absolutely *ugly*) was that it kept you from being the one to set the upper limit of your negotiation. How can you improve on it? Consider the following scenario:

> Buyer: "How much do you want for the property?"
>
> You: "Please, make me an offer."

Now you're cooking! You've put the burden entirely on the buyer. At the same time, you've taken a much more direct, confident stance. If your potential buyer tries to wiggle out, tactfully repeat your position: "Please, make me an offer." In most cases, if the buyer is really interested, you'll get one. If it's not what you want to hear, you can start bargaining up from there. You've made no personal commitment to an upper limit, so you're not operating under any limitations.

Dealmaker

Be clear in explaining the reasoning behind your offer or counteroffer. If you make no explanation, you force your opponent to guess what you're up to—and he'll likely imagine the worst.

The Use of Counteroffers

Once you've heard your opponent's offer, you're ready to try to improve upon it. That's where counteroffers come into play. Counteroffers serve a number of important functions that can help you get what you want:

➤ They keep the bargaining alive and breathing when you seriously want to do the deal. While it's true that you can reject your opponent's offers without making counteroffers of your own, it's generally not a good idea if you want to keep the negotiation alive. Your opponent will most likely just walk away from the deal.

➤ They demonstrate how serious you are about the bargaining and how you are trying to reach a mutually favorable agreement. By making a counteroffer, you show that you're not just stringing your opponent along or rejecting every proposal you don't like.

➤ They place your terms and conditions under a magnifying glass. Your opponent may not have thought of some of the suggestions or compromises you incorporate into your counteroffer. She may even like them.

Guidelines for Making Offers and Counteroffers

As mentioned in the introduction to this chapter, there is an art to effectively determining appropriate offers and counteroffers. Here are some important rules you should remember when you start to make offers and counteroffers:

➤ *Never appear too anxious.* Your eagerness may suggest that you desperately want to cut a deal. Your opponent will smell your fear and drive a harder bargain.

➤ *Be prepared for any reaction from your opponent.* This could range from "Whadda you, crazy? I wouldn't pay 10 cents for that pit you call a house!" to "How does $3 million sound?" Don't be caught off-guard, even if your opponent's reaction isn't what you expected.

➤ *Always get offers and counteroffers in writing.* If you negotiate a good deal and your opponent tries to back out, you've got a written record to prove that you had already reached an agreement.

➤ *Be specific when you state your offers and counteroffers.* "I'll give you $3,000," is better than "I'm thinking somewhere in the area of $3,000." The vague approach invites your opponent to try for more.

➤ *Explain the reasons for your offers and counteroffers.* Say you're interested in buying a used car that you're willing to pay $10,000 for. You have the car checked out and discover that it needs $1,000 worth of repairs. You should pass that information on to your opponent when you make a $9,000 counteroffer. That makes it clear to your opponent that you have a legitimate reason for offering $9,000— you're not just trying to chisel away at his price.

➤ *Don't get angry if your offer or counteroffer is rejected.* You don't want to offend your opponent. Ask him why he's rejecting your offer—perhaps he has legitimate reasons that you can equalize.

Why Highballs and Lowballs Are for Screwballs

Making outrageously highball or lowball offers is a foolish bargaining strategy. If your price is too high (if you're the seller) or too low (if you're the buyer), you risk losing your credibility unless you can give your opponent some reason for your position. That credibility damage will spill over onto every bargaining position you take from that point forward in the negotiation.

Even worse, if you negotiate regularly and develop a reputation for coming in with highballs or lowballs, many of your opponents will automatically discount your proposals, no matter what they are. That's much too heavy a price to pay for those few situations when you might get an inexperienced opponent to swallow a highball or lowball offer.

> **Negotiable Terms**
>
> **Highballing** means naming a figure or term in a negotiation that is obviously too high for your opponent to accept. Its opposite is **lowballing**, which means setting a figure or term unreasonably low.

Catching a Highball or Lowball

When your opponent makes offers or counteroffers that you know are too high or too low, don't be too quick to write him off as a crank or a fool. Ask for an explanation. Maybe your opponent is misinformed or just made a mistake.

On the other hand, if your opponent is deliberately coming in too high or too low, requesting an explanation will call your opponent's bluff. That puts your opponent on the defensive and swings the bargaining momentum to you.

Handling Your Opponent's Offers or Counteroffers

It's not enough to know how to determine a realistic offer or to present it effectively. You also have to know how to evaluate your opponent's offers or counteroffers. Always look at your opponent's suggestions objectively, even if they're obviously too high or too low. If you're not happy with your opponent's offers or counteroffers, explain why. Once again, that puts your opponent on the defensive, which is precisely where you want him to be.

Dealmaker

Deadlines are an important element of the offer/counteroffer process. Be sure to set deadlines that you can live with; whenever possible, make your deadlines another contributing element to your overall negotiating strategy.

Be gentle when you reject an offer or counteroffer. Remember, your opponent has a lot of her self invested in her offer or counteroffer. If you don't explain why you can't accept the offer or counteroffer, you run the risk of offending her.

Then again, if you like your opponent's offer or counteroffer, don't tip your hand! If you appear too pleased (by grinning like an idiot, singing a merry song, or leaping up and performing a victory dance on the table), your opponent will have second thoughts on the wisdom of her offer or counteroffer and may withdraw it. Keep a level, calm, and passive attitude. Tell your opponent you'll get back to her within the deadline period (if one has been set) or very soon. Or, you can accept on the spot if you feel it's the right thing to do.

Identifying Dealmakers and Dealbreakers

Many negotiators throw "dealmakers" or "dealbreakers" into the negotiation at the offer or counteroffer stage.

A *dealmaker* is anything that's thrown onto the bargaining table that clinches the deal. For example, say that you are negotiating to buy a house and you and the seller have agreed on all the details, but you're still $5,000 apart on the price. Then you offer to split the difference and pay $2,500 more for the house. The seller, finally pleased with all the terms of the deal, accepts. Your split-the-difference suggestion was the dealmaker.

A *dealbreaker* is the opposite of a dealmaker. It's anything thrown onto the bargaining table that kills the deal. With the home-buying example, say that when you offer to split the $5,000 difference, the seller refuses and insists that you pay the entire amount. If you walk away from the deal at that point, then the seller's insistence on the $5,000 was the dealbreaker.

The Legalese of Offers and Counteroffers: A Cautionary Tale

Here's the scenario: You want to buy a house. The sellers—let's call them Joe and Jane Jones—are asking $200,000. You make a counteroffer for $150,000 and add the following conditions:

> ➤ The Joneses' lawnmower comes with the deal.

> ➤ The large doghouse comes with the deal. (Fido will love it.)

> ➤ The Joneses will pay for a water-quality test. (You're very health-conscious.)

> ➤ Three living-room chairs come with the deal, and furthermore, the Joneses will re-upholster them in that precious blue chintz pattern you saw in *Martha Stewart Living*. (I know, I know . . . that's a ridiculous condition. But I've included it to better illustrate the way the law treats offers and counteroffers. Work with me here.)

Negotiable Terms

A **dealmaker** is any provision, offer, or consideration that clinches the deal. A **dealbreaker** is anything that kills the deal.

The Joneses are intrigued but not yet convinced. They make another counteroffer: They agree to all your conditions except the price and the absurd upholstery job. They will sell for $190,000 and will have nothing to do with chintz.

You decide to make a counteroffer. You raise the price to $160,000 and propose that they reupholster only two of the chairs.

The Joneses smell a deal, so they aren't going to walk away yet. They propose splitting the price difference at $175,000. They still refuse to reupholster the chairs.

You want that house. So you make a counteroffer. You accept the $175,000 compromise price but insist on getting at least one chair reupholstered.

And the verdict is: you goofed! By insisting on that one chair, you modified the seller's counteroffer and thus rejected the counteroffer. The seller can now reject the entire deal on the basis of that one chair. For example, what if someone comes along after you make your counteroffer and offers the Joneses $175,000 with no stipulations about the reupholstery of the chair? The Joneses can accept that offer and kiss yours good-bye.

Dealmaker

If you alter an offer or counteroffer, you are effectively rejecting the entire thing. No matter how tiny the change is that you make, it legally invalidates the whole deal.

The rule is: Any alteration of an offer or counteroffer, no matter how trivial, is a rejection of the *entire* offer or counteroffer.

You can't accept an offer in little bits and pieces until you have a deal. It's an all-or-nothing game. The same rule applies to your opponent. In that way, the law tries to treat both sides equally and fairly.

In negotiations in which more than one issue is involved, agreements must be reached on all issues, or there's no deal. Tentative agreements in multi-issue negotiations are not binding (unless the parties involved agree to accept tentative agreements before the negotiation has begun).

Devastation via Concession

Just as good strategy dictates that you shouldn't make the first offer, it also dictates that you should never be the first to make a large bargaining concession. To do so will make you appear weak in your opponent's eyes and can destroy your bargaining power. But if you're really hungry for a deal, how can you avoid major concessions if your opponent won't budge from his or her position?

Dealmaker

On the rare (I hope) occasion that you're forced to make a major concession, be sure that you can provide a convincing reason for doing so. That way, you retain your credibility as a good negotiator.

The first thing you can do to avoid making a large concession is to make sure all your negotiating positions are fully supported by facts and documentation. Of course, that puts the burden on you to prepare for the negotiation, but by now you're ready for that, right? (Head back to Chapter 2, "Bargaining Essentials," if you need a refresher course in doing your homework.)

After you've clearly presented all the supporting data you need to make your case, if your opponent still demands a large concession, ask why. If he comes up with a legitimate reason that you hadn't thought of, you have a genuine basis for making the concession, and your concession probably won't cost you your credibility (although you do risk looking unprepared for the negotiation).

On the other hand, if your opponent can't come up with a legitimate reason, you should resume negotiations, beginning with a new presentation of the basis for your position. In most cases, if your opponent has any interest in making a deal, he will drop the demand for a large initial concession.

The Least You Need to Know

➤ Always try to get your opponent to make the first offer.

➤ Use counteroffers to keep the negotiation alive and to indicate your serious interest in the negotiation.

➤ Get any offers or counteroffers in writing.

➤ Don't use highballing or lowballing strategies. They risk your credibility and make your opponent suspicious.

➤ A counteroffer that alters an offer or counteroffer in any way is a rejection of the entire offer or counteroffer.

➤ Always explain your reasons for proposing or rejecting an offer or counteroffer.

➤ Never make the first large bargaining concession.

Chapter 20

Closing with Class

In This Chapter

➤ It's closing time!

➤ Closing do's and don'ts

➤ Techniques for effective closings

Congratulations! You finally made it. You prepared thoroughly, negotiated ferociously, and skillfully maneuvered through the offers and counteroffers. Both you and your opponent are ready to say "yes!"

The final step you're now approaching is called closing the deal. It, too, is a special skill, and one that you'll need to master if you want to become an effective negotiator. This chapter shows you how to successfully conclude a bargaining session.

When Is Closing Time?

No two negotiations are alike, so it's impossible for me to predict the perfect time for closing that will work in every negotiation. The key question you should ask yourself is: Do I think my opponent is ready to say yes? If you're sure, then go for it. You might, for example, simply shake hands and say, "Okay, it's a deal."

Dealmaker

Skilled negotiators develop almost a sixth sense for the best time to move on to close a bargaining session. You, too, will gain that sense of judgment after you've gotten a few successful negotiations under your belt.

But it's often the case that the best time to close your bargain isn't so clearly marked. If you're unsure if the time is right, continue the bargaining a little longer, perhaps by re-explaining your last counteroffer or by asking your opponent for more details on her offer or counteroffer. At some point, it will become clear that there's nothing more to be said. That's when you know the time's ripe for closing the deal. The more bargaining experience you gain, the easier you'll be able to pinpoint the best time to close.

When Your Opponent's Body Language Tells You Not to Close

Still, there are some tell-tale clues that closing time is near. One such clue can be found by observing your opponent's body language. Chapter 6, "Getting Physical," gave you a basic primer on body language and how to interpret it. When you approach closing, it's especially important that you closely observe your opponent's physical movements—it pays great dividends. You want to stay alert and notice your opponent's body movements to help you gauge whether the time is right for you to close the bargaining.

Certain gestures or movements suggest that your opponent is not yet ready to say yes. When you see one or more of the following signs, hold off the closing until you get your opponent in a more receptive mood:

➤ Arms folded tightly against the chest. This is a classic defensive position. Your opponent is subconsciously telling you that he is not ready to say yes.

➤ Turning his body slightly sideways, even while facing and looking at you. By presenting the side of his body to you rather than openly facing you, your opponent is protecting himself from fully accepting your bargaining position.

➤ Looking away, even though his body is facing you. If your opponent can't look you in the face, he's not ready to agree to your terms.

➤ Crossing his legs and leaning back, away from you. Your opponent is putting distance between the two of you. He is resisting.

➤ Rising from her chair and moving away from you. Here again, your opponent is trying to distance herself from you.

➤ Rubbing or shielding her chin or face. By putting her hands in front of her face, your opponent is shielding herself because she's having doubts about the negotiation.

If you see one or more of these postures, you know your opponent is subconsciously not ready to commit to closing the negotiation just yet—regardless of what he is actually saying to you. Keep pointing out the worth and value of your proposals until he stops using defensive, shielding postures. Then—and only then—will he be receptive to saying yes.

What to Expect at a Closing

Most informal negotiations, such as resolving family matters or buying small items of personal property, don't require any ceremonial closing agreements: A simple verbal assent will usually do.

Dealmaker

Ignore your opponent's body language at your peril! If you're getting all sorts of rejecting or non-receptive cues from your opponent and press on with the close anyway, you're bound to fail.

Other types of negotiations, such as buying or selling real estate, do require extensive closing arrangements. Part 7, "Real-Time, Real-World Negotiating," covers the details of closing procedures for particular real-life negotiating scenarios; for now, here are a few pointers to keep in mind at any closing in which you must sign on the dotted line:

➤ Use a lawyer, if you can afford one. Real estate and lease agreements are usually long-term and involve a lot of money. You should be sure you are signing something you can live with—including all the small print written in legalese. It's better to be safe than sorry, and a lawyer can help to keep you safe.

➤ Always read the document you are asked to sign, clause by clause, and seek an explanation for anything that's not clear. Don't worry about seeming naive or foolish. There's nothing more naive or foolish than signing a document you don't fully understand.

➤ Documents prepared by your opponent are usually loaded with provisions that heavily favor your opponent, and thus are very unfavorable to you (this is very common in leases, for example). If your opponent prepares the document, many of these provisions will go unchallenged, so it's always better to prepare (or have your lawyer prepare) the document and submit it to your opponent for his or her signature, if that's possible. That way, you can insert provisions that are favorable to you—and they'll be less likely to be challenged by your opponent.

➤ In most cases, each party should receive a signed original of the closing document or contract. This document is often your only legal safeguard to make sure that you can enforce the provisions contained within it. Keep your original in a safe place, and keep it for as long as the object of the agreement is subject to the contractual agreement.

Closing Do's and Don'ts

As with other stages in your negotiating process, there's a right way and a wrong way to go about closing a deal. I've discussed several of the pointers here in previous chapters, but they're important enough to mention again:

➤ Do make good eye contact when you make your closing pitch. That tells your opponent that you believe in the deal. Looking away conveys the impression that you lack confidence in the deal, and your opponent may refuse to go along.

➤ Do use the magic words "fair and reasonable." You want your opponent to know that a truly fair and reasonable person would seal the deal.

➤ Don't be too anxious to close. If you appear too eager to get your opponent to say yes, your opponent may get suspicious of you and ask for more time to reexamine the deal.

➤ Don't beg and plead with your opponent. This will also make you appear anxious. Stay calm and repeat the merits of your position. At some point, your opponent will concede.

➤ Don't try to bully your opponent into saying yes. The more you bully, the more your opponent will resist. You'll also risk making your opponent angry.

Dealbreaker

Never give your opponent a chance to reopen bargaining issues that have been resolved. This can toss all your hard negotiating work away. Funnel the bargaining so that closed matters stay closed.

Four Words That Can Devastate a Closing

I once watched a negotiator bring a long, arduous negotiation to what should have been a spellbinding close. He presented his case beautifully, deftly navigated the offer and counteroffer stage, and remained respectful and pleasant throughout. He had his opponent ready and willing to say yes.

But then he made a cardinal bargaining mistake. He said, "Please, think it over." With those four words, he lost a golden opportunity to get what he wanted. He gave his opponent an open invitation to rethink his bargaining position and aim for ways to improve it. And that's exactly what his opponent did: He came back to the bargaining table with new ideas and new proposals.

When you give your opponent time to think over a negotiation that is ready to close, you offer her time to regroup, to rethink her bargaining position, and to concoct new positions she had lost sight of during the negotiation. When she comes back to the bargaining table, she'll be eager to present her new positions—not to say yes.

The moral is, when you sense that your opponent is ripe for saying yes, make the deal right there and then.

Effective Closing Techniques

A closing technique is a cue to get your opponent to say yes. It's not a device to trick your opponent to say yes if he isn't ready. If your opponent isn't ripe to say yes when you use a closing technique, no amount of skill will succeed in getting your opponent to close the deal.

Use the following techniques when the issues have been thoroughly discussed and you sense your opponent is ready to say yes to the deal. These techniques will get your opponent off the fence and ready to agree to a deal.

Dealbreaker

If your opponent keeps reinventing the wheel—going back time and time again to renegotiate issues that the two of you have already resolved—you can be pretty sure that he's not serious about coming to any final resolution to the bargaining. You may want to consider cutting your losses and finding a better deal elsewhere.

Prompting Action Technique

You can encourage and motivate your opponent to say yes by asking her to take some simple form of action that signifies that you have a deal. For example, you hand her the closing papers and say, "Please sign here." Or, you can simply ask, "Does this mean we have a deal?" In either case, you are suggesting that your opponent take an action—sign a paper, or verbally commit to an agreement—that will prompt the closing of the deal.

The Art of the Deal

Good television commercials use the prompting technique with maximum effectiveness. They'll end with the overenthusiastic announcer yelling, "Order now!" or "Call now!" The same is true of direct-mail campaigns that ask you to fill out a quick survey or try a free sample issue of a magazine. They're encouraging you to act, to say yes to their product. That's exactly what the prompting action technique is designed to do: motivate your opponent to say yes and close the deal.

Assumption Technique

With the assumption technique, you assume that your opponent will say yes, so you prompt the closing action: "I'll call the bank and ask them to go ahead with the loan," or "I'll call the title company and ask them to check out the title to the property" are examples of this closing technique. If your opponent is in a "yes" mood, he will nod or say okay. Even if he wasn't quite ready to close yet, the momentum you establish with your prompting may be enough to carry him along to closing of deal.

Summarizing Technique

When you employ the summarizing technique, what you do is briefly summarize your understanding of the deal. This serves to prompt your opponent to say yes to it in its entirety.

When you use this technique, your goal is to reaffirm issues that you've both already decided. But be careful! You don't want to open up old issues for further discussion. To avoid this, phrase your summation in positive sentences rather than questions, and never use this technique if your opponent hasn't already agreed to any of the points you plan to mention in your summation.

Dealbreaker

While maintaining control is important at all stages of the negotiation, it's especially true during the closing. Be vigilant during this delicate part of your bargaining process, or you can lose all the benefits you've worked so hard to achieve.

How does the summarization technique work? Say you're working with Smithers from Wonder Widgets to close a special deal. You're ready to close, but you realize that Smithers needs a little nudge to get him to the finish line. You summarize the discussion by saying, "So we're looking at a rush order of 5,000 widgets with the company logo engraved on the handle. They'll be delivered to the Chicago office on the 28th, and the price is 50 cents per widget." To this Smithers agrees. Note that nowhere in the summary have you posed a question—you're presenting your summary as a series of settled agreements.

The Final Word on Closing

Once your opponent says yes and the details have been wrapped up, don't discuss anything related to the bargaining. You don't want to run the risk of reopening discussions. Make small talk about the weather, sports, the news, your Aunt Edna's kidney stones—anything that's not connected with the subject matter. When your opponent has said yes, stop.

The Least You Need to Know

➤ Close the bargaining when you sense from your gut instinct and your opponent's body language that your opponent is ready to say yes.

➤ Make sure you have all the necessary paperwork correctly prepared and ready for the closing.

➤ Don't bully or plead with your opponent to close.

➤ When you sense that your opponent is ready to say yes, close. Never ask your opponent to think it over.

➤ Use closing techniques to prompt your opponent to act.

➤ Once you and your opponent have agreed on a deal, don't continue to discuss the deal. You risk reopening the bargaining if you do.

Part 7
Real-Time, Real-World Negotiating

Now that you've got the basics of successful negotiating down pat, it's time to put them into practice. Let's look at how to negotiate everyday matters you'll deal with many times as you wind your way through the trail of life.

Buying a home, a car, or real estate; asking for a raise, a loan, or a refund—many people dread these common negotiating situations. But not you! Once you know how to negotiate them smoothly and powerfully, you'll be able to save a lot of time, money, and trouble. And with the knowledge you'll get in this part, you'll not only lose your fear—you'll actually enjoy the process.

Chapter 21

Real Estate Negotiations

In This Chapter

➤ Dealing with the middle man: agents and brokers

➤ Pulling your home-buying information together

➤ Making offers and counteroffers

➤ Closing in on the closing

➤ Commercial and investment property deals

Whatever your dream house—a grand Victorian mansion or a small bungalow with the proverbial white picket fence—you probably envision yourself owning a home at some point in your life (if you don't already). It's a cherished part of the American dream—and will continue to be, despite the soaring costs of home ownership. In fact, you'll probably own more than one home during your lifetime.

But buying—or selling—a home is one of the biggest financial negotiations you're likely to face. With that in mind, it's easy to see that there are a few basic pointers you should follow to get the best deal. And that's true about any real estate negotiation—whether you're buying a private residence or a commercial or investment property, there are certain strategies that will help you to get the deal you want. This chapter shows you how to conduct a hassle-free real estate negotiation, no matter what type of property you're buying or selling.

Dealmaker

Some of the material presented here was adapted from *The Complete Idiot's Guide to Buying & Selling a Home,* by Shelley O'Hara. It's a great resource for home buyers or sellers.

You Can't Tell the Players Without a Scorecard

Once you jump into the market to buy or sell a home, any number of real estate experts will offer their services. Here are the key players you may deal with:

➤ The *seller* is the actual property owner. Some owners do try to handle the sale of their home privately, hoping to realize more money from the sale by saving on broker's commissions. Most often, however, you'll be dealing with a middle man—a broker or agent.

➤ *Brokers (or agents)* are licensed to sell real estate in their state (and can be licensed to sell it in other states). Brokers usually are agents who work for the seller, and they charge the seller a commission (usually a percentage of the sales price). The amount of the commission is negotiable and is decided when the seller agrees to hire the broker. Brokers can also open their own real estate offices.

➤ *Salespeople* or *sales associates* are licensed to sell real estate in their state. They cannot open their own real estate offices or conduct business on their own. They must work for a broker. They also are agents of the seller.

Do You Need an Agent?

For both buyers and sellers, agents can help define your search and serve as your representatives to the other side. Agents can help with these issues:

➤ *Financing.* Agents can analyze your current financial situation, estimate the costs involved with a home you are interested in buying, or help you set the listing price on the home you are selling.

➤ *Finding a home.* If you aren't sure what kind of home you'd like to buy, an agent can help define your terms. She will have information about communities, schools, taxes, and neighborhoods. She will also arrange all your visits to homes and will tour them with you. (But, today, prospecting for properties on the Internet is becoming more and more popular—reducing your need to rely on agents.)

➤ *Preparing your home.* Agents have a good idea what home buyers look for. If you are selling your home, your agent can often tell you which repairs and renovations will increase its sales value and eye appeal.

➤ *Negotiating.* Home buying and selling is an intricate deal with plenty of concessions and fine print. Even though you're a negotiating whiz because you've read this book, you may still want an experienced attorney or real estate agent to assist you at the bargaining table.

Negotiable Terms

In many states, the **listed price** or **asking price** is considered the seller's offer for the house.

If you are selling a home, I'd suggest that you almost definitely need an agent. Some home sellers, though, choose to go it alone.

For Sale by Owner: Selling Your Home on Your Own

If you want to sell your home by yourself, you'll have to become an instant expert in a number of professions. You'll need to be a market researcher, a smart advertiser, an enthusiastic salesperson, a shrewd financier, and a master negotiator. I can help you with that last part, but as for the rest, you're on your own.

You will also have to be on call any time someone wants to see your place. You probably won't have the luxury of showing it only on evenings and weekends.

The Downsides of Dealing with Agents

If you want to avoid handling all the details of buying or selling your home yourself, you'll need to deal with an agent. But there are some negatives attached to doing so. For one, agents cost money. *Buyer's agents* usually get a flat fee or a commission based on the purchase price of the home. *Seller's agents* usually get a 5 to 7 percent commission of the selling price. (Commissions are negotiable, too.)

Remember, however, that agents usually represent the seller. They therefore want to get as good a deal from the seller's perspective as possible. Still, because the agent is generally working on a commission arrangement, he or she will desperately want to push the deal through, which gives you some bargaining room.

Dealmaker

In complex negotiations such as real-estate purchases, you may find it advantageous to enlist the services of a lawyer. You'll particularly want legal advice when it comes time to close the deal.

If you're the buyer, you should offer less than the listed (or asking) price. In many cases (unless the house is a hot property with a lot of interested buyers), you'll get the house for a reasonable price—less than the seller originally asked for. That's because the agent will want to make a commission and will recommend that the seller accept any reasonable offer.

On the other hand, if you're the seller, you must prevent your agent from pushing for a sale that's lower than your asking price. The time to do that is when you first list the price with the agent. Make it clear to the agent at that time that you'll stand firm on the listed price unless a buyer comes up with a genuine reason why you should take less. (If you sell your house yourself, of course, none of this applies.)

What to Look for When You Buy a Home

There are literally hundreds of factors you should consider when you evaluate a home, far too many to list here. But some major standard considerations that can affect the price, including these:

➤ The size of the property

➤ The size—in both dimensions and number of rooms—of the dwelling itself

➤ The popularity of the style of the dwelling

➤ The condition of the building—the standard of maintenance or upkeep

➤ The desirability of the neighborhood

➤ The school district

While these are all significant considerations when evaluating a house, in terms of actually negotiating the purchase, there are a few additional factors you should investigate.

Nobody Wants It

No matter how good the house looks from a physical standpoint, keep in mind that a fresh coat of paint and other cosmetic tricks can cover a multitude of sins. You should find out how long the house has been on the market. If the For Sale sign has been up for a while, the house may have defects, or the neighborhood may be changing for the worse.

On the other hand, perhaps the house is fine but the asking price is too high. Frequently, homes that are sold by their owners stay on the market longer because owners tend to let their emotions rule when they set the price. This usually means that they price their homes too high because they are unfamiliar with the real estate market in their area or are simply unable to set an unbiased price.

It's a Buyer's Market

While a good seller (or agent) won't disclose how anxious the seller is to make the sale, you may be able to gauge his desperation level by asking a few key questions:

➤ How long has the house been on the market? If it was only recently listed, chances are the seller isn't particularly anxious just yet. If it has been on the market a while, he may be more than ready to make a deal.

➤ Has the selling price been reduced? That's a sign that the seller is facing the hard facts of the real estate market and is willing to be more realistic about an appropriate price for the property. If the price has been reduced several times, you have the opportunity to do some real negotiating.

➤ Why is the house on the market? Has the owner already bought another house? If so, he or she is going to want to reduce expenses by selling this house relatively quickly. Is the owner getting divorced or transferred? If so, there may be time-sensitive considerations that will impel him or her to negotiate a quick sale.

But beware: On occasion, an unscrupulous agent may advertise, "Must sell. Owner transferred," or something similar. If you see a listing like that, first make sure that the owner really *is* being transferred. Some less than ethical agents advertise false information just to make the house seem like a better deal. To be sure the information is true, ask the agent for specific details about the transfer: who the seller's employer is, where the seller is being transferred, and when. A legitimate agent will fill you in.

If the information is legitimate, you can usually make a much lower offer than the selling price.

It's a Money Pit

When you first view a house, it's easy to be swayed by appearances such as a well-kept garden or new deck (or, to the opposite extreme, by peeling paint or five trashed autos sitting in the yard). But what really counts is the infrastructure: the pipes, wiring, heating system, and foundation.

You can ask questions about the house yourself. In many states, sellers are required by law to disclose in writing all details concerning the property, including any existing problems. But you should also arrange to have a professional inspection done. (You can make the deal contingent upon receiving a relatively clean bill of health from the inspector.)

Should you discover any large faults with the house, such as an unstable roof or an antiquated heating system, you may be able to deduct the repair costs from the selling price of the house. Or, the seller may agree to arrange and oversee the repairs for you.

Dealmaker

Remember that old real-estate agent's trick? These agents recommend that the owner bake cookies just before a potential buyer is brought to view the house. The smell of baking goodies sends a subliminal message to the buyer: "You've come home."

But you can do this only for large, necessary repairs—don't nit-pick: Wanting to re-cover the toilet seat in fake fur does not qualify as a necessary expense, no matter how much you want it done. If the seller gets the impression that you are hung up on petty details, she will get angry—and that will make any further negotiation difficult.

Terms Every Home Buyer Should Know

So you've found the perfect home. What kind of issues can you negotiate? You may think only about the selling price, but in fact there are many other conditions you may want to specify in the deal:

Dealbreaker

Try not to get too attached to any house you look at. If you do, you make yourself vulnerable to emotional manipulation and may make a bad deal. As disappointing as it is to lose a deal on a house you like, remind yourself that there is no one perfect house for you. If you stay in the market long enough, you'll find several houses that you like.

➤ *What else the seller will pay for.* Closing costs, inspection, appraisal, title search, and document fees are some costs you can ask the seller to pick up.

➤ *Contingencies (what must happen for the deal to close).* You can make the deal contingent upon getting financing, on securing a clear deed and title for the house, on the results of a professional inspection or appraisal, or any number of other items, such as necessary structural repairs that must be cleared before you sign the deal.

➤ *Deadlines.* You most certainly want to negotiate a time by which you must have a response to your offer or counteroffer. Equally important, you want to make sure you negotiate the time when the seller must be out of the house.

➤ *Extras.* What else comes with the house: appliances, furniture, fluffy dog, those cookies baking in the oven (just kidding about those last two).

➤ *Condition of the house.* If the seller agrees to any necessary repairs, you will want them completed *before* you move in.

Making the Offer

Once you've decided on your terms, you must include them in a written (not verbal) offer form, sometimes referred to as a purchase agreement. You can draw up (or have an agent or lawyer draw up) your own offer form, but that isn't recommended. It's time-consuming, and there's a good chance you might forget something important.

Your offer form should include the following information:

➤ The address and legal description of the property

➤ The price, down payment (often called *earnest money*), and when and how the balance will be paid

➤ A time limit for response to your offer (see Chapter 7, "Timing Is Everything," for more on setting deadlines)

➤ The conditions and contingencies that must be met before the deal is finalized: getting a loan, making any repairs or improvements to the house, having the house inspected, and so on

➤ Who pays the property taxes as the deal is in progress

➤ The date of closing

Dealmaker

Most states have written offer forms that you can get from agents, your local real estate association, or from stationery or office supply stores. Use a form: It's easier and safer than trying to cover all the necessary legal points by drafting your own.

What Should Your Offer Be?

Once you've selected your dream house and have decided on the terms you're comfortable with, there are several different approaches you can take to making your offer (or counteroffer, in states that consider the listing price to be an offer):

➤ *The lowball.* As I said in Chapter 19, "Offers and Counteroffers," I don't recommend making lowball offers—it's too easy to find yourself closed out of the negotiations before you've really gotten started. If you must go the lowball route, make one only if you are not completely committed to the house.

➤ *The highball.* If you are anxious to seal the deal, you can make your first offer your best. But never make it higher than the seller's asking price, unless another buyer has already offered that price and you want to top it.

➤ *The bidding war offer.* If other buyers are interested, you may have to bid for the house like you'd bid on a hand of poker. That's not a desirable situation, so be careful you don't go too high in your effort to beat the competition.

➤ *The negotiable offer.* You make what you believe to be a reasonable offer, but make it clear that there's room for wheeling and dealing. It's often the best approach and the one that can lead to closing the deal.

Making Concessions

Unless your deal is accepted or rejected on the spot, your offer will probably be met with a counteroffer from the seller. This, too, should be in writing—and there is usually a space reserved on the purchase agreement where you can enter your counteroffer.

On receiving the seller's counteroffer, you're faced with one of three choices: You can accept the counteroffer, you can reject it outright, or you can respond with yet another counteroffer. Here are a few pointers to keep in mind as you maneuver through the offer/counteroffer stage of your negotiations:

➤ Small financial concessions can equal a lot of money. If you can chip away at even $1,000 on the sales price, you can save over $2,642.40 (assuming you finance the house with a 30-year, 8 percent interest loan).

➤ If you find yourself making many changes to a counteroffer, you may want to draw up an entirely new form. A marked-up original covered with crossed-off and written-in items points out all too clearly how many concessions you are asking for. A clean copy may be psychologically easier for the sellers to sign.

➤ Don't agree to *any* verbal offers. Get everything in writing.

➤ Don't split hairs. Remember, you are there to get a house, not pummel the sellers into submission. You'll make better progress if the sellers feel comfortable with the deal.

➤ If you don't like a counteroffer, or if a contingency isn't met, you're free to walk away from the deal.

Dealbreaker

If you're the seller and you're not prepared to respond to and equalize any questions the buyer raises about flaws in the house, your chances of getting the price you want will be slim.

Signing and Closing the Deal

Once you and your opponent both agree on an offer or counteroffer and sign it, it is a legally binding document. For this reason, you might want to have a lawyer look over the agreement before you sign.

After you sign, you will have to handle financing, insurance, and the inspection—each of which could be covered in its own *Complete Idiot's Guide*. You should also conduct a final walk-through of the property, to make sure that the house is in good condition and that the seller has done everything he was obligated to do under the agreement. If everything falls into place, you will approach the closing. Here are some issues you'll face on closing day:

➤ Determining who will hold the title (in other words, who will own the house). Will it be you alone, or will you hold the title with your spouse or someone else?

➤ Bringing along the money you need to close the deal. (You will know the amount in advance of closing day.) You'll need a cashier's check for the amount.

➤ Bringing along a homeowner's policy, and any other insurance documentation required by the lender.

➤ Reviewing so many documents that you'll feel like the prosecutor at the Lewinsky hearings. These include lending statements, notes, mortgages, affidavits, deeds, title policy, disclosure statements, IRS forms, compliance agreements, and sanity documents to prove that the process hasn't driven you completely crazy. (Just kidding on that last one!)

After payments have exchanged hands and all the paperwork has been signed, you'll walk out of the closing with the keys to your new kingdom. Congratulations!

For Sellers Only: Evaluating an Offer

When *you're* the one wearing the seller's hat, your perspective on negotiating the deal is obviously going to be different from that of a buyer. Your first decision will be whether to hire an agent or to sell the house yourself. (See the section "You Can't Tell the Players Without a Scorecard" earlier in this chapter.) Whatever you choose, you should have a firm idea of what you would like to get for your house, what you are willing to settle for, and what is unacceptable. Keep in mind that these figures may change after you test the market.

Once you've snagged an interested buyer, she will present you with an offer (or counteroffer, if you're in a state that legally defines the listing price as the initial offer) in the form of a purchase agreement, as was discussed earlier in this chapter). The terms mentioned in the offer are listed in the earlier section "Making the Offer." Ask yourself the following questions as you evaluate the offer:

➤ Has the buyer offered a price within your range of acceptability?

➤ How much of a deposit is the buyer willing to put down? This indicates how serious the buyer is about your house.

➤ What contingencies and terms did the buyer specify?

➤ How much time do you have to consider the offer before you must respond?

At this point, you have the same three choices a buyer would have: You can accept the offer, reject it, or make a counteroffer. Remember, if you're selling, financial concessions are the least beneficial to make. If you cut $1,000 off the selling price, you lose that $1,000 *plus* any return you could make from investing it. So, whenever possible, suggest concessions on non-financial matters: extras, a different moving date, and so on. Make financial concessions only when absolutely necessary.

Read through the earlier section "Making Concessions" for more information about the offer/counteroffer phase.

No One Wants My House!

Remember, selling a house takes time—sometimes months or even more than a year. If you've waited a suitable time and still aren't getting any offers, you may want to sweeten your terms. Now's the time to reconsider the following questions:

➤ Should you lower your asking price?

➤ Are there improvements you should make, or agree to make, as part of the deal?

➤ Are there incentives you can add to make the house or property more attractive?

➤ Should you offer to help interested buyers with financing? (Be especially careful with this one. You must understand all financial terms and understand your liability, should the buyers not be able to hold up their end of the bargain.)

Negotiating to Buy or Sell Commercial or Investment Property

You might want to increase your worldly estate by buying a piece of land or a building, either as a site for your business or as an investment down the road. Buying property, whether for commercial or investment reasons, has a lot in common with buying a home, but there are a few notable differences. In this section, you'll learn the special tips and tricks of the trade when buying real estate as an investment.

Negotiable Terms

Commercial real estate is property used for business, such as a restaurant or a store. **Investment real estate** is property of any kind—whether or not it produces income—that you buy and hold onto in hopes of eventually selling it for a profit.

Dealing With Commercial or Investment Brokers

A major difference between buying commercial or investment property and buying a home is the price tag. Most commercial or investment properties are more expensive than residential properties (unless you're looking to buy a home like Buckingham Palace).

Along with that, brokers who sell commercial or investment property usually make higher commissions (anywhere from 8 to 15 percent) than brokers who sell homes.

Because a commercial or investment property broker deals with both higher-priced properties and a higher commission, he has a lot more to lose than might be the case with residential property if he can't sell a piece of commercial or investment property. That means that in this market, buyers have the advantage—brokers will usually encourage sellers to accept any reasonable offer to make the sale.

Buyer's Market: Figuring Out What a Property Is Worth

Property assessment is a specialized science, particularly when it comes to buying a business or investment property; I could write an entire *Idiot's Guide* on the subject. For now, I'll give you a brief overview of how you should think about the process. The first thing you should determine is the intended purpose of your purchase—as a commercial location for your own business, or as a straightforward investment.

If you're buying property as a place to put up your business, you will have to determine the maximum cost you can absorb without lowering your profits or placing your business in jeopardy.

If, on the other hand, you're buying the property strictly as an investment, you'll want to figure out how much profit you expect to make (in the form of rents, for example) compared to how much the building will cost you (in the form of taxes, insurance, or loan payments, for example). Negotiate the asking price until you can realize a rate of return you are comfortable with.

Researching Real Estate

As you prepare to negotiate for commercial or investment property, get as much information as you can about the property. As with any negotiation situation, the more you know, the more successful you'll be. Here are some sources you can tap to get information:

➤ *The seller, or the seller's broker*. Ask for profit and loss statements and information on expenses related to the property (taxes, insurance, and so on). If you are refused any of this information, you should probably think twice about investing in the property.

Dealmaker

Real estate purchases for investment purposes can be tricky to handle on your own. This is definitely a time when you'll want to enlist the services of professionals, to make certain that your interests are protected.

➤ *Public records*, such as the Register of Deeds (find them at the county building or courthouse in the county in which the real estate is located). You can examine the deed and the history of the property.

➤ *Title*. Insurance companies will check out the title to the property to be sure it is free from defects so that the title company can insure the title. Defects might include liens (unpaid taxes on the property) or conflicting claims of ownership on the property.

➤ *A professional examination of the property*. This is a must. Have an experienced person evaluate the plumbing, wiring, heating and cooling systems, roof, and basic structure of the property and advise you of any significant problems or any repairs the property will need.

➤ *A personal examination of the property*. Check the place out yourself. Talk to tenants and find out if they are happy there. (You don't want to deal with a mass exodus of tenants after you buy the place.)

Negotiable Terms

Net rent is the money you get after payment of all expenses associated with the property (taxes, insurance, maintenance, loan payments, and so on).

219

➤ *Existing leases for all tenants who occupy the property.* Check out their rents, what expenses they pay for, and when their leases are up for renewal.

Opening the Negotiations

Once you've evaluated a property and have decided to negotiate for it, some tips can help you work out a good deal. The following table breaks them down for you.

Negotiation Tips for Commercial and Investment Property

Buyers	Sellers
List any defects you discovered during your inspection. If the roof leaks or the place needs a paint job, those are factors that justify a lower asking price.	Acknowledge and prepare to equalize any defects a potential buyer might notice and mention.
Never tell the seller why you want the property. Just offer a general, plausible reason: "I'm shopping around for an investment," for example. If you tip off the seller that you have an important need or desire to buy the property, you're giving her extra reason to insist on a higher price.	Avoid tipping off a buyer if you're in a hurry to sell. You want to protect your negotiating position so that you can get the best possible price for your property.
The offering or listed price of most property is almost always too high. Don't fall for it. Decide what you can afford to pay to make the investment a profitable one for you. Then make a counteroffer.	Any buyer will seek to bring your asking price down, so make certain that your price (both your preferred price and the least you're willing to accept) is reasonable and justified by the property's condition, location, and the local market for similar properties.
Make concessions on small items, if that helps you get the property for the price you want. For example, you can offer to pay for the title insurance or have the property surveyed. Or, you	Offer to make small concessions that make the property more attractive to a potential buyer. Consider making certain repairs or paying particular fees. This may influence an uncertain buyer to go ahead and make a deal.

Buyers	Sellers
might consider taking possession of the property at a date more convenient to the seller. Sellers are often influenced by these concessions.	
Decide in advance the maximum amount you will pay, and stick to it. But be flexible when you bargain. There's always more than one way to close a deal. For example, if you and the seller are $5,000 apart on the price, you can propose other ways to get your total cost reduced by $5,000, such as by requesting that the seller make $5,000 worth of repairs on the property.	Be prepared for your potential buyer's counteroffer—you know there'll probably be at least one. If you anticipate a counteroffer, you can respond without giving the appearance of unreasonableness or inflexibility.

A special note for both buyers and sellers: Don't rush into the deal. Remember, real estate deals often involve a tremendous financial commitment. Make sure you're happy with the deal before you commit yourself.

The Least You Need to Know

➤ Use the broker's fear of losing the deal to drive a better bargain for the property: if you're the buyer, aim for a price below the asking price; if your the seller, make it clear to the broker that you won't lower your asking price without a good reason.

➤ Negotiable terms in the buying or selling of real estate include the price, contingencies, condition of the property, and any extras the seller may include with the sale.

➤ Inspect the property for defects: if you're the buyer, you can use such information to ask for a reduction in price, if you're the seller, you'll want to address these defects prior to setting your listing price.

➤ If you're a buyer, shoot for financial concessions. If you're a seller, suggest any concessions other than financial ones.

Chapter 22

Negotiating a Lease or Sublease

In This Chapter

➤ Renting, rationally

➤ The subletting option

➤ Negotiable lease terms

➤ Dealing with the landlord

You may not be ready to make a commitment to buying a house or a piece of property. If that's the case, renting is probably the way you'll want to go.

Renting has become increasingly popular for a number of reasons. For one, when you rent property, you usually don't have to plunk down a huge payment and take out a loan. For another, it's more flexible—it's easy to pick up and move when you need more space or want to relocate. In today's highly mobile society, that kind of flexibility can be very important.

If renting is for you, read on. In this chapter, you'll learn how to negotiate for the best terms when you rent.

Lease or Sublease?

When you rent property or an apartment, you'll usually be asked to sign a document called a *lease* (if you're dealing directly with the property owner or landlord) or a *sublease* (if you're dealing with someone who already rents the property or apartment). In either case, you have the right to occupy the property, but there is a major difference between the two types of documents—with significant implications for you, as tenant.

Dealbreaker

Before you want to sublease property, read the prime lease and make sure that the sublessor has the right to sublease to you. That's the only way you can be sure you won't get kicked out if the property owner decides to terminate the prime lease.

The difference between a lease and a sublease is this: When you sublease property, you have no legal connection (in legalese, this is called "privity of contract") with the property owner. Your only legal connection is with the person who subleased the property to you. If you damage the property or default on any payments, you have to answer to the sublessor, who in turn has to set things straight with the property owner.

In addition, if you have a lease, you have direct recourse to the landlord if there are problems that need fixing. With a sublease, you may have to go through the sublessor for such things. And, of course, if the sublessor fails to fulfill his or her own obligations to the landlord, you may find your status in the property jeopardized.

There is a third alternative: Leases can be assigned rather than subleased. When a lease is assigned, both the person assigning the lease and the person to whom the lease is assigned are liable to the property owner.

Negotiable Terms

When you sign a lease, you become the **lessee**; the property owner is the **lessor**. The **lease** determines the rights and responsibilities between you and the property owner. A **sublessee** rents property from another person, who holds the primary lease and is known as the **sublessor**.

You and Your Lease

Whether you lease or sublease, you should have a written contract that covers your rights as a renter. Verbal agreements—however well-intentioned—can and often do break down, and without a written contract, renters can face a long stay in tenant court or even eviction. Obviously, then, your lease is an important document, and one that you should carefully consider before signing.

Many landlords rely on standard, store-bought leases to which they write in any changes, additions, or deletions. Others may write their own leases. Whatever form your lease takes, it should mention the following provisions:

➤ *Rent.* This is the biggie. Make sure that both the amount of the rent and the method of its payment are clearly stated in the lease. And make sure you know what happens if your payment is late.

➤ *Term.* How long will you be leasing? How much notice do you have to give before you end the lease? Do you have any options to continue the lease for another term? If so, what provisions of the lease are likely to change? (Usually, rent increases are applied at the time of renewal.)

➤ *Security deposit.* Many landlords require a security deposit to ensure you don't destroy their property during your stay. When and how will the deposit be refunded? Make sure you get a written reciept of any money you pay up front.

➤ *Last month(s) rent.* It is a common practice for landlords to require the final month's rent (sometimes the final two months) paid at the time that you sign the lease.

➤ *Condition of the property.* Both you and the owner should agree on the condition of the property at the time you move in so that you aren't blamed for damages you weren't responsible for. Ideally, both of you should tour the property, make notes of any damages or defects, and specify in the lease that those damages are not your fault or responsibility. (Some rental agencies have their own standard forms on which renters are asked to note any damages.) The lease should also specify who is responsible for any improvements or repairs that are needed during your stay.

➤ *Pets.* Usually, if it's not expressly forbidden in the lease, little Fluffy or Fido can move in with you—although some rental agencies charge extra rent or an additional security deposit (or both) to cover any damage your pet might cause. Keep in mind, though, that if your pet constantly barks or menaces your neighbors, you might be in violation of other terms of the lease, which require you to not interfere with the safety and security of other tenants.

Dealbreaker

If you're planning on subleasing an apartment, make sure you read the prime lease (the lease held by the sublessor). If it forbids subletting, you may find yourself in a very difficult situation if the landlord objects to your presence.

➤ *Sublets.* Are you allowed to sublet the property? Some leases expressly forbid subletting; others allow it, but only after potential sublessees have been screened by the landlord.

➤ *Default.* What can the landlord do if you don't comply with any of the terms of the lease? The lease should specify what legal action the landlord will take if you are in default of the lease.

➤ *Breaking the lease.* What if you have to move out before your lease is up? Are you penalized? If so, how much?

The terms listed here just cover the basics; you may need to add more provisions to cover special circumstances. Are you allowed to have a waterbed in your apartment? Can you run a tap-dance studio out of your fifth-floor apartment? Does your landlord mind if you cram five roommates into a two-bedroom apartment? Make sure any and all special provisions you need are not forbidden in the lease.

When Renters Rent

Let's say you've got to be out of town for awhile—you're going away for the summer, perhaps. But you don't want your apartment to stand vacant all that time, and you really wouldn't mind easing the burden of paying rent while you're away. You might choose to sublet the property during your absence. You check your lease and discover that subletting is allowed, so you run an ad.

Keep in mind that if you decide to sublet your place, you are still held accountable for all the terms in the lease. You are still responsible for the rent, for example. For this reason, you might charge a sublessee more (to make some extra money) or less, if you desperately want someone to cover at least part of the rent while you're gone.

This is not a responsibility to take lightly. For example, if you sublet your place to Derek Destroyer, who doesn't pay up, converts the apartment into a rehearsal studio for his thrash metal band, and wrecks the place while you're gone, you are still responsible for all the rent money and repairs.

Negotiable Terms

An **option** in a rental agreement is your right to renew a lease. You're not required to exercise your option, but you have to be offered the chance.

For all these reasons, you should consider drafting your own agreement with a sublessee before you hand him the keys to your castle. And don't forget that even if your primary lease (the one between you and your landlord) allows you to sublet, it may contain a provision that stipulates the owner's right to screen all potential sublessees.

Terms to Negotiate in Your Lease

The power you have to negotiate over a lease largely depends on the rental market in your area. Apartment dwellers in smaller cities, for example, can get much better terms than their counterparts in tight markets such as New York City. Still, if you have room to maneuver, you might be able to negotiate the following terms:

➤ *Rent.* If the landlord's rent is not regulated by law (as it is in some cities, under certain conditions), you may be able to cut yourself a deal if you promise to sign a longer lease, for example, or plunk down more money up front, or even do odd jobs around the place, such as cutting the grass or shoveling snow.

➤ *Condition.* Is the owner willing to make any improvements to the property before you move in? Will the landlord replace the old fridge or paint the place? If the owner does agree to make any improvements, be sure to get those promises included in writing in the lease.

➤ *Dates of occupancy.* Can you move in a few days sooner or later without forfeiting rent? Will you get better terms if you sign a longer lease?

➤ *Options.* Will you be able to renew your lease on the apartment or property? You don't want to set up a cozy apartment or build up a nice business and then get kicked out when the lease runs out. Protect yourself by having the right to renew when the lease expires.

For retail space, try to lease the space for two years, with three options to renew for an additional six years (two-year renewal terms for each of your three options). If business is good after the first two years and you need more space, you can shop around without being forced to stay for two more years; you're not locked in. If, on the other hand, you want to stay longer, you can exercise your two-year option.

For business property, a two- to five-year initial lease term is good, along with three options to renew. For example, you lease the property for three years with three options to renew, all for three years. At the end of the first three-year term, say you like the place and business is good. You can exercise your first option and stay another three years. You can stay for a total of twelve years, reconsidering your location after every three-year period.

Dealmaker

For residential property, a one-year lease is adequate, especially if you can get a couple of options to renew if you want to stay longer. If you simply can't stand the place, you can kiss it good-bye after your one-year term is up.

Five Tips for Negotiating Leases

Again, your negotiating power largely depends on the rental market in your area. But you can increase your odds of renting the space you want by following these tips:

➤ Never rush into a lease. Approach it carefully and neutrally, and remember that there is more than one apartment or property out there that's right for you. When you sign a lease, you're entering a legal contract that obligates you to conform with all its terms. So don't rush into signing unless you're happy with the deal.

➤ If you are using a rental agent to find a place for you, remember that many rental agents

Dealbreaker

Make certain that you understand the terms of your lease agreement thoroughly. Violation of your lease can make you vulnerable to eviction.

work on commission and will get paid only if they successfully pair you up with a property. That means they are motivated to find you the deal you want. Make it clear that you will walk away if the agent doesn't find you a deal you can live with. The agent may be able to sweeten the deal.

➤ Have a lawyer draw up a lease. It's in your favor to have an attorney involved, as most property owners heavily stack the terms of their leases in their favor. When you start the bargaining with a lease drafted by you or your lawyer, you can do the same.

➤ By all means, try to reduce the rent (like you needed an expert to tell you that!). Even $50 a month can add up to $600 a year for every year you lease the property. That's money you can pour into improving your apartment or your business. And if you can't get the dollar amount reduced, at least try for a longer-term leasing period. A two-year lease means that, once your rent has been set, it can't be increased for another 24 months.

➤ Emphasize what a good tenant you are (you are, aren't you?). Many property owners have had bad experiences with tenants who were unreliable, who were difficult to live with, or who damaged the property. The more you impress the owner with your cleanliness, professionalism, reliability, and all-around niceness, the better your chances of negotiating a better deal.

The Least You Need to Know

➤ If you want to rent property, you should have a written lease that states the rent, the term of the lease, the deposit, the condition of the property, subletting arrangements, what happens if you default on the lease, and any other provisions you deem necessary.

➤ If you decide to sublet your property, use a written agreement to protect yourself from any damages or costs incurred by the sublessor.

➤ If you are interested in a sublet, make sure the primary lease permits your sublessor to sublease the property to you.

➤ Lease property for a short period of time, with plenty of options to renew the lease if you want to continue to occupy the property.

➤ Never rush into a lease. Don't sign unless you're happy with the deal.

The Art of Auto Negotiations

This is a culture that's downright infatuated with automobiles. So it's likely that at some point in your life you're going to take the plunge and buy one, if you haven't already. Negotiations for a car can range from the relatively casual (selling your old clunker to a neighbor for a little pocket money) to the frantic (listening to a salesperson yammer over a 283Z with all the trimmings).

This chapter covers the high points of negotiating for any car, whether you're buying or selling, and whether it's a new Lexus or an old lemon.

Five Car-Buying Focus Points

Before you walk into a showroom or scour the classifieds, you should do your homework and know what you're looking for. (See Chapter 2, "Bargaining Essentials," for a refresher course in preparing for negotiation.) It's not enough to decide that you just adore that snazzy sports job with all the extras—before you walk into the showroom or call the private seller, you need to have a firm idea about what you want to achieve on the financial side of the deal as well. When you buy a car, you should concentrate on five key areas:

➤ The gross sales price (including extras).

➤ The trade-in value of your car.

➤ The financial terms, if you want to finance the deal.

➤ The warranty. Most new cars are warranted, and the details vary from each manufacturer and make and model. Used cars rarely come with a warranty, so if you get one, consider yourself lucky. Make sure all warranties are in writing.

➤ The condition of the car, if it's used.

Only *after* you've got a clear idea of what you're looking for on all these five points is it time to take the plunge.

Dealmaker

Get as many dealers into the picture as possible—it improves your odds of getting a good deal. Each dealer that's competing for your business will experience fear of losing you as a customer, so they'll all compete with each other on price and extras.

How to Get the Best Deal from a Dealer

Ever watch car salespeople in action? They run through as many emotions in a single session as an entire theater company in a Shakespearean play. They may be hawk-eyed and shark-faced when you first enter the show-room, jokey and friendly as they make introductions, solicitous and concerned while you look at different models, disappointed when you finally admit what you're willing to spend. It's enough to give anybody pause. But shopping for a new car doesn't have to be an intimidating experience—if you do it right.

Beat the Competition

Once you've found the model you want, present the dealer with the highest price you are willing to spend—which should be lower than the dealer's offering price or the sticker price. If you're buying the car outright, think in terms of the highest price you will pay. If you're financing, determine what you'll accept as your highest monthly payment.

Let's say you tell the salesperson that you'll pay no more than $200 a month for five years. You're not making an offer; you're simply stating a fact. Now the burden is on the salesperson to juggle the price of the car, your old car's trade-in value (if applicable), and the financial terms to come up with an arrangement that meets your price.

Use the same approach with a minimum of two to three dealers. Don't make a deal with any of them on the spot. Give them your name and phone number, and ask them to either call or write you with a proposal. And be sure to let all of them know you'll be checking on the competition for a better deal. You want to create a fear of loss to motivate the dealer to give you the best deal possible.

Let's assume that one dealer meets your $200-a-month ceiling and the other two are close. Inform Dealers 2 and 3 that Dealer 1 has met your terms and that you're going to do business with her unless they can do better. In many cases, they will. And if they don't, you still got the deal you wanted.

Use the Dealer's Language

Car dealership advertisements are full of bold statements like, "Nobody sells for less" or "We'll beat any deal." Believe it or not, once a claim like that appears in print, the dealer is actually obligated to follow through on the promise. If you feel that a salesperson isn't living up to those claims, use the language as it appears in the ad. Quote the exact words. Put the burden on the salesperson to stand by the dealership's claims. That puts pressure on the dealer's reputation, which can motivate the salesperson to give you what you want.

Don't Get Attached to Any Car

For most of us, our cars are part of our self, (we even name them and talk to them), so it's easy to get emotionally attached to our wheels. That's fine once you've got the title in your hands, but it's a liability while you're *shopping* for a car. Do your best to avoid getting emotionally attached to any one make or model. You don't want to seem overeager to the salesperson, who can spot an anxious customer like a shark smells blood in the water. Remember, there will always be other models that can fit your needs. You don't want to be the salesperson's next victim.

Dealbreaker

As with any negotiation, you don't want to appear too eager—that's not the way to get a good deal. Keep that poker face, even if you suddenly see your dream car in the middle of the showroom floor.

Signing and Closing the Deal

Once you've negotiated the deal you want, you still need to finalize a few particulars before you can drive your car off the lot:

➤ Ordering a registration and license plates. Usually, the salesperson will do this for you.

➤ Deciding in whose name the title will be held.

➤ Providing proof of insurance.

➤ Checking the car title to be sure it's correct.

➤ Knowing how much money you'll need to bring in for a down payment.

➤ Discussing dealer financing with the salesperson, if you are interested. Many dealers and car makers now offer their own financing plans.

Buying a Used Car

The fundamentals of buying a used car are the same as those for buying a new car—you want to consider the same five focus points carefully. But buying a used car involves a few additional considerations. When you decide to go with a used car, here are some things to keep in mind:

➤ *Greater price negotiability.* You have much more flexibility in negotiating the price of a used car because chances are that the dealer got a good deal on the car (whether through a trade-in or at a used-car auction). You can safely assume that the asking price of any used car you're interested in is set on the high side; you've got plenty of room to bargain downward.

The Art of the Deal

Whether you're buying or selling a used car, take a look at two books that list prices for most makes and models: The *N.A.D.A. Used Car Guide* (published quarterly by the National Auto Dealers Association) contains information on cars up to 7 years old. There's also the *Blue Book Used Car Guide* (Kelley Blue Book Company). Both are great references for guidelines to car prices and can be found in your local library.

➤ *Higher probability of mechanical problems.* Because used cars may have serious physical flaws, it's a good idea to have it checked by a mechanic *before* you buy. (You can usually have this done for less than $100.) If the mechanic discovers any flaws (bad brakes, transmission problems, rust, and so on) and you still want the car, you can use those flaws to bargain for a lower price. Or, you can insist that the dealer or seller repair any problems before you will buy the car.

➤ *Limited or no warranty coverage.* Warranties are a key consideration when you buy a used car. Some dealers give them; most private sellers don't. Recently, a number of large used-car dealerships that do give warranties have sprung up, and this trend will likely grow because the used car market is so good. Make sure any warranties you negotiate are in writing.

While we're on the subject of warranties, here's a useful tip: Try to get the dealer or seller to put any promises about the car's excellent dependability or fine running condition in writing. Then, if the car proves to be something other than greased lightnin', you can use that language against the dealer or seller.

Selling a Used Car

What about when you're on the other side of the dealing table? Let's say you've got the family sedan to unload, and you think you'd do better if you sell it privately instead of using it as a trade-in on a new car. It's tough to get a top price when you sell a used car. Most buyers are leery of paying a lot of money because used cars traditionally have a lot of problems. Here are some tips to maximize your chances of getting a good price on the old heap:

➤ Be prepared to answer any questions or comments made by prospective buyers, such as how well the car has been maintained and how many miles it gets on a gallon of gas (which you can estimate). If you've kept records of repair work, oil changes, lube jobs, and so on, offer to show them to potential buyers.

➤ Remember, you must equalize every position taken by any prospective buyer to get the price you want.

➤ Be sure your old clunker is cleaned and polished—you want it to have plenty of eye appeal. You might even consider "nose appeal"—there's an aerosol product on the market today that sprays the "new car smell." It's amazing how big a difference that can make for some buyers.

Leasing a Car

Car leasing has become increasingly popular these days. If you're not ready to buy a car outright, you might want to consider a lease. Leasing offers a couple of advantages over buying:

➤ The money you have to put up for a loan is small compared to the amount you have to plunk down for a new car.

➤ You have a few nice options when the lease is up: You can drop off the keys and leave (if you have a closed lease), or you can buy the car for the amount specified in the lease.

➤ If you're using the car for business purposes, you can deduct the lease costs as a business expense.

Dealmaker

For the price of a run through your local car wash, you can increase the odds of selling your used car immensely. And a can of touch up paint can hide any little dings that mar its appearance.

Negotiating a lease is similar to negotiating to buy a car. Keep these points in mind as you negotiate a lease:

Dealbreaker

Leases are not always the best choice for every individual. Do your research beforehand, and read all the fine print about fees and hidden costs—it may be that your best option is to buy rather than to lease.

➤ Set an upper ceiling of what you can afford to pay per month. Take that figure to at least two (preferably three) dealers. See if they can meet your monthly ceiling on a make and model you like.

➤ Don't set a ridiculously low monthly payment amount that gives the dealer no room to work with. Be realistic.

➤ Many auto makers (Ford, GM, and Mazda, to name a few) frequently run lease specials that are good deals. Keep your eye out when you watch TV or read the newspapers.

➤ When you negotiate, try to get as many free miles as you can. A good target to shoot for is 15,000 miles each lease year.

➤ Car leases vary from two to five years. I recommend a two- to three-year lease because that's the period most new car warranties cover. Check out the warranty period of the car you're interested in and try to peg the term of the lease to the warranty.

➤ As with all documents, read the lease carefully. (You might even want to ask the dealer for a blank copy to take home and examine before you sign.) Be sure you understand every lease provision before you sign it.

The Least You Need to Know

➤ When you're shopping for a new or used car, tell the salesperson exactly what you're willing to pay. Let the salesperson come up with a deal that best meets your price and needs.

➤ Always get two or three dealers to bid against each other.

➤ Always have a mechanic check a used car before you buy it. If the car has any problems, use them to drive down the asking price.

➤ When you sell your used car, be prepared to answer any of the buyer's questions or comments about your car.

➤ When you lease a car, use the same approach as buying a car. In addition, get the most free mileage you can and take a lease whose term matches the term of the warranty.

Chapter 24

After All, You're Worth It: Pay Raises

In This Chapter

➤ Timing is everything

➤ Getting your boss into the mood

➤ Avoiding the classic pay-raise pitfalls

➤ Turning a "no" into a "yes"

You're a star employee, the Sultan of Sales, the MVP of marketing. For nearly a year, you've come in at the crack of dawn and left after the cleaning crew has gone home. You've knocked yourself out on the Smedley account, and you oversaw the development of the world's first aerodynamic widget. It's time you got what you deserved. You'll suggest . . . no, you'll request . . . no, you'll *demand* a raise.

Throughout this book, I've touched on many of the tips and techniques that will help you convince your boss to give you a raise. In this chapter, you'll get a more focused, up-close-and-personal view of the art of negotiating a pay raise.

There's a Right Time for Everything

Given the tightfistedness that's sweeping most companies these days, you just can't wait around for your boss to notice that you deserve a bigger paycheck. It's probably up to you to request a meeting with your boss to discuss a raise. Lots of people are uncomfortable about having to take the initiative, but you shouldn't be. If you're the one to set up the meeting, it means that you have the advantage of picking the best place and time for *you*. Pick the time of day when you're raring to go: If you're sharpest early in the morning, set the meeting for then. If you don't get cranked up until late afternoon, that's when you want to meet.

Where, Oh Where, Shall We Meet?

Just as you want to pick the best time for your purposes, you also want to give some thought to where you do your negotiating. The last place you want to bargain with your boss is in his office—his home field. But because he's the boss, you may run into a little difficulty about setting the meeting place. If you can, though, try to get him to meet you in your office, or suggest a neutral spot such as a local restaurant or quiet conference room. (For more on securing the home field advantage, see Chapter 4, "On Your Mark . . ., Get Set . . ., Negotiate!".)

Setting the Mood

Your raise is important to you, right? So, it's worth taking a little care in setting up the negotiations. One important issue to consider is the *mood* of the meeting—that means not just getting your boss into a receptive frame of mind, but psyching yourself up as well.

Dealmaker

Make good eye contact with your boss when you ask for your raise. If you look down or away at that critical time, your boss will conclude that you lack confidence in yourself and in your belief that you deserve a raise. (See Chapter 6, "Getting Physical," for more information on body language.)

Suiting Your Boss's Schedule

Obviously, you don't want to arrange a meeting a few hours before the Third International Widget Manufacturers Gala Convention is slated to begin. Your boss will be too frazzled to give your request the attention it deserves. He may even resent you for asking at such a bad time.

Try to set your meeting for a time when your boss is in a good mood. Maybe the company's earnings just shot up or a big deal was just completed. Maybe the annual conference is finally over and the entire office is relaxed. Or, maybe something personal has happened—he's just come back from vacation, or his son just got married, or he was nominated for an industry award. Anything that puts him in a good mood is a good time because he will be more receptive to your request for a raise.

Gearing Yourself Up

Your own fabulous accomplishments can also have a large impact on both your boss's mood and your own confidence. Try to hit up your boss for a raise when you've just finished an important project. Maybe you finally completed that onerous filing overhaul that no one wanted to do. Or, maybe you closed a big deal, or won an important account. Maybe your department just won an award for being the most efficient or most productive.

Don't be reluctant to call the good news to your boss's attention when you open the meeting. ("Just got off the phone with Mr. Smithers. He says he's anxious to get started on that ad campaign. I'm so glad I snagged him for a client.") That makes a nice opening into your raise request and makes it very difficult for your boss to turn you down.

Keep a Compliment File

Whether your company is large or small, in today's overheated business climate it's all too easy for the boss to take your performance for granted. That means she may not have a firm idea of all the good things you've been doing for the company. But you can change all that. Starting today, begin setting up a new file in your already over-flowing drawer. Call it your compliment file, or anything you like. No matter what you choose to call it, use it to stash any and all compliments you receive on your work. That includes these:

➤ Thank-you notes from clients or customers

➤ Acknowledgments of a job well done from coworkers

➤ Sales figures on projects you've spearheaded

➤ Impressive reports or charts you've put together

➤ Results from surveys you've overseen

➤ Industry awards or honors

Dealbreaker

When negotiating for a raise, avoid confronting your boss during a time of high pressure or negative business news—you want him to be in as receptive a mood as possible, not distracted by trouble or looming deadlines.

When you finally set up your meeting with your boss to discuss your raise, take your compliment file with you. Invite your boss to flip through it, or use it to highlight some of your more fabulous accomplishments. Your boss can't be expected to remember how smoothly you handled the infamous Smedley fiasco of a year ago—no matter *how* important it was at the time. But your compliment file will jog her memory. Besides that, it's a great confidence booster for you.

Have a Specific Target

If your boss is amenable to the idea of giving you a raise, her next question will most likely be, "How much do you have in mind?" Don't let that question catch you unprepared: You should have a specific goal decided on beforehand. You can express your goal in either dollars or percentages. You might ask, for example, for $100 dollars more a week, or $1 more an hour, or a 10 percent annual increase—whatever you feel is reasonable.

Of course, deciding what's "reasonable" can be tricky. How can you determine what's right to ask for? If you fish around, you can find a number of comparative figures that may help you set a goal. Some sources of information you might consult would include these:

➤ The *Occupational Outlook Handbook*, published by the U.S. Department of Commerce, offers information on occupational trends and lists average salaries for particular fields and occupations. You can ask for this at your local library.

➤ Industry newsletters and magazines often run salary surveys on particular jobs.

➤ Through the office grapevine, you may be able to discover how much other people in the position you hold (or are seeking) earn.

Why Most People Fail to Seek a Raise

The two major reasons most people fail to ask for a raise (besides being lousy at what they do) are fear of losing their jobs and fear of being turned down. But there are definite things you can do to reduce or eliminate these fears.

Dealmaker

If you're afraid that your boss will fire you if you ask for a raise, get yourself a little insurance. Make some discrete inquiries about other possible job options *before* you begin negotiating. It will have the added benefit of giving you some leverage with your boss if you can say that XYZ Company has expressed interest in hiring you.

You're Fired: Fear of Job Loss

Usually, the longer you've worked for your employer and the more benefits you have (such as medical and pension benefits), the more attached you'll be to your job and the more you'll fear losing it. Fear of job loss is an especially potent inhibitor that keeps people from "rocking the boat" by asking for a raise. That's why timing is especially important: you don't want to ask for a raise at an inappropriate time. Don't ask for a raise under these circumstances:

➤ Your performance hasn't been up to par.

➤ Your company or industry is in a dangerous slump.

➤ Rumors of layoffs or downsizing are wafting through the company corridors.

➤ You've seen evidence of layoffs or firings in your department.

Do keep in mind, too, that just as you've invested a great deal of time in your job, so has your employer invested time and money in you—in your training, in particular. Most likely, if you're good at what you do, the company will see that it's to their advantage to keep you rather than starting from scratch with a new hire.

"Raise? Ha!": Fear of Failure

Unless you're a billionaire like Bill Gates, you'll probably also fear getting turned down. That's only natural. You don't want the embarrassment, and you might be afraid that if you ask for but fail to get a raise, that means your boss is unhappy with your work. But, assuming that you haven't been falling asleep on the job, there are a number of legitimate reasons why your boss might tell you no. These might include the following:

➤ "There's no money in my budget."

➤ "Our company has set salary levels, and you're already at the top of your range."

➤ "There's a company-wide wage freeze in effect."

You can't directly challenge reasons like these, but you *can* prepare in advance by putting together a backup plan that will salvage a bad situation. If your boss says no to a raise, you can suggest other ways to reward your performance. Here are some alternatives to a direct raise that you might suggest:

➤ Performance-based bonus

➤ More vacation time

➤ Flexible working hours

➤ The ability to work at home part-time

➤ Better benefit options

➤ Reimbursement for continuing education

➤ Reimbursement for attendance at a job-related seminar, conference, or workshop

➤ Reimbursement for membership in a professional organization

➤ A promise to reopen salary discussions in a set period of time

Dealmaker

When negotiating a raise, you can use the "Vinegar and Honey" technique explained in Chapter 10, "Top Negotiating Techniques." As you recall, you ask for a raise much higher than your ultimate goal (the "vinegar") and then gradually reduce your high request (the "honey") until you arrive at the amount you're really after.

What's most important is recognizing your fears and refusing to let them immobilize you. You can ward off fear by using mental practice, as explained in Chapter 15, "Taking Control." Visualize yourself talking with your boss. Imagine your boss's response. Run through your reply. Do an entire dress rehearsal—several times, in great detail, until you have your approach down pat. You'll find that when you're actually sitting down with your boss, the mental practice will have largely eliminated your fears.

The Least You Need to Know

➤ Try to get your boss on your home field (in your office or work area) or, if that's not possible, at a neutral spot.

➤ Pick the time of day when you're sharpest.

➤ Try to catch your boss when he is in a good mood and when your performance has been particularly good.

➤ Be specific on how much of a raise you want.

➤ Think of other benefits you can ask for if your boss says he can't give you money but would like to reward your performance.

➤ Mentally rehearse every detail of asking your boss for a raise.

Chapter 25

Brother, Can You Spare a Dime? Negotiating a Loan

In This Chapter

➤ Looking into lenders

➤ What's negotiable?

➤ Pre-negotiation information gathering

➤ The special art of loan negotiating

Sooner or later, you'll need to borrow money, if you haven't had to do so already. Maybe you'll find that dream home or decide to finally indulge in a new car. Maybe you want to start a new business or go back to school.

Whatever your reason, you'll need to—you guessed it—negotiate! In this chapter, I show you how to get the best possible deal when dealing with a lending institution.

Understand Why Lenders Make Loans

Lenders aren't charitable institutions. They loan you money for one reason only: to make a profit. When you borrow from a lender, you must return the money you borrowed *plus* an additional amount: the interest. If lenders don't loan money, they won't make money. So approach any lender with confidence—you know that the lender *wants* to make you a loan.

My Momma Told Me, You Better Shop Around

All lenders aren't created equal. You should shop around for a lender just like you shop around for a car, house, clothes, and everything else. You're looking for the best possible terms you can get. Just keep in mind that the competition to loan you money is fierce, so take advantage of it.

Dealmaker

Tactfully let each lender know that you'll be shopping around for the best deal. It creates the fear of losing your business, and thus it helps motivate the lender to give you the best deal.

But how do you "shop" for a lender? First, you want to do a little preliminary homework.

If you're shopping for a home loan, start out by checking the Yellow Pages. Lenders are usually listed under "Mortgages." You may also want to check with your bank, other local banks, savings and loans, and credit unions. In addition, many newspapers print a weekly list of lenders and the rates they charge for home loans. Some lenders—for example, The Money Store—even advertise on TV.

Once you've got a list of likely lending institutions, it's time to make your first contact. Call several different lenders and arrange for an appointment to discuss a loan. Don't be reluctant to visit as many of the lenders as you feel necessary to get a loan arrangement you're happy with.

Choosing a Lender

There isn't enough room here to get into the many complex financial arrangements that lenders are willing to work with. (But, if you're interested, you might want to check out *The Complete Idiot's Guide to Managing Your Money, Second Edition,* by Robert and Christy Heady.) You'll have to do some legwork to decide what kind of loan you want and what kinds are available. For the purposes of this book, though, here's a simple checklist of questions that will help you evaluate a lender:

➤ *What types of loans are offered?* Many large lenders, such as banks, will offer any type of loan you need: business loans, personal loans for vacations or medical bills, educational loans, home-buying loans, and so on.

➤ *What are the payment schedules?* Loan payments can vary in terms of how often you make payments (monthly, quarterly, or biweekly) and how long you have to pay off the loan. These schedules are negotiable and are based on your desires and your ability to pay.

➤ *What is the current interest rate for the type of loan you are interested in?* There's no set interest rate—it depends on your negotiating ability and how much you shop around. If you encounter a lender who quotes you a fixed rate and refuses to negotiate, don't do business with that lender. Plenty of other lenders will do business with you.

➤ *What is the prime rate?* You've probably heard the term *prime rate* in the news and have been told that the prime rate is the rate that lenders charge their best customers. That's baloney! Most strong customers borrow at rates well below the prime rate. If you have bargaining skills and financial clout, you, too, can probably get a better rate than the prime rate.

➤ *How many points are charged for a particular rate?* Points are a disguised way of referring to interest. Points are usually associated with real estate loans, especially home loans. The more points you are charged, the higher the cost of the loan—so shop around.

Dealbreaker

There's an astonishingly wide range of interest rates, depending on the type of loan you're looking for, your credit rating, and the lender you choose. Don't settle for the first rate you're quoted.

➤ *What fees are charged?* Lenders (again, especially home lenders) charge a variety of fees, such as closing costs, loan application fees, loan processing costs, and similar charges. They all add to the costs of your loan, so get a complete list of the fees before you commit to the loan.

➤ *How long does it take to get the loan?* Each lender has its own processing schedule. Usually it takes from 30 to 60 days to process a loan. Sometimes it's possible to negotiate an expedited processing schedule.

➤ *Are there any penalties on loans that are paid off early?* Some lenders charge prepayment penalties if you pay the loan off before its due date. My advice is to avoid those lenders, because those penalties narrow your borrowing options. For example, if you agree to a loan with a prepayment penalty, and a better loan deal comes along later, you may be unable to take advantage of the better deal because the amount of the prepayment penalty may offset or even exceed the better loan deal.

➤ *What is the fee for late payments?* Ask the lender and read the fine print to find out what late charges are assessed. Credit card companies, for example, frequently charge steep penalties for every late payment.

➤ *Whom do you deal with if you have a problem or question?* Usually, the person you negotiate the loan with—called the *loan officer*—is the person you contact for more information.

Dealmaker

When you meet with a loan officer, make sure you have all the documentation you need. Being organized and prepared suggests that you are confident that you will get the loan (and that you'll be reliable when it comes to paying it back).

Everything Is Negotiable

When you meet with a loan officer, you'll be able to discuss and negotiate on the following terms:

➤ *The amount of your loan.* Do you want $10,000? $20,000? $100,000?

➤ *The interest rate and points.* Rates can range anywhere from 4 to 15 percent, or higher.

➤ *The term of the loan.* How long will you be paying the loan? 30 years? 15 years? 1 year?

➤ *The amount of security, if any.* This is how much money or other collateral you have to put up to secure the loan.

The High Cost of Lending

Before you set your terms, you should explore all your lending options. Small differences in interest rates make a big difference in terms of your wallet. This table, taken from *The Complete Idiot's Guide to Buying & Selling a Home*, shows you what I mean.

How Interest Rates Affect Payments

Example 1		Example 2	
Loan amount	$100,000	Loan amount	$100,000
Interest rate	8%	Interest rate	13%
Term	30 years	Term	30 years
Monthly payment	$733.76	Monthly payment	$1,106.20

The length of time during in which you'll be making payments will also affect the amount you need to plunk down every month. Generally, the faster you pay off the loan, the less interest you will pay. The following table (also taken from *The Complete Idiot's Guide to Buying & Selling a Home*) compares the amount you pay on a 30-year, 15-year, or 30-year biweekly (26 payments a year) loan.

Comparing Mortgages

	30-Year	15-Year	30-Year Biweekly
Interest rate	8%	8%	8%
Monthly payment	$844	$1,099	$422
Principal paid	$115,000	$115,000	$115,000
Interest paid	$188,779	$82,820	$135,195
Total interest paid	$303,779	$197,820	$250,195

Information, Please!

While you have questions for the lender, the lender will also have questions for you. You should be prepared to reveal the following information—and provide documentation if the lender requests it:

➤ Your current income

➤ Your debt obligations

➤ Your current and past employers

➤ Copies of bank statements

➤ Copies of stock accounts, 401(k), IRA, insurance, and other assets

➤ Copies of pay stubs

➤ W2 forms

➤ Tax returns

➤ Addresses and account numbers for all credit cards and other debts

➤ An explanation for and documentation of credit problems, if you have them

➤ Specific information related to the reason for the loan (for example, a copy of a purchase agreement for a loan on a home)

If you go into the loan interview with all the information your lender may request at your fingertips, you can significantly expedite the process. This also presents a strong, competent image to the loan officer, which is always an asset when you're negotiating.

Dealmaker

One frequently neglected piece of homework you can do before asking for a loan is to check out your own credit rating. Get a copy of your credit report and check to make sure that all the information on it is current and correct. You don't want to be turned down because of a typo on your credit history!

Negotiating with a Loan Officer

Let's face it: Negotiating with a loan officer can be scary. Most people are reluctant to discuss their finances with strangers, and many don't have unblemished financial histories.

But you don't have to be intimidated about asking for a loan. Most loan officers are fair, reasonable people who want to work with you. And always remember, lenders *must* loan money, and the competition for borrowers like yourself is fierce. To reduce your loan-negotiation jitters, prepare yourself, know what to ask for, act confidently, and remember the following tips:

➤ Prepare for the interview as if it were a job interview. Dress professionally, organize your paperwork, and arrive early.

➤ Make good eye contact with the lender. Lenders prefer confident borrowers because they feel that a confident person is more likely to succeed and pay off the loan.

➤ Start the process early. You'll need plenty of time to shop around for a lender. When you find one, you'll need to allow time (usually one to two months) for the loan to go through.

➤ Be truthful about your financial history, even if it isn't unblemished. With all the credit reporting services available today, you can be sure that the lender will find out—and you'll hurt your own position if you appear to have tried to keep negative information from the lender. Instead, explain all credit problems and how you have addressed them.

What if You're Rejected for a Loan?

If your loan request is turned down, the loan officer will tell you why. In some cases, you may be able to remedy the situation.

For example, the loan officer may have found that you have a sketchy credit rating (a computerized file of your credit history). There could be a mix-up on your credit report, which you can remedy by calling the credit agencies and asking for a copy of your credit report. (For more on this subject, see *The Complete Idiot's Guide to Managing Your Money*.)

Or, maybe you've had some unforeseen expenses—such as steep medical or car repair bills—that have temporarily damaged your financial standing. In that case, if you explain and discuss the situation with your loan officer, you can probably still work out a deal on a loan.

If the loan officer is still not convinced, shop around for another lender. Many new loan agencies specialize in lending money to people who traditionally have problems getting loans—for example, people with unfavorable credit histories or other financial troubles. If you look around, you'll be able to find someone who will give you a loan.

The Least You Need to Know

➤ Shop around for lenders the same way you shop around for a car or a house.

➤ Evaluate a lender based on what kind of loan the lender offers, the terms of the loan, the interest rate, the processing time for the loan, and the fees added to the loan.

➤ Be prepared to give the lender all the information requested, including current financial status, financial history, and credit, bank, and employer information.

➤ Be sure you understand the amount of down payment, the interest rate, and the loan term you want.

➤ When you deal with a loan officer, be truthful about your finances, make good eye contact, and dress professionally.

Chapter 26

Becoming a Savvy Consumer

In This Chapter

➤ Winning with a good warranty

➤ Getting them to take it back

➤ Reaching a refund agreement

➤ Oops! I lost my receipt!

➤ Getting the service department to serve you

If your home is like mine, it's packed with appliances and gadgets such as vacuums, toasters, CD players, and TV sets—all those items that make your life easier and more enjoyable. When these goods break down, it's more than a nuisance to have them fixed or replaced—it's also expensive! This chapter teaches you how to demand—and receive—customer satisfaction, whether by securing a refund, getting repairs, or returning a defective item for replacement.

Check Out the Warranty Before You Buy

A warranty is a promise from the manufacturer that the product you've bought will work as you expect it to work for a certain amount of time. But beware! Not all warranties are alike, and some items (which are bought as is) don't come with warranties at all.

Negotiable Terms

A **warranty** is a written guarantee that goods or property will be repaired or replaced if not as represented. Some purchases are protected by an **implied warranty** (not written, but assumed when you buy the product) or an **express warranty** (an oral or written statement by the seller). Implied and express warranties are not honored in all cases.

You should check out a company's warranty policy before you plunk down hundreds of dollars on a new computer or stereo system. Read it closely—a good warranty will answer the following questions:

➤ How long is the product covered? Two months? One year? A lifetime?

➤ Which parts of the product are covered?

➤ What will the company pay for? Will it pay for replacement parts only, or will it also cover the cost of labor and repairs on those parts?

➤ What is the repair procedure? Do you have to ship or lug your stereo to the company's repair center? Or will your local retailer cover shipping and handling costs?

➤ How do you begin coverage? With many products, you must fill out a registration card or customer questionnaire to begin coverage. You don't want to find this out the day the product breaks.

➤ What is and is not covered under the warranty? If you try to repair your computer yourself with tape and glue, the company may not be responsible for fixing the damage you've done.

Once you buy a product, you should keep all paperwork related to the purchase—store receipt, credit card slip, warranty, and owner's manual—together in a safe place in your files. I know, I know—this is easier said than done. But it's worth the effort: A little efficiency up front can save you lots of dough down the road.

Never Pay in Advance!

A word of caution: Whenever you're buying expensive equipment—or paying for expensive repairs—try not to pay the entire amount until you're completely satisfied that the product and services are worth the money. Once you've handed over the cash, you've got little leverage if something goes wrong. Protect yourself by following these tips:

➤ Choose a financing option so you can pay in installments rather than all at once. If you choose to go this route, however, make sure that you check the interest rates and late fees.

➤ Pay by credit card rather than cash or check. Many credit card companies will withhold payment to a particular store if you aren't happy with the product or service.

➤ Place as small a down payment as possible on repairs or home improvement jobs. By withholding as much money as you can, you give yourself extra bargaining power if you're not happy with the work.

Finding the "Yes" Person at the Store

Let's say that one fine day, the screen on your computer freezes up, and no matter what you do, you can't get it working again. Uh-oh, your hard drive crashed! If you've got a receipt and warranty, your next step is to head back to the store and explain your situation to the person who can give you what you want.

Usually, cashiers and salespeople are not authorized to handle returns or refunds, especially for large items. They may also be too harried to give your request the attention it deserves. If you hold up the line blathering to Suzy Salesperson about how you lost your computerized grocery list file, there's a good chance that she will escape to the office of Melissa Manager, do a slipshod job of presenting your case, and then come back and gleefully inform you that Melissa rejected your request for a refund.

Dealbreaker

Most employees lack the authority to give you satisfaction when your warranty has run out. Insist on dealing directly with the "yes" person—usually, a store manager or owner.

To prevent this from happening, don't waste your time—or anybody else's— and head straight for the "yes" person (see Chapter 3, "Scoping Out the Other Side," for more on identifying the "yes"). Usually, this means finding the customer service department— most major department stores have these. If you're dealing with a smaller store, you'll want to speak to the manager, assistant manager, or store owner.

And *how* you request service or a refund is just as important as *who* you talk to. Unless you want to be taken for a crank or a crackpot, I suggest not storming into the store shouting, "I demand to see the manager!" Instead, politely explain that you've got a refund situation and that you want to speak with the person who is authorized to give you a refund or replacement.

Making Your Case

Once you've located Melissa Manager, greet her cordially and make good eye contact. Don't just launch into a litany of complaints—first take the time to tell her how often you and your friends and family shop at her store.

Speak slowly and clearly as you reveal why you're there. I suggest telling your story as a chronological narrative and presenting any paperwork you have as it becomes relevant. Here's how you might start out:

"I bought this Smarto computer from your store a month ago. (Show the receipt.) I've been using it to store personal files and browse the Internet—maybe an hour or two a night. Last week, when I went to open a particular file, the screen froze up on me. I checked the troubleshooting guide in the manual, but there's nothing like this in there." (Show the owner's manual.)

End by stating exactly what you want and producing the warranty as you do so. Say, "I want my money back," or "I want the computer serviced with no additional cost to me," or "I want a new computer."

If you present yourself calmly and professionally, and if your paperwork is in good order, Melissa should accede to your request. (If she doesn't, see the later section, "If All Else Fails.")

If you're a frequent customer and want to maintain a good relationship with the store employees, you should head over to Suzy Salesperson after the situation has been resolved. Tell her that you dealt with Melissa because you thought it would hasten the process and not waste Suzy's time. Suzy will understand—trust me.

Winning Without a Warranty

If you don't have the paperwork, or if your Smarto computer waits until the day after the warranty expires to break down (they usually do), you should still approach Melissa as described in the previous section. Because you don't have a receipt or warranty, your next best ally is the brochure or owner's manual that came with your computer (if you have it). Like most manuals, it probably brags about how durable, reliable, and easy the computer is to use.

If you've lost the brochure or owner's manual, ask for a replacement copy from the store before you approach the manager about your complaint. Most stores have or can get a copy from the manufacturer.

Once you've got a copy of the brochure or owner's manual, you're ready to go in and discuss the problem. Quote all the highfalutin' language in the owner's manual to Melissa Manager. If she's at all concerned with providing good customer service, she'll find it very difficult to refuse you. If she does argue, be prepared to equalize her statements:

Melissa Manager: "This computer looks worn out. Did you abuse it in any way?"

You: "I used the computer normally—only about an hour or two a night. That doesn't constitute heavy use."

Melissa Manager: "But your warranty has run out."

You: "The computer doesn't live up to the promises made in the brochure and owner's manual." (Quote any promises that relate to the longevity or dependability of the computer.)

Melissa Manager: "You don't have a receipt for this computer. I have no way of proving you bought it here."

You: "I bought it last year. You should still have a computerized record of the transaction, because I paid with a credit card." (Show the credit card statement if you have it. If you don't, you can probably order a copy from your credit card company.) Or: "Here's a copy of my canceled check, made out to Erratic Electronics." (Again, if you don't have a canceled check, you can order one from your bank.)

If All Else Fails

Because most stores value customer satisfaction highly, they usually won't hesitate to give you what you ask for: a refund, a replacement, or free repairs. Some will even throw in extra products or services to restore your faith in their product and company. But sometimes you face an obstinate employee who just won't give you any satisfaction. What can you do then? Here are some suggestions:

➤ *Stay calm.* Don't lose your cool in the store. You'll only give your opponent more reason to dig in his heels and refuse your requests.

➤ *Take it to the top.* Try moving higher up the company ladder. If the store manager won't help you, try contacting the company president, by letter, if necessary. (Most executives take customer complaint letters very seriously and will route your letter to a person who has authority to deal with you.) Make sure you mention the model number, when you bought the product, and the location of the store from which you bought it. Include copies of any and all paperwork that documents your purchase.

Dealmaker

Respectable retailers are concerned about their reputation. Refunding or replacing your defective product will help promote the retailer's reputation. Don't hesitate to suggest that to the retailer.

➤ *Take it outside.* If you're still not satisfied, you may want to send a similar letter to the local Better Business Bureau or your state's consumer affairs division. (You can find addresses for these organizations in your phone book.)

➤ *If necessary, bring in the law.* If you feel strongly that a lawyer should be involved, you can contact an attorney and see if you have a case. Before you go this route, be sure to let the store manager and company president know that you are discussing the issue with a lawyer. This may motivate the dealer or manufacturer to give you what you want.

The Least You Need to Know

➤ Keep all receipts, warranties, and manuals that come with any product or service you buy.

➤ Make sure you fully understand the warranty before you buy a product or service.

➤ If you want a repair, replacement, or refund, ask the "yes" person for help.

➤ Be prepared to equalize every argument your opponent may raise.

➤ Use your opponent's written literature against him. That puts your opponent on the defensive and gives you the bargaining momentum.

Chapter 27

Dispute Settlement

In this Chapter

➤ Keeping the peace

➤ Explosive emotions, and how to defuse them

➤ Dispute settlement basics

My first important negotiation as a young attorney fresh out of law school was a dispute. My client, a building owner, had a problem with a major tenant. The two locked heads and horns and got nowhere.

My job was to undo the stalemate and get the sides to reach a fair solution. During that process and throughout my professional negotiating career, much of my work has involved settling disputes.

Settling disputes is a special kind of negotiating, one that is much more vulnerable than most to get bogged down in emotions. But the basic principles of general negotiating apply in this, as in other kinds of bargaining—they simply need a little fine-tuning to address the kinds of problems that are likely to arise in disputes. In this chapter, you'll learn how to custom tailor all the skills you've learned so far to most effectively use them in dispute settlement.

The Need for Skilled Dispute Settlers

Settling disputes is a major bargaining area. We all have differences with family, friends, employees, employers, neighbors, sellers, buyers, school officials, and many, many others. Resolving these differences means bargaining, and the more skillful you are at bargaining, the quicker and more successful you'll be at settling these disputes.

Talking Points

"You can't see clearly if you insist on smoking up your glasses."

—Amos Parrish

Burying the Hatchet

Native Americans believed that evil spirits in the air caused people to quarrel. The hatchet or tomahawk was a symbol of hatred because it was used for violence. To resolve quarrels without violence, the Indians would literally bury a hatchet in the ground, and the quarreling parties would stand over the hole and work out their problems.

It's not that simple these days. Unless the disputing parties resort to the courts (which is costly and time-consuming), they have to work out the problem themselves. That's where being a skilled negotiator can pay enormous dividends. Disputes with family and friends are usually not serious enough to warrant court action, although plenty of family disputes (especially those with a lot of money involved) wind up in court because the parties are not able to work out the problem. It's almost like a fog has descended over them, blocking their ability to reason out a solution. Often that fog originates within them.

The Common Sense Approach

One important key to successfully settling disputes is using common sense. People respond to positions of common sense even though they may not want to admit it at the time.

Negotiating positions based on common sense have the virtue of keeping the discussion calm: Your opponent will find it difficult to continue arguing if you insist on employing the voice of reason. And by basing your position on common sense, you make it difficult for your opponent to come up with a counterargument that doesn't make her look (and feel) unreasonable.

While common sense is always a good tactic to use, it's especially effective in disputes where the basic facts of the issue are not subject to debate. For example, say your child wants an advance on his allowance that your budget this week can't easily handle; or say your teenager wants to borrow the car, just when you need it to run necessary household errands.

The Art of the Deal

Say your teenager asks for $20—for the second time this week. You could say "No," but that likely will fall on deaf ears. You could say, "I already gave you $20 a few days ago." That might make a slight impression, but not much. Your teenager might still press you for the money, and the matter might become heated. What if you said, "I don't have $20 to spare this month. Your braces just cost me $250." That's a good common sense position. You're informing him that you've already laid out $250 on something he needed. Your teenager now knows that you've been spending money for his welfare, and he may even feel a little sheepish for asking for more.

Abolishing Anger

People who are involved in a dispute are highly prone to anger. In fact, some dispute settlement situations can turn into mud-slinging sessions that only succeed in driving the parties further apart. Chapter 16, "Don't Get Your Dander Up!", explains in detail the danger of letting anger intrude upon your negotiation. Here, we deal specifically with anger in dispute settling.

Provocation Pitfalls

If you make your opponent angry, you can kiss settling the dispute good-by. An angry person is confident of the rightness of his or her position, and likely to be bent on retaliation, not on reason. In that state of mind, there's no way your opponent will be receptive to your efforts to settle the dispute.

Hold Your Temper

If you become angry during a dispute, you're just as likely as your opponent to lose sight of your goal and to focus solely on retaliation. You will not be receptive to your opponent's efforts to resolve the dispute, even if those efforts are reasonable or favorable to you. When you're angry, you're reacting—not acting. You stop listening to the other side. That can be devastating to your efforts at resolving your dispute.

Talking Points

"Anger is the wind that blows out the light of reason."

—Benjamin Franklin

257

Hold your temper, count to 10, and, if necessary, count to 10 again, if that's what it takes to keep your temper in check. If that doesn't work, take a recess or even a postponement until you get yourself under control.

Cooling Off a Hot-Headed Opponent

Sometimes disputes erupt into anger unexpectedly. Your opponent might simply have been spoiling for a fight. Or, you might inadvertently say something that rubs your opponent the wrong way and suddenly find yourself in the middle of an emotional blow-up.

Dealbreaker

Pride is dangerous to indulge when you're trying to resolve a dispute. When you can't admit to an error, you've closed the door to reasoning with your opponent.

Once that happens, you can still bring the dispute back onto reasonable turf. If you've caused the anger, take immediate steps to remedy the situation. If that means an apology, go for it. Don't let your ego or pride stop you.

Keep your apology light, something like this: "I'm sorry. I was out of line." In most cases, your apology will be accepted and you can get back into the business of settling the dispute.

Successful Settlements

Dispute settlement is a specialized kind of negotiating. Unlike other negotiations, such as making a purchase, selling something, or entering into a contract, dispute settlements are always based on some underlying argument or disagreement between you and your opponent. There's therefore going to be some degree of tension present when you meet. You want to relieve that tension as soon as possible.

That's why it's very important to get off on the right foot when you're negotiating to resolve a dispute. You want to set the stage for reason to prevail. You accomplish this by keeping the discussion on an unemotional plane. That means striving to maintain a humble, tactful posture; keeping calm; and taking the following steps:

➤ Getting the facts

➤ Communicating the facts clearly

➤ Keeping the discussion focused and on track

➤ Involving your opponent in every stage of the discussion

Let's take a closer look at these elements of successful dispute settlement.

Getting the Facts

It's been said that "facts, when combined with ideas, constitute the greatest force in the world." The major reason why disputes arise is a difference of opinion regarding the facts. For example, you plunk down $10,000 for a house you intend to buy. Before the deal is closed, you discover a bad crack in the foundation that's going to cost $5,000 or more to repair. The seller claims you knew of the problem. You deny it. You want the purchase price reduced by the cost of repairing the problem.

What are the facts (as opposed to emotionally based opinions) of this dispute? First of all, there's the central issue to your dispute: Whether or not you knew about the cracked foundation before you paid out your $10,000. If you can factually show that the crack was covered when you inspected the property (perhaps you have photos of that part of the wall showing that the crack was hidden by an obstruction) or that the showing broker steered you clear of the cracked wall (maybe you had a witness with you during your inspection tour), you have a solid factual basis to get the price reduced.

A second fact of the case is the cost of the necessary repairs to the foundation. You might get an estimate, in writing, from a contractor. This supports your case for reducing the purchase price by a specific dollar amount.

Communicating the Facts

Once you've marshaled the facts, your next step is to be absolutely certain that your opponent is aware of them. If he isn't, he won't be influenced by them and thus he'll be unlikely to agree with your bargaining position. He may simply believe you're trying to pull a fast one to reduce the price of the house. He can hardly be expected to go along with your bargaining position if he doesn't know what it's based on.

Let's go back to our earlier example. If the owner wasn't present at the time that the broker took you on your tour of the property, he might not know that you were steered clear of the foundation crack (or that a strategically hung wall rug covered it up). Or, he might be unaware that the crack is anything more than a cosmetic flaw in the building. By presenting him with indisputable facts, he's likely to be more receptive to your appeals to his sense of fairness and honesty when you ask for a reduction in the selling price.

Talking Points

"Behind every argument is someone's ignorance."

—Louis D. Brandeis

There's another great benefit to informing your opponent of the facts: It gives your opponent an opportunity to dispute them. That's healthy. If you can substantiate the facts as you know them, you've strengthened your position. If your opponent points out some portion of your facts that is

Dealmaker

It's really marvelous to see the response when you concede an obvious point: It opens up your opponent. Your opponent may even visibly relax, as if a burden has been lifted from them. She'll become more receptive to your position—and definitely to reaching a solution.

in error and you're convinced that your opponent is right, concede the point. That shows that *you're* a fair and reasonable person who's interested in resolving the dispute, not merely trying to arbitrarily gain the edge.

When you concede an obvious point, do it quickly yet casually. If you make a big deal out of your concession, you'll risk losing its beneficial impact. If you suggest later in the bargaining that your opponent concede a point, you can at that time tactfully remind your opponent of your earlier concession. You're using it as a trade-off. Usually, your opponent will respond with a concession.

Just the Facts, Ma'am

Stick to your facts throughout the settlement process, and—*tactfully*—keep your opponent fully aware of them as well. If your opponent raises an argument or a position contrary to the facts, recite the facts again to bring her back to reality.

It's virtually impossible to refute accurate facts—and if you're keeping the discussion on a calm, reasonable level, your opponent will have no choice but to at least acknowledge that your position is reasonable. This means that the only dispute left to resolve is how to accommodate those facts.

Let's go back to that home-buying example. You enter the dispute with a photo you took during your tour of the property that shows thick shrubs concealing the portion of the foundation that had the crack—clearly you couldn't have spotted the defect at the time of your tour. You back this up with a copy of an estimate by a local contractor, detailing that repairs will cost approximately $5,200. Your opponent has little wiggle room—except maybe in setting a dollar value on the needed repairs.

Dealbreaker

If your opponent is a skillful negotiator and has a weak factual position, you can be sure that she's going to try to steer you away from the fact. Don't let that happen! Keep your eye glued on the factual ball—that's your road to successfully resolving the dispute.

Involving Your Opponent

Nobody likes to feel railroaded into a dispute settlement. That's why you want your opponent to feel as if his position is fully understood and respected. Questions are a marvelous way to do this (see Chapter 8, "Questions, Questions, and More Questions," for additional details). Questions are useful because of these points:

➤ You can gain valuable information. The chances are great that your opponent will respond—people have an urge to answer questions even when it's against their interests.

➤ When responding, your opponent is on the defensive. Your opponent must think of the answer, then respond. That deprives him of the opportunity of concentrating on his own bargaining position.

➤ Questions show you're genuinely interested in resolving the dispute.

If you learn of new information that alters your view of the case, don't be reluctant to change your strategy or bargaining position. As John H. Patterson once said, "Only fools and dead men don't change their minds. Fools won't. Dead men can't."

As long as you explain fully the reason for your change, no harm's done—in fact, you've strengthened yourself in your opponent's eyes. By being open-minded enough to acknowledge new information, you're essentially saying, "I wasn't aware of that point. I'm glad you brought it up." That lifts your image in your opponent's eyes.

Talking Points

"No man really becomes a fool until he stops asking questions."

—Charles P. Steinmetz

Contrast that to a situation in which you refuse to consider new facts raised by your opponent. By being so inflexible, you appear closed-minded and unreasonable. Now you're dead in the water. You've substantially lowered your opponent's perception of your integrity, and you can kiss any real chance of getting a favorable agreement good-bye.

Watch Your Attitude

How you conduct yourself during a negotiation is as important as the words you say and the facts you present. A smug, superior attitude can be as disastrous to your position as an angry, unreasonable one.

Humility Helps

Using humility in your dealings with an opponent is often called the "Ben Franklin" approach. Franklin frequently employed self-deprecation to score points with an adversary—and for good reason: It works.

For example, say your teenager got into some school trouble and you find yourself sitting before the principal. You think your kid got a bum rap, but you don't want to

Talking Points

Humility leads to strength, not to weakness.
—John J. McCloy

anger the principal by coming on too strong. All you want to do is get the dispute resolved with no penalty to your kid. You might start the discussions by relating how tough it is to be a parent in this modern day and age. That puts you in a sympathetic position, especially if the principal is a parent.

Now you're in a good position to get into the details of the dispute. The principal should be in a very receptive mood and thus willing to cooperate with you in working out a favorable solution.

The Diplomatic Touch

Dispute resolution is no time for being rude, sour, or excessively forceful, even if you feel that such an approach is fully justified. You're confronting a situation where tempers can easily flare, so your approach should be diplomatic, tasteful, and balanced—even if your opponent is not. Why? It's tough for anyone to sustain an unreasonable and uncooperative attitude if you refuse to fight fire with fire. Your tactfulness will have a calming effect on your opponent and will make him much more receptive to your side of the dispute.

Dealbreaker

Being overly anxious is almost always unwise when negotiating. Your opponent may read it as a lack of confidence, in your bargaining position, even when your position is strong. Be patient. Be deliberate. That'll convey confidence in your bargaining position.

Don't Push!

Because disputes are personal, you may find that you're impatient to bring them to a close—you're prone to becoming very anxious to achieve a quick settlement. But be careful. The major drawback to displaying this anxiety is that it makes you look as if you have a weak bargaining position—even if you're holding all the aces.

You're most vulnerable to becoming anxious and impatience during the critical time when it appears that your opponent is about to agree with your position—but jumping the gun at that point can blow your deal. Be careful. Keep your cool.

Be Persistent!

Our old friend persistence pays big dividends during dispute settlement. You have to stay at it. When you hit a roadblock, look for ways around it, over it, under it—whatever it takes to keep moving forward toward a favorable result.

Coming Around to a Compromise

As with politics, most disputes end up with a compromise—rarely does one side get all the loaf. In most cases, you'll have to leave a slice or two for your opponent—after all, disputes are the most personalized of all negotiation situations. Before you begin to bargain, therefore, it's wise to think out what compromises you're willing to accept. Use them to your advantage to show your opponent you're a fair and reasonable person who's willing to give an inch if your opponent will, too.

Humor Always Helps

Because of their personal nature, disputes can get pretty serious. If that seriousness is carried into the discussions, it becomes more difficult to reach a favorable agreement. If the opportunity presents itself, it's wise to relieve the seriousness with a little humor—a lighthearted moment can take the edge off when emotions threaten to intrude on your discussions. Find a way to insert a gentle anecdote that has some bearing on the situation you're presently in. You might draw upon a personal experience or the experience of a friend or relative.

Your goal is to relieve the tension of the dispute. Try to keep your humor remotely relevant to the subject matter of the dispute. For example, if you're attempting to resolve a dispute over a repair bill on your refrigerator, any humorous story involving appliances will be relevant. But avoid anything that might cause your opponent to take offense or that gives the appearance that you are trivializing the subject under dispute.

Dealmaker

Humor can ease a tense point in the discussion. But remember that humor doesn't mean telling jokes. Jokes can be offensive, and normally have no place in negotiation, especially when resolving disputes.

The Least You Need to Know

➤ Be particularly careful not to let the discussion become personal—it can quickly escalate to an angry confrontation.

➤ Use common sense—it's hard to resist.

➤ Get the facts, and stick to them—then be sure your opponent is fully aware of them, too.

➤ At every appropriate point, ask questions so that your opponent will feel like an active and valued participant in the negotiation.

➤ Humility, patience, and tact are important qualities to cultivate when negotiating a dispute.

➤ Difficult points in dispute resolution can sometimes be eased by the use of humor—but make sure that it's relevant to the negotiations.

Chapter 28

Negotiating on the Internet

In This Chapter

➤ Getting wired

➤ Bargaining opportunities on the Internet

➤ Electronic negotiating basics

➤ Wheeling and dealing on the World Wide Web

Looking for a job? You can do it online. Want to buy a car? Just log onto the Net. Thinking about moving cross-country? You can find house or apartment listings in your new community through—you guessed it—the Internet. How about research? Need to get information on a potential employer or a business competitor? They probably host a Web site online. Looking for information on a service you need? You'll find it on the World Wide Web.

The Internet has become a major resource for everything from scholarly research (for which it was first designed) to online shopping access. That makes it an important negotiating arena. As more goods, services, and just plain people go online, the need for good negotiating skills on the Internet can only increase. In this chapter, you'll learn about this important new part of the modern commercial and communications landscape, and you'll discover how best to take advantage of its resources and limitations in your negotiations.

Adventuring Online

The word "Internet" is relatively new, but it's one that's destined to be around for a long, long time—perhaps forever. At the date of this writing, it's estimated that more than 100 million people use the Internet. As rapidly as the Internet is growing, it won't be too long before billions of people around the world will be using it. Whenever so many people have access to each other, there's bound to be bargaining.

What Is the Internet?

In its simplest form, the Internet is just a bunch of computers linked together by telephone lines so that they can communicate with each other. It began when university research departments were looking for an easy way to share information, and it quickly expanded to include government researchers and departments as well. Major corporations came next, but it was the explosion of popularity for the home PC that really kicked off the growth of the Internet—especially once online services made accessing the Internet simple for everyone.

Negotiable Terms

The **Internet** is the world of information made available through the interconnection of millions of computers and their users.

Today, all sorts of computers—and computer users—are linked by the Internet. All it takes is a telephone connection to an ISP (an Internet service provider), and you're just a mouse-click away from going online!

Walking Through the Web

When your computer has access to the Internet, you have access to what are commonly called Web sites, which are nothing more than information made available by anyone on the Internet to any other person. Everybody from university professors and students to retail companies now maintain Web pages.

The late-comers to Web sites have been businesses—it took awhile for them to truly grasp the commercial potential of establishing a presence on the Internet—but now just about anybody or any firm looking for a means of selling something has a Web site that you can visit.

For example, through the Sears Web site, you can see what the department store is selling. And, if you're interested, you can now even make a purchase through your computer, using your good old credit card.

Harnessing the Internet

The possibilities of the Internet for communication and for commerce are only just beginning to be explored. But the use of the Net is clearly on the rise, and that means it's becoming a more important resource—and venue—for negotiating. People work, play, and buy on the Internet, and each of these activities gives rise to negotiating situations.

Jumping into the Online Experience

Buying and selling aren't the only things you can do on the Web. Let's say you're getting ready to negotiate with your boss for a pay raise. How could the Internet help? Well, by now you know that you should always do your homework before a negotiation. One part of that homework might be to research the average payscale for your particular job. You might search the Internet for government labor statistics. Or, say you're in the market for a new computer—you could go online to research the best systems available, and then you could research comparative prices and even make your purchase—all without leaving your den.

Searching Every Which Way

Of course, you have to know how to find the information or companies you're interested in. There's no inherent organization on the Internet—though some service providers have tried to make things a little less confusing by providing partial directories of Web sites for their users.

Most of the time, though, you must search the Web sites on the Internet to find what you're looking for by using what's known as a *search engine*. A search engine allows you to type in key words—names or descriptive terms—and then goes hunting to find Web sites that fit your search request. Then the search engine reports back to you with the site addresses that might suit your needs.

If you're a newcomer to the Internet, The following table provides a basic sampler of terms you'll find useful.

Dealmaker

One major advantage of using the Internet for negotiation research is the timeliness of the information available online. You can get information that's far more up-to-date than anything available in your local library or other, more traditional sources.

Internet Basics

Internet Terms and Phrases	Definition
address	The way you contact a particular Web site or e-mail recipient. E-mail addresses include your ISP name (AOL, CompuServe, and so on). Web site addresses begin with the designation "www."
chat	Real-time communication with someone else, conducted over the Internet. You type a question or answer, and your recipient sees it appear almost instantaneously on his computer screen. There is a brief time lag, however, which can sometimes lead to confusion.
download	The process of copying information or files from the Internet directly onto your own computer's hard drive.
e-mail	"Electronic" mail—communications sent from one computer to another through the Internet.
homepage	The first page of a Web site.
ISP	Internet service provider—a company that provides you with your link to the Internet. Popular ISPs are AOL (America Online) and CompuServe, but there are thousands of smaller, locally based ISPs to which you can subscribe.
search engine	A program on the Internet that makes it easier for you to locate a particular Web site. Yahoo! and Excite are well-known search engines.
telecommuting	Working from home via your commuter terminal.
Web site	Information posted on the Internet by an individual or an organization. Web sites can be simple, single-screen affairs, or they can be vast, multipage sites. Many—particularly the commercial ones—are interactive: A visitor can directly enter an order for a product or service and can even make payment online by entering a credit card number.

Honing Your Internet Negotiating Skills

Why is it important to be a skilled Internet negotiator? The reason is simple: The Internet is going to be such a major form of business activity that those who know how to negotiate on the Internet will have a decisive advantage over those who do not.

Everything from Soup to Nuts

As you can probably guess from what's been said so far, you can get almost anything through the Internet: cars, clothes, books, and even real estate. You can buy or sell stock, make travel reservations, and get financial advice. You can even buy or sell through Internet auctions.

Daily, more products and services are being added to the Internet. Large department store chains, for example, are adding more merchandise to their Web sites as the number of potential customers using the Internet dramatically increases. Eventually, you'll be able to get almost everything on the Internet that you can get now through traditional means.

Talking Points

"Business on the (Internet) is booming. And from retailers to brokers to suppliers, it is destroying old habits and creating opportunities."

—*Business Week,* June 22, 1998.

How Negotiating on the Internet Is Different

Many of the skills you've already developed by reading this book apply to Internet transactions. But there's one fundamental difference between negotiating on the Internet and the usual way of bargaining face-to-face: It's done by the written word alone. You can't yet see your opponent, although someday you will see him on your computer screen or television screen.

Dealing in the Dark

Throughout this book I emphasize the importance of keeping your attention (and sight) on your opponent. Reading the subtle clues of body language is a powerful component of your negotiating arsenal. By his body actions, tone of voice, and facial expressions, your opponent is constantly conveying important information that you can use to your advantage during the bargaining.

For example, if you're making an offer to buy a car and the seller's arms are folded tightly across his chest, that's a clear sign that the seller is not receptive to your offer. (The importance of body language is discussed in Chapter 6, "Getting Physical.") You won't be able to see that important body language when you're bargaining on the Internet.

Dealbreaker

Brush up on your written communications skills if you're likely to do much Internet negotiating. It's far too easy to give offense to your opponent by being careless in your use of the written language. Make certain that what you write is exactly what you mean to say.

However, this does have an upside: Your opponent will not be able to see *your* body language, either. You can literally laugh at your opponent's price, offer, or whatever, and he won't be the wiser. And there's another upside as well—you have a ready record of every word of your negotiating exchange when you're bargaining online. If you're working through e-mail, you can keep copies of every message you send to or receive from your opponent, and even print them out in hard copy. If you're working with a Web site, you can print the screen contents (or save it to your hard disk), so there's never any confusion about the terms you've agreed to.

There's an additional, commonly underestimated problem of Internet negotiating: Unless you're very careful in how you word your communications (say, through e-mail), it's very easy to give a false impression. Your opponent can't see the friendly grin on your face as you type in what you mean to be a gentle jest—and he may easily get offended. Your telecommuting coworker can't see that helpful expression you're wearing as you type in a suggestion, and she might think you're being bossy or insulting.

This means that you need to take extra care in how you word your Internet communications. If you've given unintended offense, you may never know it until long after you've passed the point of no return and can no longer correct the bad impression you've made.

Limitations to Internet Bargaining

Most of the commercial transactions done on the Internet at this time don't really offer legitimate bargaining opportunities. That's because the Internet is relatively new, and many companies or persons with Internet Web sites just offer a product at a set price—you can take it or leave it. But that's changing rapidly, and soon bargaining on the Internet will be as common as face-to-face bargaining. As it is, it's common that you begin a transaction by visiting a Web site, but carry it through to completion by contacting a service or sales representative on the telephone—so you're actually combining two modes of negotiating in one transaction.

On the other hand, the rise in telecommuting means that there's an increase in the number of negotiations about job specifications, work flow, and payment (of salaries or invoices) on the Internet. So, this area of Internet negotiation is already well established.

How to Negotiate on the Internet

You bargain on the Internet the same as you bargain face to face. Use all the bargaining tools, strategies, and techniques in this book. The only major difference is that you must compensate for the lack of immediate visual feedback between you and your opponent. This means being extremely careful about wording your position and any related communications so that there is no possibility of misunderstanding.

Comparison Shopping Made Internet Easy

Product price comparison is one area of the Internet in which you can truly bargain, whether you're bargaining for yourself or your company.

Here's How It Works

Let's say you own a business—a kitchen supply store—and need coffee grinders, one of your best-sellers. You check the Internet and locate three sources for the grinders. One seller's price is $20 per grinder, plus shipping costs. If you buy a dozen or more, you get a 10 percent discount. The second seller's price is $19.50 per grinder, but you pay the freight. The third seller's price is $19.00 per grinder, and he will pay shipping if you order a dozen or more. The last two sellers offer no volume discount.

Dealmaker

The vast array of information on the Internet can make your pre-negotiation research quick and thorough. Take the time to familiarize yourself with the search engines and how they work—the knowledge you gain will pay huge dividends in saved time when you engage in traditional, face-to-face negotiations.

This is a classic competitive situation that you run into almost every time you buy anything. Car dealers, for example, will vary—sometimes substantially—in price and terms for the same car. The same is true with clothes and even groceries. The cost of the same loaf of bread varies with each store.

Getting to Your Goal

You're after the best deal. Of the three, if you need a dozen or more, the first seller will give you a 10 percent discount for a per grinder price of $18.00 ($20.00 per grinder less 10 percent). You can get that without bargaining. But that's just your starting point. Here are your next steps:

➤ You contact the other two sellers and let them know right up front that you can get a better deal with their competitor, advising them of the terms of the deal. (They'll probably know that because they, too, can check out their competition on the Internet). Then ask if they can give you a better deal. What you're doing is creating fear of losing your business, and as explained in Chapter 17 "Fear and Trembling," fear is a very powerful motivating emotion.

Dealbreaker

Just because information appears on the Internet doesn't mean it's true. Check your sources, whether they're retail outfits or private individuals offering a service or product. Use the same consumer savvy and caution you'd use in face-to-face negotiations.

➤ You repeat the process until you get the price you're happy with. Assume, for example, that the second seller agrees to meet the $18.00 per grinder price and cut off half the shipping charges. In addition, that seller points out that his shipping charges will be lower because he's located closer to your business.

That's the kind of give and take you can already experience using the Internet—and we haven't even scratched the surface yet. Many companies, even very large companies, are playing one supplier against another (using fear of loss of business) and are saving literally many millions of dollars. For some large companies, the savings will reach the billions as the Internet continues to mature.

Another Advantage from Bargaining on the Internet

By negotiating on the Internet, you'll be able to reach more sellers (if you're buying) and more buyers (if you're selling). The time and money you save doing so can be substantial. All you need to do is literally click on your computer and search for what you're after—it's right at your fingertips. As an additional help, some magazines even list Internet Web sites by product.

Talking Points

"The Internet is ushering in an era of sweeping change that will leave no business or industry untouched."

—*Business Week*, June 22, 1998

The Bottom Line

You'll have fantastic bargaining opportunities on the Internet. The face of online communications is changing every day, as graphics become more sophisticated, as modem speeds increase, and as new ways of integrating technology (voice capabilities and real-time video transmission) become perfected. If you hone your bargaining skills as explained in this book, you're on your way to saving tons of money and having fun doing it. And, like most everything else in life, the more you bargain on the Internet, the better you'll get at it.

The Least You Need to Know

➤ The Internet is simply computers linked together. It's growing rapidly and will change the way we do business.

➤ With the rise of telecommuting, negotiations on the Internet go beyond simple consumer interactions and include many of the bargaining issues that arise from the workplace.

➤ One major difference between negotiating on the Internet and normal negotiating is that you can't read your opponent's body language.

➤ Negotiating on the Internet requires that you take particular care in choosing your words when you communicate with your opponent, to avoid inadvertently offending or alienating him and ultimately blowing your deal.

➤ Use the bargaining strategies, techniques, and tools in this book when you bargain on the Internet the same way you use them when you bargain face to face.

Glossary

Arbitrator   A neutral third party who resolves a controversy between two or more parties.

Assumption   A negotiating technique in which you prompt a closing action.

BATNA (Best Alternative To a Negotiated Agreement) The outcomes or alternatives that remain if no negotiated agreement is reached.

Bidding offer   The offer you make if you are bidding against other interested parties.

Body language   A series of gestures that reinforce or display what you are thinking, feeling, or saying verbally.

Brokers   People who are licensed to start and run their own real estate offices.

Building Block   A negotiating technique that permits you to parcel out facts during the negotiation so that they have a greater impact on your opponent.

Choice question   A negotiating technique meant to pin your opponent down to a definite course of action.

Closing   The process of finalizing all the dealings related to a negotiation.

Commercial real estate   Property used for a business, such as a restaurant or health food store.

Concessions   The compromises both you and your opponent are willing to make in order to reach a deal.

Conduit   A negotiating technique used when you are facing more than one opponent or you want to use your opponent to reach the "yes" person.

Contingencies   Events that must happen in order for a deal to close.

Controlled anger   A negotiating technique used to express your displeasure at something an opponent has said or done.

Counteroffer   A subsequent offer that makes changes to an original offer or counteroffer. Can be made by either opponent.

Dealbreaker   Any proposal, offer, or counteroffer that kills a deal.

Dealmaker   Any proposal, offer, or counteroffer that clinches a deal.

Earnest money   The down payment on a house.

Equalization   The ability to answer your opponent's argument with an equally compelling argument of your own.

Exhausting   A negotiating technique used to wear down your opponent.

Express warranty   An oral or written warranty given by a seller or a seller's associate.

Extrapolation   Stating facts in a manner that can only lead to one inescapable conclusion.

Funneling   Setting aside points once they are resolved. The points may be returned to later in the negotiation for review or summation, but not for renegotiation.

Gear Shifting   A negotiating technique in which you shift from issue to issue. It works best on large, complex negotiations.

General question   A broad question, best asked early in negotiation to uncover new facts and information.

Goodwill   The trust you build up with your opponent.

Highballing   Making an offer or counteroffer that is obviously too high for the negotiation.

Home field   Any place that you are intimately familiar with, such as your office or home; the best place for you to conduct a negotiation.

Implied warranty   A warranty that is not written but is assumed when you buy a product.

Investment real estate   Property you buy and hold onto in the hopes of eventually selling and making a profit.

It's a Shame   A negotiating technique best used when the negotiation is nearly settled and only a few points remain.

Jargon   The specialized language of a particular organization, occupation, or group.

Lawyer   A person licensed by the state in which he or she works to represent and advise people in legal issues.

Leading question   A statement turned into a question. Used to get an opponent to say "yes."

Lease   A contract that determeines the rights and responsibilities of a renter and a property owner.

Lessee   A person who rents property from a property owner.

Lessor   A property owner who rents property.

Listed or asking price   A homeseller's offer for a house.

Lowballing   Making an offer or counteroffer that is obviously too low for the negotiation.

Manipulation   Using unfair or underhanded means to reach your goals.

Mediator   One who tries to resolve disputes between two or more parties.

Motivator   Anything that influences someone to act.

Negotiable offer   An offer that leaves room for wheeling and dealing.

Negotiation   A way to get what you want, deal with people, and increase your skills in human understanding and interaction.

Net rent   The money received after all the expenses associated with a business property are paid.

New elements   People, ideas, or issues that are foreign to the negotiators or the subject under negotiation.

Obvious question   A negotiating technique designed to get a favorable response from your opponent.

Offer   A proposal to pay, do, or give something such as money, goods, or services in return for other money, goods, or services.

Opponent   The person with whom you negotiate.

Option   In rental agreements, your right to renew a lease.

Personality   The distinctive individual qualities of a person, considered collectively.

Position paper   A written offer presented at the beginning of a negotiation.

Primary base   The most important issue you negotiate for; your objective or goal.

Principle   A fundamental truth or law upon which others are based; a rule of conduct; adherence to such rules; integrity.

Prompting Action   A negotiating technique that motivates your opponent to take a simple form of action that seals the deal.

Props   Any extra materials, documents, charts, or accessories you bring to the negotiating table.

Purchase agreement   An offer form used to make an offer to buy a house.

Salespeople or sales associates   People who represent property owners (usually sellers) and who handle the sale of a home or commercial or investment real estate.

Secondary bases   The positive factors that support your primary base.

Self-Deprecating   A negotiating technique in which you tactfully play down your merits or the merits of your bargaining positions. Used to form a bond with your opponent.

Specific question   A negotiating technique that calls for confined answers from your opponent.

Sublessee   One who rents property from another renter.

Sublessor   A renter who rents property to another.

Successive question   A negotiating technique used to maintain control of the negotiation and develop positive bargaining momentum.

Suggestive question   A negotiating technique that suggests a specific course of action.

Summarizing   A negotiating technique in which you summarize your understanding of the deal to prompt your opponent to say "yes" to it in its entirety.

Talk-Show Host   A negotiating technique used to uncover personal or private information from your opponent.

Vinegar and Honey   A negotiating technique used to make a bad negotiating situation or concession seem better than it really is.

Warranty   A written guarantee that goods or property will be repaired or replaced if not as represented.

"Yes" person   The person who has the authority to resolve the issue you are trying to negotiate.

Index

"Exhausting", 98-99
"Gear-Shifting", 99-100
"It's a Shame", 103
"Self-Deprecating", 102-103
"Talk-Show Host", 101-102
"Vinegar and Honey", 97-98
professional negotiators, 18. *See also* lawyers
property-appraisal jargon, 47
property. *See* commercial property; homes; investment property; real estate
props/visual aids, 59
guidelines, 60
key item in negotiation, 61
proper use, 59-60
timing usage, 60-61
Proverbs 17:2: comment on listening, 49
psychological perspective in negotiations
opponent's emotions, 122
desire for wealth, 123-125
need for self-preservation, 124-126
thirst for recognition, 123-126
using strongest emotion, 124-126
opponent's self-image appeals, 120
learning interests/ values, 119
negative appeals, 121-122
positive appeals, 120-121
remaining aloof, 126-127
self-images, 117-118

Q

questions in negotiations
aimed at you by opponents, 80-81
dispute settlements, 260-261
source of power, 144
types, 73-74
choice, 79
general, 74-75
leading, 76-77
obvious, 78-79
specific, 76
successive, 80
suggestive, 78

R

real estate negotiations
agents
negative aspects, 211-212
selling without using, 211
services provided, 210-211
buying/selling homes
actions if no offers are being made, 217-218
anxiousness-level of seller, 212-213
consideration affecting prices, 212
evaluating offers, 217-218
making offer, 214-216
need for repairs, 213
negotiable issues, 214
reasons not moving quickly, 212
signing and closing process, 216-217
commercial or investment property, 218
assessing value, 218-219
dealing with brokers, 218
negotiation tips, 220-221
research sources for assessing value, 219-220
leases/subleases, 223-224
negotiation tips, 227-228
provisions needed, 224-227
terminology, 210-212
registered mail, 90-91
rent for leases/subleases, 224
repair contracts, guidelines for handling, 92
restricted delivery of mail, 90-91
Rogers, Kenny: comment on strategies in song, "The Gambler", 152
Roosevelt, Franklin D.: comment on fear, 172
Rusk, Dean: comment on being good listener in negotiations, 38
Russell, Bertrand: comment on fear, 176